SCIENCE IN THE FOREST,
SCIENCE IN THE PAST

HAU
Books

SCIENCE IN THE FOREST, SCIENCE IN THE PAST

Edited by Geoffrey E. R. Lloyd and Aparecida Vilaça

HAU Books
Chicago

Originally published as a special issue of *Hau: Journal of Ethnographic Theory* 9 (1): 36–182.
© 2019 Society for Ethnographic Theory

Cover photo: Carlos Fausto. Used with permission.

Cover design: Daniele Meucci and Ania Zayco
Layout design: Deepak Sharma, Prepress Plus
Typesetting: Prepress Plus (www.prepressplus.in)

ISBN: 978-1-912808-41-0 [paperback]
ISBN: 978-1-912808-79-3 [ebook]
ISBN: 978-1-912808-42-7 [PDF]
LCCN: 2020950467

Hau Books
Chicago Distribution Center
11030 S. Langley
Chicago, Il 60628
www.haubooks.com

Publications of Hau Books are printed, marketed, and distributed by The University of Chicago Press.
www.press.uchicago.edu

Contents

List of Figures

Preface

Geoffrey E. R. Lloyd and Aparecida Vilaça

The present volume stems from a workshop that the editors organized at the Needham Research Institute in Cambridge from May 31 to June 2, 2017. We observed that in recent years investigators in a number of different disciplines have been questioning the ontological presuppositions of whatever branch of inquiry they are engaged in. The problems are particularly acute in two areas especially: (1) in the history of ancient science; and (2) in the cross-cultural ethnographic study of the knowledge and practices of living Indigenous peoples. In the case of the history of ancient science, one key question is how and why Greco-Roman and Chinese science in particular developed in the ways they did, a topic of particular importance in the context of the work currently undertaken at the Needham Research Institute and in the Classics Faculty at Cambridge University. In the case of Indigenous peoples, the focus is on the ontological clashes related to their contacts with Euro-Americans and the subsequent transformations brought by new political movements, insertion in the market economy, monetarization, Christianization and schooling, themes well-developed by the Brazilian and Cambridge organizers and collaborators.

The underlying problem in both types of case can be expressed like this. When different individuals, groups or whole societies evidently adopt markedly divergent views on the objects in the world around them, on the proper relations among humans and between humans and other living things, and on how knowledge on such matters is to be obtained, what are we to say? On one view there is a single objective reality, correct access to which is secured by philosophy, science and mathematics, which accordingly supply reliable criteria by which more or less accurate accounts are to be judged. In this view it is generally assumed that modern Western science holds a privileged position, although this is often in ignorance of alternative traditions. It follows that this is one reason why it is so important to study science in such other cultures as China and in India. On the diametrically opposed view, there is no such single objective reality. Rather, we should allow that divergent knowledge and practices relate to different realities and that those who adopt and live by them should be seen as, in an important sense, inhabiting different worlds.

Reflecting the aims of the workshop this volume brings together specialists from several different disciplines to tackle different aspects of these fundamental problems. Historians of mathematics examine the commonalities and the divergences in mathematical practices and concepts in different cultures separated in time or space or both, and they pose questions to do with the very framework within which the history of mathematics can be undertaken. The questions of the status of the objects that mathematics presupposes and the characteristics of the modes of reasoning it deploys are taken up, also, by those whose training is in computer engineering. Philosophers and historians of science here revisit the problems of mutual intelligibility posed by apparently incommensurable scientific paradigms. Anthropologists who have studied Indigenous cosmologies in the field comment on the problems of understanding they pose. Several who have direct experience of how both schooling and missionary activity effect Indigenous beliefs discuss how modern Western scientific ideas impact on the traditional ideas and practices of the peoples to whom those ideas are presented as correct solutions to the question of what reality consists in and how to investigate it. A particular feature of our approach is to stress the importance of intercultural knowledge exchange in the context of Indigenous and local understanding on biodiversity matters, an issue that has obvious potential consequences for policy-makers everywhere in the world as we face the more and more pressing challenges of climate change, the over-exploitation of natural resources and ecological degradation.

Each of our participants brings a particular set of skills and experience to bear, but all are united by the sense of the importance of the task. To achieve greater mutual understanding across peoples, cultures, religions and indeed across intellectual disciplines is as urgent now as it has ever been in human history. Past societies and contemporary ones alike are a precious resource contributing to this crucial goal. The aim of bringing together leading scholars in a wide variety of disciplines is to pool our expertise in a bid to throw light not just on current academic problems in each field (such as the ontological turn or the incommensurability of rival scientific paradigms) but also on issues of global practical concern. In the event not all of those who gave papers to the workshop were able to contribute chapters to this volume. But in rewriting our papers we have all been able to draw on the valuable points that were made in our wide-ranging discussions. The full list of participants in the workshop is as follows:

Mauro William Barbosa de Almeida (Social Anthropology, Universidade Estadual de Campinas)

Alan Blackwell (Computer Sciences, University of Cambridge Computer Laboratory)

Matei Candea (Social Anthropology, University of Cambridge)

Manuela Carneiro da Cunha (Social Anthropology, University of Chicago)

Karine Chemla (Sinology, Université de Paris)

Serafina Cuomo (Ancient History, Durham University)

Giovanni da Col (Social Anthropology, SOAS, University of London)

Marina Frasca-Spada (History and Philosophy of Science, University of Cambridge)

Simon Goldhill (Classics, Centre for Research in the Arts, Social Sciences and Humanities, University of Cambridge)

Christine Hugh-Jones (Social Anthropology, University of Cambridge)

Stephen Hugh-Jones (Social Anthropology, University of Cambridge)

Dame Caroline Humphrey (Social Anthropology, University of Cambridge)

Nicholas Jardine (History and Philosophy of Science, University of Cambridge)

Agathe Keller (Indology, Université de Paris)

Tim Lewens (History and Philosophy of Science, University of Cambridge)

Sir Geoffrey Lloyd (Comparative History of Science, Needham Research Institute, University of Cambridge)

Willard McCarty (Digital Humanities, Kings College, London)

Anthony Pickles (Social Anthropology, University of Cambridge)

Joel Robbins (Social Anthropology, University of Cambridge)

Lena Springer (Sinology, Needham Research Institute, University of Cambridge)

Richard Staley (History and Philosophy of Science, University of Cambridge)

Dame Marilyn Strathern (Social Anthropology, University of Cambridge)

Tang, Quan (Sinology, Needham Research Institute, University of Cambridge)

Liba Taub (History and Philosophy of Science, University of Cambridge)

Aparecida Vilaça (Social Anthropology, Museu Nacional, Universidade Federal do Rio de Janeiro)

Wu, Huiyi (Sinology, Needham Research Institute, University of Cambridge)

Zhao, Jenny (Classics and Sinology, Needham Research Institute, University of Cambridge)

Acknowledgments

It is our pleasant duty to express our deepest gratitude to those persons and institutions without whom the workshop could not have taken place, and first of all for the generous financial support of the Chiang Ching Kuo Foundation in Taiwan. Our thanks go next to the Director of the Needham Research Institute, Professor Mei Jianjun, who allowed us to hold our meetings in the friendly and intimate environment of the Institute, and to the Administrative Manager of the Institute, Ms Sue Bennett, who oversaw all the complex detailed arrangements with impeccable efficiency. We are grateful too for the support, both financial and intellectual, that we received from the Departments of Classics, and of History and Philosophy of Science, from the Division of Social Anthropology of the University of Cambridge and from Darwin College.

CHAPTER ONE

The Clash of Ontologies and the Problems of Translation and Mutual Intelligibility

Geoffrey E. R. Lloyd

The studies collected in this volume stem from a workshop that brought together specialists in a number of different fields or disciplines who had, in recent years, become increasingly aware of facing a set of similar or analogous radical methodological and substantive problems. Those fields include, especially, social anthropology, the history of philosophy, science and mathematics, and computer science. The key problems concern, first, the subject matter of each field and the relations between them, and second, the character of the understanding within reach. Should we, in each case, presuppose that there is a single objective reality that is the proper subject of inquiry and in relation to which correct or incorrect judgments can be evaluated? Or rather should we deny any such unique objective reality and allow that divergent knowledge and practices relate to different realities, to different ontologies, different worlds? In which case, the fundamental problem is how any communication or understanding across worlds is possible.

I construe my principal task in this introduction as being to offer some suggestions concerning the rules of encounter to be adopted for fruitful cross-disciplinary investigation. First, I consider it necessary to set some limits to how indeed we should understand the similarities in the issues facing different disciplines, which is to qualify, if not to take back, what I have just written in my opening paragraph.

We are all faced with radical otherness, whether we are ancient historians or modern ones or anthropologists. But that otherness takes different forms, posing different challenges to our understanding. Alternative customs are one thing, values another, ontologies, science, and mathematics yet others.

Thus, in some cases (variety of customs) there is no pressure to suggest there is or should be just the one preferred solution (how to organize social relations, for example). In others there may be. Where values are concerned, we would do well to recognize their heterogeneity. No one has a monopoly of the right values to live by. We can and should tolerate others' views. But tolerating others' views does not mean agreeing with all of them; in particular, there is a limit to a tolerance of the intolerant.

But what about where ontologies and science are concerned? Here is where one of the major potential conflicts arises. To simplify, but I hope not too drastically, we may identify two extreme positions. On the one hand (A), there are those (I shall dub them "monists") who would insist that there is just the one world, one reality, the truth about which is delivered by science. On the other hand (B), there are those who say no ("pluralists"). The evidence (of anthropology and of ancient history) shows that ontologies—in the sense of what is entertained about reality—differ. And some of those pluralists would say that each ontology can only be judged from inside—that is, that evaluation *across* ontologies is impossible. To anticipate, my view would be to agree with the first but deny the second. But that does not settle the issue between A and B, since monists would still claim that there is just the one—correct—solution to what is the case, although that will mean ruling out other ways of knowing, other practices, other ways of being in the world, and we have all become sensitized to the dangers of doing just that.

Thus, I am used to considering the similarities and differences between ancient Greek and ancient Chinese thoughts, values, and speculations about the world around them. But those similarities and differences are not necessarily similar to those that anthropologists who study Indigenous knowledge systems encounter. They are not even the same as those that face historians of early modern and modern science. To start with, the evidence available for each of those endeavors exhibits remarkable differences. I have to rely almost (but not quite) exclusively on texts, the lacunose and biased sources that all stem one way or another from the literate elite (even when members of that elite purport to be reporting

2

others' views). Anthropologists and historians of contemporary science can and do interview their subjects and can gauge their reaction to how they have been understood. But the character of the reflections that their informants themselves engage in exhibits certain differences from the theorizings we find in ancient texts already.

But it is not just that we have to use different methodologies: the subject matter to which we apply those methodologies and that we endeavor to understand manifests deep-seated differences. We call the project Science in the Forest, Science in the Past. But how far is that repeated "science" justified? Does it not prejudge the question of whether indeed we are dealing with "science" in such dissimilar cases? In the heyday of positivist historiography the answer would have been to have asserted in no uncertain terms that those other "sciences" are incommensurable with all modern science and do not rate as "science" at all: end of project. On that view nothing that diverges importantly in any respect (either in substance or in method) from our current knowledge could count as "science" but has to be put in the trash cans of superstition or myth or the irrational or primitive mentalities or whatever.

I shall have to come back to that view, but it can and should be challenged straightforwardly and immediately by a reminder of what these other systems of knowledge comprised. If we are tempted to say that nothing before the so-called Scientific Revolution counts as science, my favorite examples to give us pause include the following: ancient Babylonian, and then later ancient Chinese and Greek eclipse predictions; Greek and Chinese attempts to determine the size and shape of the Earth; ancient and Indigenous modern understanding of the therapeutic properties of plant and mineral remedies; ancient and Indigenous modern understandings of animal behavior, of animal reproduction, and of the classification of both animals and plants. That is not to mention umpteen examples of technological mastery that imply systematic knowledge and, in many cases, presuppose repeated experimentation, in metallurgy, textiles, agriculture, navigation, and so on. Even when there was no explicit theory about the experimental method there were in practice plenty of trial-and-error procedures used effectively to increase understanding and control.

Yet am I not myself still presupposing that we can be confident about just how such examples are to be evaluated? *Can* we be confident that we are indeed dealing with an "eclipse prediction"? The assumptions that the Babylonians made about the signs in the heavens are indeed very different from those we would endorse (Rochberg 2016). The heavenly bodies for them and for the ancient Greeks are indeed heavenly, indeed divine. Calling these accounts eclipse predictions runs the risk of glossing over some major differences in how they fitted in to what else was believed about the world, including about the relations of humans to gods. Point taken: but the ancients were able on occasion successfully to predict a lunar eclipse, sometimes even a solar one, even though what they made of them reflected assumptions about the significance of signs from heaven. Interpretations of what occurred differed radically. But the fact of such an occurrence was a possible subject of reliable prediction.

Of course, there is a recurrent question of translation, not just in the sense of what the terms in the vocabulary used may mean. How far is any mutual understanding possible? The *Zhuangzi* texts from the fourth–third century BCE have a famous story concerning the person after whom the text is named (*Zhuangzi* 17; cf. Graham 1981: 123; 1989: 80–81). Zhuangzi was walking along a weir above the River Hao with his friend Hui Shi when he said how happy the fish were as they swam in the water. How do you know, Hui Shi asks, you are no fish? No more, Zhuangzi says, are you me: so how can you know what I know? Hui Shi comes back by conceding that not being Zhuangzi he cannot know him, but by parity of reasoning Zhuangzi not being a fish cannot know about them. But Zhuangzi picks him up. Hui Shi had begun by asking him how he knew the fish were happy by using an expression that more strictly equates to "whence"—that is, from where or from what. So Zhuangzi uses it to claim that Hui Shi already knew that Zhuangzi knew the fish were happy—and he answers the last question by referring to the weir above the River Hao; that is, the place at which he knew the fish were happy.

There is a bit of sophistry, then, in that exchange. But ignoring that trick, we can identify that recurrent problem of how anyone can understand anyone else, but also see that such a move is eventually self-defeating. If we go down the solipsist route, there is no more to it. But persuading anyone that he is right is impossible for the solipsist, for there is no one for him to persuade. We are not solipsists and we have to tussle with acute problems of understanding others. Yet we do so, generally, in the belief that *some* understanding is possible, however incomplete, provisional, and revisable that is.

Whatever our specialist field of inquiry we are all familiar with the experience of terms that have no exact equivalent in our ordinary everyday vocabulary. The historians come back with *qi* and *logos*, the anthropologists regale us with *tapu, mana, hau*, and many more. But at the same time, it is absurd to conclude that because there is no single exact equivalent in English, we can understand nothing of what those various terms mean—in different contexts, where indeed what they mean may well be much influenced by those contexts. But that process of understanding is likely to be a long drawn out one, never complete. But then our understanding of what we take to be familiar concepts is never perfect and complete either. Indeed, that understanding is constantly on the move.

It is important also to register that this problem does not just affect such highly theory-laden terms as *qi* and *tapu*. The indeterminacy of reference infects mundane ones as well. We think we can find approximate equivalents between the English word *fire* and the Greek and Chinese terms that are regularly translated like that in English; namely, *pur* and *huo*. In many contexts that seems to work well enough. But when we examine what counted as *pur* and what counted as *huo*, we encounter quite a problem. For many Greeks (but not Heraclitus, and not Theophrastus) *pur* was an element, entering into the substance of many compounds when it was combined with other elements. For the ancient Chinese, *huo* was one of the *wu xing*, but the *xing* are not elements but phases. One Chinese text from the *Shang Shu* (*Book of Documents*) is explicit (Karlgren 1950: 28, 30). *Huo*, it says, is "flaming upward" and *shui*, the term regularly translated as *water*, is "soaking downward." The five *xing* (the others are "earth," "metal," and "wood") are not substances so much as processes. Those differences gave rise to all sorts of misunderstandings when Europeans, Jesuit missionaries in the van, first got to China (Gernet [1982] 1985). But the crucial point is that they *need not* have arisen—if, that is, the Europeans had been prepared to examine Indigenous Chinese beliefs more carefully. The question that this raises for me is how far there are parallels to that when the knowledge of Indigenous peoples is confronted by the interpretations put on that by the missionaries and teachers instructing them—a theme that Aparecida Vilaça especially takes up. Misunderstandings are clearly common: but could they, can they, not be avoided, or at least mitigated?

The standard reaction, in the old positivist days, would be to set about determining which view of "fire" or "water" is the correct one and to dismiss any alternative as a plain mistake. In this context, the temptation, which still haunts us perhaps, would be to say the Chinese got "fire," *huo*, more or less right (it's more a process than a substance), but the Greeks were closer to the mark with "water," *hudor*, at least insofar as they treated it as a substance (even though, for most of them, as an element not a compound), a material rather than a process (Heraclitus again excepted).

Yet it can be argued, I would argue, that any such temptation should be resisted. Rather than say that a process-based ontology is correct and a substance-based one mistaken (or vice versa) we should ask what is to be said in favor of each of them, in different contexts, and from different perspectives. Chemistry cannot settle definitively what "water" is. "Is Water H_2O" is the title of a splendid study by Hasok Chang (2012), who explored what was and is to be said in favor of alternative analyses, HO for example, where the hydrogen component is analyzed differently. In so many scientific disputes the victory of the winning side tends to beguile one into assuming there was nothing to be said for their rivals, not only at the time, but even after the victory was secured.

What I do at that point, in response to the competing claims of different ontologies, is to insist first on what I call the semantic stretch of the term *water* (and of *hudor* and of *shui*) and then also of the multidimensionality of the phenomena in question. What is there for the terms to refer to is not just one thing or process. The answer to that "what is it?" question varies with context and perspective. But does that not commit us to hopeless vagueness and fudge? Is not the danger that pluralist ontologies lead to ontological chaos? That conclusion can be resisted provided that our expectations for synonymy are modest. Once we are prepared to examine the full range of the uses of Greek and Chinese and English terms in question, we can trace similarities as well as differences in their senses and their referents. There is no neutral vocabulary in which we can do that. But provided we are aware of just that fact, that does not constitute any fundamental block to achieving some comprehension both of the meanings of Indigenous terms and of the referents they target.

On this view, then, the difficulties of translation and of mutual understanding should not be treated as a threat but as an opportunity. When we encounter strange beliefs and practices we should resist reaching immediately for those labels of the irrational, myth, fiction, mystification, and probe further what they mean in context. In my view, a large group of problems was not solved but radically lessened when the anthropologists moved away from the supposition that the beliefs and behavior that puzzled them reflected assumptions about *causality*, to an alternative set of questions to do with *felicity* and appropriateness. And one such anthropologist, Stanley Tambiah, was certainly inspired to do so by his reading of the philosopher J. L. Austin's distinction between different speech acts (Tambiah 1968, 1973). The efficacy/felicity distinction can, in other words, be brought to bear to relocate the question of intelligibility to give it a far more manageable, if still to be sure not unproblematic, twist.

One of my favorite examples of this comes from our own Western society, the practice that used to be common in weddings in Christian churches of showering the bride and groom with confetti. When it was rice that was thrown, the thought may have been that this expressed the hope that the pair would be fertile. Yet those who engaged in this practice did not necessarily believe that this was the effect of the throwing of the rice, that the rice had causal efficacy. Rather nowadays the thought was that without the confetti the wedding would somehow not be a proper wedding. The aim was appropriateness rather than causal efficacy—which of course leaves open the question of why it came to be thought appropriate.

We should, in other words, aim for charity in interpretation, though not in precisely the way Donald Davidson ([1980] 2001) advocated, since the point he underestimated was that we must allow that our own conceptual framework will need to be revised as we learn from others. But an objector will still protest at my attempt at charity that it simply does not allow for error. But if I do not go along with Davidson, no more do I sign up to Paul Feyerabend's "anything goes" (Feyerabend 1975). Judging that the ancient Greeks or the ancient Chinese got certain things wrong is always tricky, since we have to pay attention among other things to those substantial differences in ontological preconceptions that I have mentioned. But that does not mean that they were always right and never made mistakes. The ancient Greeks and Chinese themselves were often in the business of diagnosing mistakes in other ancient Greek and Chinese theories, beliefs, and practices. They did not always get it right: but they certainly recognized the possibility and the problem of error. That is not just a feature of literate societies, of course, for one other lesson we have learned from ethnography is how widespread skepticism and criticism can be in predominantly oral communities. While sometimes we can react to those ancient Greeks by saying they should have been more charitable (a reaction I frequently have when Aristotle is, as he often is, in one of his dismissive moods) there are other occasions when we can join them in diagnosing error.

The terms in Greek and Chinese that we translate as "heart"—*kardie*, *xin*—have multiple associations and resonances, some tied up with ideas about cognitive functions, some not. But when Aristotle locates the organ on the left side in humans, and when Galen puts it in the center, it is not that both are equally correct, though in both cases more is at stake than just a point of anatomy, since symbolic associations and notions of hierarchy are deeply implicated. But what about one of the star examples usually quoted in relation to the progress of science—namely, heliocentricity? Aristarchus's view was contradicted by Ptolemy, who insisted like most Greeks that the earth is at rest in the center of the universe. But though everybody now knows that geocentricity is incorrect, we should remind ourselves that we do not *see* the earth move when the sun sets.

There are, of course, plenty of issues on which modern science would be adamant that it has the answers, but plenty where those issues may be more complex than a dogmatic science would allow. We now know that the anopheles mosquito transmits malaria. Eradicating them helps to eradicate that disease, while praying to the Malaria Goddess does not. Those prayers do not eradicate the disease: but recall my point that efficacy may not always be the goal nor the outcome but rather felicity or what is appropriate. How it gets to be thought appropriate to pray to the goddess is a formidable problem. But we should not shy away from an investigation of the origins and characteristics of ritual behavior and religious experience itself, even though I confess to taking a rather dim view of much of what passes as answers to those questions.

Whether the ontological turn has helped or not is an issue on which opinions will no doubt continue to differ, with plenty of potential for confusion about just how "ontological" is being understood. When it goes with a warning that what we might take for granted does not necessarily apply to the materials we are puzzling over, it is surely useful. When it is thought to validate the conclusion that mutual intelligibility is impossible, that there is no possible communication across worlds and that we are all imprisoned in our particular preconceptions of our particular world, it surely isn't. When it is a slogan to help the cause of enfranchising those whom we might otherwise dismiss, ancient Greeks or Chinese or Wari' or Maori, we can endorse it while remaining vigilant about its being carried to extremes.

So I think we can and should allow Science in the Forest and Science in the Past to be indeed "science" in the broad understanding of that term that focuses on aims and methods rather than on results. We find in both careful, more-or-less systematic observation, careful description, an interest in classification, in explanation, in prediction, in the use of experiment in the large sense of trial-and-error procedures. The particular challenge of these ancient and modern Indigenous materials is to see what *we* can learn from such an exposure to the strange, to unfamiliar assumptions and practices. The first thing we can learn, maybe, is simply *not* to assume that "we" (whoever) are right and "they" are wrong, to dismiss their views, as seems to happen still in some circumstances in the interactions described by Aparecida Vilaça, Marilyn Strathern, and Manuela Carneiro da Cunha, for instance. Further, apart from this first lesson in modesty—or at least antidogmatism—there are concrete points to take home from our explorations.

"Mathematics" perhaps provides a particularly interesting test case, since here the temptation to legislate has been especially strong. What ideas of quantities and shapes will be found useful for different groups is not the kind of question to which we should expect a uniform answer across the world. We cannot assume that everyone has always had exactly the mathematics they need, for that flies in the face of the fact that they often express dissatisfaction with what they have got. On the other hand, we cannot rule a priori what mathematics should be for them.

The incommensurability of the side and diagonal of the square holds wherever the issue is thought worthy of investigation. But it is not a truth that can be put to use (I dare say) in Amazonia. As for its uses in ancient Greece, one of those was simply to show how clever those who were in the know were: though the surprise among those whom they were putting down soon, in fact, wore off. The ancient Indians, too, certainly knew about it. But when it came to the construction of the altars that is such a preoccupation in the *Apastamba Sulbasutra*, they were content with measurements that gave rough approximations: they had to be.[1] The ancient Chinese, too, knew of the incommensurability of the diameter of a circle and the circumference, but again were content with the observation that closer and closer approximations of the value of what we call π can be given.[2] We should remark that this is not a matter of saying that truths vary: just that the interest in different exemplifications of truths does.

In this context, what is especially striking about some of Vilaça's materials is that while the missionaries and the school teachers tend to be stuck with the mathematics they have learned, their Indigenous pupils

---

1. For a first orientation on the problems of approximations in classical Indian mathematical texts, I may refer to my brief discussion in Lloyd (1990: 98–104).

2. One of the earliest discussions comes in the third century CE commentary by Liu Hui on the *Jiuzhang Suanshu or Nine Chapters on Mathematical Procedures* (chap. 1: 103–6; see Chemla and Guo 2004: 175ff.; cf. Lloyd 1996: 152–53).

seem to be both more imaginative and more flexible, seeing the value of their traditional ideas and practices even while they tussle with the new-fangled ones the Whites are introducing them to. The aim here of our interdisciplinary investigations would be to evaluate the case for plural, alternative mathematics, or rather to firm up what it would mean to assert or deny such. Suffice it to say for the moment that we should surely not be in any way surprised that the symbolic associations of certain numbers can continue to be important in some contexts, even while abstraction is carried to the limit in others.

My Greek-Chinese confrontations can yield further insights both about the potential objects of study and about the criteria we should adopt for their fruitful investigation. Under the first head I would count the ontological alternatives suggested—for example, by the substance/process dichotomy—and some of the problems with "nature" I do not think I appreciated until I saw the Chinese doing cosmology without any such notion. That is not as impressive as the anthropologists' problematizing person, the individual, agency, causation, relation itself, but not negligible nevertheless.

Under the second head I would reckon the advantages, as it seems to me, of exposing oneself to others' expectations for explanation and understanding, and in particular to taking on board some of the weaknesses of what was supposed to be the great strength of the Western tradition of science, an insistence on the delivery of certainty via demonstration. Modern Western science seems to have needed that ideal in some phases of its development. But I return to the key point that the West has no monopoly of the truth, not just of results but even of methods. We do not have a monopoly of the world either, though that undeniably and potentially disastrously is the direction that global capitalism is heading. So much more urgent is the task of recovering and appreciating pluralism: the Forest and the Past have much to teach us.

Let me then, at the risk of some repetition, recapitulate the position I would argue for, focusing on four fundamental points. First, we should acknowledge the multidimensionality of the explananda, and allow for that pluralism I have just mentioned. Second, we have to accept that there is no neutral vocabulary in which to do our work of interpretation; indeed, all our terminology exhibits greater or less semantic stretch. Third, we should see incommensurability not as a threat but as an opportunity. Fourth, that in turn implies that we have to accept the provisionality and the revisability of whatever results we claim. This is so much less comfortable than what until fairly recently was the customary view—namely, that clearly defined, univocal terms should enable us to identify unique problems to each of which there is a single, definitive, certain solution. Whether the advantages of my foursome outweigh the disadvantages is an issue that will become clearer in the studies that follow.

Those studies deal with a great variety of topics, whether disciplines or concepts and practices. But all seek to exploit to the full what we can learn from the rich evidence from social anthropology, ancient history, and modern developments in such fields as computer engineering, concerning the practices and conceptions of knowledge entertained at different times and places across the world.

Among the disciplines investigated, several contributions focus on mathematical traditions, where positivist preconceptions of a supposed universality of mathematics are perhaps at their strongest. Aparecida Vilaça considers the tensions and possible misunderstandings that arise when Indigenous Amazonian peoples are confronted by missionaries and educators intent on replacing their traditional practices by what is presented as the superior mathematics of Western modernity. Serafina Cuomo in turn investigates the pluralism of mathematical practices and the different aims and goals of different practitioners that can be found already within the Greco-Roman world, and in the process reveals the oversimplifications that reference to that world as a single culture commits.

Analogously Karine Chemla considers evidence for the variety of Chinese mathematics and investigates the possible divergences in the ontological implications of different mathematical operations or procedures. Agathe Keller discusses the pluralism of mathematical practices in India, noting how much has been lost through the neglect of historians who tend to concentrate on elite Sanskrit texts; however, she is able to trace interactions and what she calls the dialogue between those texts and modern Tamil elementary mathematics. Mauro Almeida similarly explores the consequences for ontology and intertranslatability of different perceptions of what "mathematics" comprises. He develops the contrast between a narrow focus on objects and a broader appreciation of the possible similarities in mathematical structures and pragmatic applications across widely divergent domains, on the one hand drawing from ethnography (Indigenous kinship systems in particular) and on the other hand on developments in the history of mathematics since the break with the Euclidian tradition.

Manuela Carneiro da Cunha looks at what we take to be one of the most basic of human activities, agriculture, and against the positivist tendency to treat it as mere technology, recovers what we can learn from its study concerning the knowledge systems of its practitioners. In the process, she is led to challenge some deep-seated assumptions concerning some supposedly inevitable and irreversible progress from foraging and swidden to domestication and to complexify the very idea of domestication itself.

Then two contributors from the field of computer science, Alan Blackwell and Willard McCarty, look critically at the claims made for what we call artificial intelligence and at where the capacities of computers leave our understanding not just about what can currently be achieved by bringing them to bear but also about what future developments might hold. The intelligence imputed to the machine depends, indeed, crucially on the humans that put it there. Studying what McCarty calls the anthropology of the artificially intelligent can throw light not just on the nature of intelligence and the variety of modes of reasoning it depends on and uses but also on what makes humans human.

Among the fundamental issues problematized in different chapters, Marilyn Strathern tackles the sense and experience of time and the concept of law in the shifting conceptual landscapes of Papua New Guinea. She explores the underlying ontological presuppositions in play and charts the understandings and misunderstandings that characterize how negotiations proceed between Indigenous groups and those who have a program to impose their notions of order upon them. Stephen Hugh-Jones confronts questions to do with the usefulness of the notion of "ontology" in relation to some complex ethnographic data from Northwest Amazonia especially. A special feature of his discussion is to contrast high-level analysis on the part of anthropologists or of Indigenous informants with the implications of the actual behavior and practices in the many different contexts that go to make up the lived experiences of the people concerned. A single underlying ontology turns out not to be so easily identifiable as some analyses would like to suggest.

Finally, Nicholas Jardine unites anthropology with history and philosophy of science in a further critical scrutiny of the usefulness and the limitations of the notion of diverse ontologies.

In every case, the contributors acknowledge that much further work needs to be undertaken. But all open up new avenues of inquiry centering on the key questions of the unity and diversity of notions of understanding and the corresponding presuppositions concerning the nature of what there is to be understood.

References

Chang, Hasok. 2012. *Is water H₂O? Evidence, realism and pluralism.* Dordrecht: Springer.

Chemla, Karine, and Guo Shuchun. 2004. *Les neuf chapitres: Le classique mathématique de la Chine et ses commentaires.* Paris: Dunod.

Davidson, Donald. (1980) 2001. *Essays on actions and events.* Oxford: Oxford University Press.

Feyerabend, Paul. 1975. *Against method.* London: Verso.

Gernet, Jacques. (1982) 1985. *China and the Christian impact.* Translated by Janet Lloyd. Cambridge: Cambridge University Press.

Graham, Angus. 1981. *Chuang-tzu: The seven inner chapters.* London: Allen and Unwin.

———. 1989. *Disputers of the Tao.* La Salle, IL: Open Court.

Karlgren, Bernhard. 1950. "The book of documents." *Bulletin of the Museum of Far Eastern Antiquities* 22: 1–81.

Lloyd, Geoffrey. 1990. *Demystifying mentalities.* Cambridge: Cambridge University Press.

———. 1996. *Adversaries and authorities.* Cambridge: Cambridge University Press.

Rochberg, Francesca. 2016. *Before nature: Cuneiform knowledge and the history of science.* Chicago: University of Chicago Press.

Tambiah, Stanley. 1968. "The magical power of words." *Man,* n.s., 3 (2): 175–208.

———. 1973. "Form and meaning of magical acts: A point of view." In *Modes of thought,* edited by Robin Horton and Ruth Finnegan, 199–229. London: Faber.

CHAPTER TWO

Inventing Nature: Christianity and Science in Indigenous Amazonia

Aparecida Vilaça

The indigenous peoples of the Upper Rio Negro have already made clear their interest in sending their children to school so that they can assimilate the sciences and bring back their benefits to the villages.
—Gersem José dos Santos Luciano (2014: 337)

Reading the literature produced by anthropologists and speaking to them, I could perceive their scientificism. They studied other cultures and other practices with a meticulous respect, but with a background of science.
—Bruno Latour and Steve Woolgar (1997: 12; my translation)

*The truth or falsehood of scientific knowledge is **known through experimentation**. It possesses the quality of **verifiability**, to the extent that claims (hypotheses) that cannot be proven do not pertain to the domain of science.*
—Intercultural high school workbook
(Érika Haese 2015: 235; emphasis in original)

The connection between Christianity and the invention of nature has been a common theme in philosophical and anthropological debates. By way of example I take two well-known contemporary authors who explore a direct relationship between them. Bruno Latour argues that it is the Christian God who enables what he calls the "constitution of the moderns," maintaining "as much distance as possible between two symmetrical entities, Nature and Society" (Latour 1993: 127). For Latour, the debates that took place in the seventeenth century, especially the dispute between Robert Boyle and Thomas Hobbes concerning the allocation of the domains of nature/science and society/politics, gave added impetus to the long endeavor to separate these domains, a process first begun during the sixteenth-century Reformation (Latour 1993: 33–34; see also Lenoble 1969; Viveiros de Castro 2004b: 482).[1]

Philippe Descola (2005: 540) also identifies Christianity—and more specifically, Creation—as the key event characterizing so-called modern peoples, positing them as paradigmatic examples of the naturalist mode of identification that characterizes Euro-American thought and founded, according to him, on an "apartheid" regime separating humans from nonhumans. He argues that a first operation of purification, related to the Greek concept of *phusis* and its developments by Hippocratic writings and Aristotle, was insufficient for men to become exterior and superior to nature in Greek thought (Descola 2005: 99–100). A second and definitive operation of purification took place with the advent of Christianity and "its double idea of a transcendence of man and a universe created *ex nihilo* by divine will. From this supernatural origin, man assumes the right and mission to manage the Earth, after being created by God on the last day of genesis to exert control over Creation" (103).[2]

Despite the many important differences existing between processes occurring in such distinct times and places, I believe that exploring a number of ideas concerning the so-called rationalization—or, in Roy Wagner's terminology (1975), conventionalization—of the world, can help elucidate the radical transformations experienced by an Amazonian people, the Wari', over a relatively short period of time. Until seventy years ago, the latter had never had peaceful contact with White people

---

1. See also Strathern (1980: 216n29). Stephen Hugh-Jones (pers. comm., September 20, 2016) told me that a Barasana man asked him to explain the difference between the social sciences and the natural sciences, which he was unable to grasp.

2. For an overview of the discussion on the existence of a concept of nature among native peoples, see Wagner (1975, 1977); Strathern (1980); Descola (1986); Lévi-Strauss et al. (1991); Descola and Pálsson (1996); Dwyer (1996); Ellen (1996); Ellen and Fukui (1996); Howell (1996); Ingold (2000).

or other Indigenous groups. Today they are Christians and take biology, physics, and math classes in their schools.

My wish is to examine a point seldom explored by ethnographies of Amazonia. Despite the intrinsic historical relation between Christian churches and school teaching (Jackson 1995: 315; Vilaça 2014)—among the Wari' and several other Native peoples around the world, the missionaries were also the school founders—these ethnographies tend to take Christianization and schooling as distinct and opposite processes, the first leading to culture loss and the second to the preservation or recuperation of culture and to political and economic empowerment.

I have no intention of questioning the pertinence of this empowerment, of recognized success throughout the world. Furthermore, my focus is not on the schools dedicated exclusively to the transmission of traditional culture but rather on those that aim to transmit Western knowledge, whether or not they assume a relativist perspective, as occurs in so-called intercultural teaching in Brazil. I look to show that the transformations in school experiences are in many ways analogous to those associated with Christianization, which, as happened in the historical past, also introduced the conceptual foundations sustaining the idea of nature and its study among the Wari'.

I wish to analyze these as transformations to their conceptions of world and personhood, with an emphasis on the systems of knowledge and morality associated with them. I begin by introducing the Wari'.

The Wari'

One of the central features of the expeditions to pacify the Wari', organized by the federal government in the 1950s, was the participation of fundamentalist Evangelical missionaries from the New Tribes Mission (NTM), an entity then just recently formed in the United States. Well drilled in military-style camps and trained for linguistic studies, these missionaries quickly assumed control of the organization and logistics of the expeditions and the first contacts with the Indigenous people.

The expedition members carried with them germs to which the Wari' had no immunity, provoking devastating epidemics. Combined with the deaths caused by armed attacks by local rubber bosses, this led to the extermination of around two-thirds of the population. Frightened and disorganized by their losses, but also very interested in these new Whites from a far-off land who had brought them metal tools, effective medications, and food, the Wari', from 1956 onward, gradually relocated from their residences to live near the houses of the Evangelical missionaries (Vilaça 2006, 2010).

In 1969, a section of the Wari' population declared themselves converted for the first time, telling the missionaries that they believed in the latter's God. Some of them had learned to read and write over the course of the decade and were able to help the missionaries translate various books from the Bible. For a decade, most of the Wari' who lived with the Evangelical missionaries attended church services conducted entirely in their own language. Translated excerpts from the Bible were read, prayers were offered to God, and people confessed their sins in public. According to the Wari', at the start of the 1980s, as a consequence of the many fights between affines that were still breaking out, combined with the deaths caused by sorcery and the attacks of animal spirits, the Wari' "abandoned God" and resumed their traditional practices and rites, with the exception of cannibalism.

This was how I first found the Wari' when I arrived in 1986. In 2002 I was surprised by a strong Christian revival movement, prompted, they said, by a fear that the world would end after seeing images of the attack on the World Trade Center on the community television. This left them with the certainty—confirmed by the missionaries living among them—that the apocalypse was imminent, set to follow the global war that was clearly looming. They resumed the church services, prayers, and confessions, and began to demonize shamans, who gradually stopped accompanying their animal partners in order to follow Jesus instead. Everything was ready and waiting for this revival: the local churches, Bible translations, pastors, hymns, and the missionaries still present in many villages. But above all, the Wari' were nostalgic for the Christian life they had once led, which during its boom period had quelled rivalries and put an end to food restrictions (Vilaça 1996, 1997, 2009, 2013, 2016). To grasp the transformations arising from this process, we need to turn briefly to examine pre-Christian Wari' thought.

Perspectivism and Shamanism

Wari' is the term for the personal pronoun "us" but also means "person" or "human being." Although known in the region as Wari', this is not an ethnonym per se, therefore, but a position, that of humanity, one that can be occupied by the Indigenous people and by animals. Just like the Wari', animals see themselves as people, *wari'*, living in houses and holding festivals, and see the Wari' in the same way that they are seen by them—as prey, *karawa*.

Although we may seem to be presented with a typically animist ontology in which human attributes are extended to animals, a flaw in this model was revealed by Eduardo Viveiros de Castro (1998: 474) in posing the following question, grounded in Amazonian ethnographic data: "If animals are people, then why do they not see us as people? Why, to be precise, the perspectivism?" (see also Viveiros de Castro 1998: 484n10; 2004b: 474). Why the difference? This involves precisely what the author calls Amerindian perspectivism. In contrast to our own relativist multiculturalism, the ontology informing perspectivism, dubbed multinaturalism by the author, presumes a series of worlds and a single culture, taken here as a set of social practices.

Among the Wari', for example, although all humans drink chicha socially, for themselves it is made from maize, while for jaguars it is made from blood, and for tapirs from clay. The most important point is that for each of the groups it is chicha that they are drinking, a social drink par excellence, characteristic of relations between humans. What varies is precisely the material substrate from which it is made. Communication between these worlds involves not cultural exchange but bodily transformation. The Wari' say that if someone encounters a person in the forest who offers them chicha and they perceive that rather than maize drink they are being proffered blood, they concluded that the person is actually a jaguar and refuse to drink. Were they to accept the drink without realizing the difference, it would be a sure sign that they share the viewpoint of the jaguar (which sees the blood as drink) and that they themselves, therefore, have become jaguars. This implies that although they continue to see themselves as a person—that is, someone with a human body (which is how jaguars see themselves)—their Wari' coresidents henceforth no longer see them as persons: in their eyes, they have acquired the body of a jaguar and are living in the houses and families of these animals.

The shaman is someone able to circulate between different perspectives and thus different worlds using his capacity for controlled bodily transformation, acquired through a process of initiation. Thereafter his body becomes double, both human and animal, allowing him to transit between different relational contexts, shuttling continually back and forth. This is what enables him to talk to the animals that accompany him and ask them to return the people captured or preyed upon by them, triggering a state that the Wari' recognize as disease (see Vilaça [1992] 2017, 1999, 2000, 2006).

What we could call someone's identity, the kind of person he or she is, depends on an external observer, since the former always sees him- or herself as human: any transformation is perceived by him- or herself merely as a change in relational context. In this sense, unlike ourselves, the Wari' used to have no notion of an inner self, a stable person with an internalized self-perception of the kind presented to them later by Christianity. So rather than an inner self, they had an outer self (see Robbins, Schieffelin, and Vilaça 2014).

Given the constant risk of metamorphosis due to the predatory attacks by animals, people were always compelled to make their own viewpoint clear. Any demonstration of strange behavior, like the refusal of food offered by kin, indicated a process of transformation underway. For the Wari', the only possible explanation for someone spurning food was that their vision had transformed, implying that they were recognizing other foods, distinct from those of the Wari', as edible: the person was eating with animals and becoming one of them. In sum, there did not exist anyone without relations, only persons with the wrong relations. Isolation and antisocial behavior were evidence of this.

Divine Creation and the Desubjectivization of Animals

Given this background, it is no surprise that the Wari' became especially interested in one particular aspect of Christianity, the same recalled by Descola (2005) and mentioned above, and coincidentally the aspect that the missionaries themselves considered the basis of all their teaching: divine creation, which implies the establishment of a new kind of relationship between humans and animals. Excerpts from Genesis, translated into the Wari' language, are found not only in the catechism books but also posted on the village church walls and are continually mentioned in their prayers to God.

I provide two examples of translations into the Wari' language:

Genesis 1:28. He spoke contentedly. Reproduce yourselves many times. . . . Spread across all the other lands. Be leaders. Be leaders of the fish, the birds and all animals. [Bible text in English: *Then God blessed them, and God said to them, "Be fruitful and multiply; fill the earth and subdue it; have dominion over the fish of the sea, over the birds of the air, and over every living thing that moves on the earth."* (New King James Bible online, March 2017)]

Genesis 1:30. Eat all the animals, all the birds, and all the strange animals that crawl across the earth too. [Bible text in English: *Also, to every beast of the earth, to every bird of the air, and to everything that creeps on the earth, in which there is life, I have given every green herb for food; and it was so.* (New King James Bible online, March 2017)][3]

It is worth mentioning that the Wari' did not have a demiurge or any idea of a created world. Paletó, my Wari' father told me:

We don't know from where our ancestors came. The oldest ancestors did not know from where they came. When the youngsters asked the elders: "Where did we come from?" "I've no idea." "Who made us?" "Nobody made us. We exist for no reason.". . . We never thought about God. We never thought: does God exist? No, never.

And his daughter Orowao Karaxu added:

In the past nobody knew that it was God who had created everything. We met the Whites and learned about him. For the elders, the animals always wandered around pointlessly. There was no reason for the animals' existence, they thought.

The fact of creation in itself implies the imposition of the perspective of the creator, God, who made men the masters of animals—that is, predators. The Wari' enthusiastically recount the moment when they began to eat various animals that had previously been prohibited. In the words of Paletó:

They used to avoid armadillo, coati. When we encountered the Whites, the Christians told us to eat all animals since it was God

---

3. On the subjugation of animals, see also Genesis 9:2–3, where God speaks to Noah: "2. And the fear of you and the dread of you shall be upon every beast of the earth, and upon every fowl of the air, upon all that moveth upon the earth, and upon all the fishes of the sea; into your hand are they delivered. 3. Every moving thing that liveth shall be meat for you; even as the green herb have I given you all things" (New King James Bible online, March 2017).

who had made them. They didn't cause sickness. Pregnant women can eat armadillo, eagle. The latter animal became a true bird (prey) for us. They eat electric eel and nothing happens. Why? "I created the animals," said God. "Oh, so that's how things are, then!" we said.

Conceiving humanity and animality as essentially reversible positions— since both the Wari' and their favored prey could be located either in the position of humans (*wari'*), defined as predators, or in the position of animals (*karawa*), prey—the Wari' experienced life as a constant struggle to define themselves as human and thus stay alive. Establishing a single direction to predation coincided, therefore, with what the Wari' sought in their day-to-day lives, a movement analogous to generalized brotherhood, also fostered by Christianity. The latter worked to deter another type of predation, namely the attacks perpetrated by affines in the form of sorcery (see Vilaça 2016: chap. 5).

Moralities

Albeit diverse authors have shown important coincidences between Christian and Indigenous moralities, others have demonstrated that such coincidences are partial insofar as they are limited to the spectrum of morality that Michel Foucault (1990: 266) called moral codes or laws, such as do not kill, do not steal, and so on. Other aspects of morality taken in a broader sense, like technologies of the self or forms of producing people, become profoundly altered (Foucault 1990: 29; 1997: 266; Robbins 2004).

Among the Wari', one of the techniques used, confession, was central to the production of an inner, secret self, visible only to the person concerned and to God, an idea clearly opposed to a conception of the person determined from the outside, by the other's perspective, which I call the outer self. Crucial to this operation was a transformation in the meaning of the Wari' notion of heart, the center of feelings, morality, and thought, previously intrinsically associated with the body, its locus of expression. A sad and tearful heart, for example, was inevitably visible in the form of an emaciated and sick body (see Robbins, Schieffelin, Vilaça 2014; Vilaça 2016: chap. 8).

Traditionally associated both with morality and with thought and cognition—the Wari' would say, for example, that a person who learned a task quickly had a good heart—these attributes, shared by animals too in the past, became separated in Christian experience into two distinct sites: moral conscience and feelings remained seated in the heart, while knowledge related to cognitive processes was relocated to the "head" (*winaxi'*), a place previously without meaning for the Wari'. This separation, however, remains ambiguous within the Christian universe and only becomes concrete through schooling, where knowledge obtained from the world of White people tends to become amoral and disconnected from relations. We can turn now to this question.[4]

School, Science, and Morality

Although the Wari' undoubtedly possessed a vast ecological knowledge, a sophisticated science of the concrete in Lévi-Straussian (1962) terms, and knew how to utilize this know-how and exploit diverse species of beings for their own sustenance (see Berlin and Berlin 1977; Berlin 1992; see also Lévy-Bruhl 1952, [1926] 1985: 79; Alexiades 1999), there were no intrinsic properties that differentiated a priori a subject or object in a perspectivist context and the Wari' found themselves open or exposed to surprises all the time. In his first visit to the city of Rio de Janeiro, in 1992, Paletó updated the myth of the carrying baskets: after the women started laughing at the funny way the baskets walked at the trail, the baskets decided to stop walking by themselves, and the women were punished by having to carry them at their backs. Seeing a mechanical digger at work, without noting the operator inside, Paletó remarked that White people had been wise enough not to laugh at their objects, which had thus kept their agency. Another time he asked me whether the electric door to my garage "had a heart"—that is, thought and agency—since, unaware of the remote control in my hand, he presumed that not only had it opened by itself, it also knew the precise moment to do so.

The subjectivity of objects has been explored by Viveiros de Castro (2004b) in an analysis differentiating our own scientific knowledge from shamanic knowledge. For the so-called hard sciences, to know involves objectifying as much as possible, stripping subjects and objects of all subjectivity and ideally transforming them into a set of chromosomes

4. According to Geoffrey Lloyd (pers. comm., 2017), where different cognitive and affective faculties were to be located was a much-disputed topic in pagan Greek. Also plenty of translations from Chinese take the word *xin* as "heart-mind."

or atoms. As Bruno Latour and Steve Woolgar (1979, 1997) showed in their study of a laboratory, even the subjectivity of the researcher ideally must be eliminated. Shamanic science is the symmetrical opposite: to know involves subjectifying as much as possible. Hence an object by itself offers no interest to investigation unless it can be associated with a subject, whether human or animal, through the shaman's own subjective and relational experience (see Lévy-Bruhl [1926] 1985: 63). A piece of wood in the forest only becomes an object of research when, for example, it is seen by the shaman as a tapir seat, used by the animal-person to sit in its home (see Viveiros de Castro in Sztutman 2008: 40–43).

Knowledge based on myths experienced through the transcorporal experience of the shamans—who could see other worlds with their own eyes and transmit this knowledge to other people in the villages—was essentially relational and multiple: in other words, there was no search for a single truth. Different shamans gave their version of events, whether these involved the appearance of a band of peccaries or an illness, depending on the events experienced during their journeys and encounters with animals. These practices did not involve the conventionalization of diverse understandings into a single body of knowledge through dialectical argumentation. Rather, to use Wagner's terminology (1975: 116), they evinced a differentiating tradition, one that sought precisely a multiplicity of visions, ignored the idea of contradiction—as indeed Lucien Lévy-Bruhl ([1926] 1985) had already observed—and did not valorize linear thought.[5]

Sitting on school benches, especially in the more advanced levels of secondary education and university, the Wari' have begun to engage more closely with scientific epistemologies in which the process of objectification that leads to knowledge is intrinsically related to the notions of truth, rationality, and linear argumentation.

---

5. It is important to note that the use of the term "contradiction" by these two authors refers, by opposition, to the paradigms of the philosophy of science dominant in the first half of the twentieth century (Carneiro da Cunha 2012: 457) rather than being determined by the debates between Aristotle and Heraclitus on the Law of Contradiction. In the latter case, attributes said to be contradictory must be "predicated of the same subject at the same time, in the same respect and in the same relation" (Lloyd 1966: 87; see also 86–102). See Vernant (1983: 470–72) on Parmenides (515 BC) and noncontradiction.

The foundation to this epistemology is a naturalist ontology—whether universalist or relativist—that comprises the polar opposite of perspectivism or multinaturalism, which supposes a diversity of worlds, or "natures," experienced by different types of subjects with distinct kinds of bodies (Viveiros de Castro 1998). For the Wari' to be able to accompany scientific thought, even basic mathematics or the principles of physics or biology, a stable and single world needs to be created, a world given a priori, work carried out to perfection by the Christian God, and further enhanced by the heirs of Newton, a well-known advocate of parsimony and elegance in explanations (Rossi 2001: chap. 17). As Jean Pouillon (1993: 28) observed, "science is monotheist," reflecting, among other factors, the Christian foundations of its development.

The contrast between Wari' and scientific-Christian epistemologies is even clearer when we recall that Christianity and scientific thought were brought to the Wari' by fundamentalist Protestant missionaries and teachers, who emphasized the veracity of Biblical events, taken literally. As one NTM missionary stated in the organization's catechism manual: "What we announce here is precisely what happened literally in time and space. It is real, it is a fact, it is history" (McIlwain 2003: 39; my translation).

The mathematical problem of quantities among the Wari' seems to me an interesting line of inquiry for thinking about this scientific-Christian transformation.

The Intercultural University and Amoral Mathematics

In 2009 the Brazilian state of Rondônia introduced a university-level intercultural teacher training course, along the lines of courses already running in other regions of the country. The course is devoted exclusively to training Indigenous students to become teachers and is taken by a diverse range of Indigenous peoples living in the region. This specific case brings together students speaking unrelated languages, like Wari', Tupi-Mondé, and Nambikwara. The classes are taught in Portuguese by nonIndigenous lecturers specialized in various areas of knowledge. The mathematics classes, which form part of the core curriculum, provide some interesting examples of the kinds of transformations we have been analyzing. Here I focus on the translations of quantities into numbers that return us to the principles of conventionalization of the missionary translations.

Like many South American (and Australian) Indigenous peoples, the Wari' do not have a developed numerical vocabulary, limited to the terms for one, two, a few, and many.[6] The absence of Native terms for different quantities was never a problem for the Wari', since they would traditionally express them by showing the fingers of their hands to list the names of participants in a war expedition, for example. Quantities higher than ten, or even before reaching this number, would automatically be classified as "many" (see OroAt 2013; OroNao' 2013). On one occasion, Orowao Xik Waje, using her hand fingers to name her grandchildren, stopped at ten saying: "I have no more fingers." Differently from some other Native peoples, the Wari', though using their fingers while enumerating, do not use the names for the fingers as numbers and do not equate a hand or two hands with precise quantities.[7] After contact with White people, the Wari' had their first experience of the commodity economy and quickly learned to use numbers in Portuguese, both in the village school and in commercial exchanges in the nearby town. The issue arises when, in the classrooms, they are encouraged by the lecturers to speak and write down numbers in their maternal language, which, given the multilinguistic context in question, only they would know.

The Wari' have been led to invent their own numerical system, then, since it was no longer enough for them to have learned our own and used it for around three decades to conduct transactions with White people and among themselves. Now it is necessary to translate, and demonstrate that their system is equivalent to ours, an idea that only makes sense through an alien conception of the world in which quantities are defined a priori and detached from the relational context in which they are embedded. It was in this situation that the Wari' found themselves poor in numbers.

---

6.   See Pica et al. (2004) on the Amazonian Munduruku and Seeger (1981: 62) on the Syuá/Kinsêdje. For an overview in relation to South America, see Lévi-Strauss (1968: 277). On Australia, see Dixon (2002); Pawley (2005: 639); Wierzbicka (2005: 641).

7.   The Wari' ask "How much?" or "How many?" through the question "Where does it stand (*main ka xat na)*"? The answer will be "like that/here." On the equation between numbers and body parts, see Biersack (1982: 813) and Mimica (1988: 31) on the Paiela and the Iqwaye from Papua New Guinea, respectively. On the opposite situation, closer to the Wari', see Carrier (1981: 468) on the Ponam from Papua New Guinea. According to Lloyd (pers. comm., 2017), modern Chinese still express numbers on their fingers and hands.

Fazed by the lack of numbers for precise quantities beyond two, the Wari' translated the number three using one of the two terms for a few (*parik*)[8] while for four to ten they used a variety of different terms for "many," traditionally applied to distinct kinds of objects. Hence, for example, the term used for many things/persons became the number four, while the term for full, referring to a large quantity of liquid, became the number five. Predictably, perhaps, the translation tables diverged among the students—differences sometimes conventionalized as differences between the various Wari' subgroups—and in fact the same student may use various terms for the same numbers on different occasions (K. Leite 2013: 120, 154, 170; Cao OroWaje 2015).

It is not my intention to discuss here the many questions posed by the literature on Native numerical systems, from which we can highlight the polemic on the absence of numerical terms among another Amazonian people, the Pirahã.[9] Emphasizing the fact that I disagree with any association made between numerical limitations and cognitive limitations, I shall focus on a question that appears to me insufficiently explored given its apparent centrality in Wari' thought: the moral and relational character of quantities, something already identified by Stephen Hugh-Jones (2012: 79; 2016) when he observes that "like Quechua numbers, the numbers of the Tukano (Northwest Amazonia) are also conceptualized in terms of social relations" (see also Carrier 1981; Lave 1988; Mimica 1988; Urton 1997; Verran 2001 on other ethnographic contexts). This is the exact opposite of the mathematical acceptance found in the schools, grounded in the idea of a given world constituted by objective quantities extrinsic to subjects and their relations.[10]

When 1 = -1

There are various points worth highlighting in the Wari' translations, which go beyond the inconsistency in the numerical equivalences

---

8. The other one is *pije*, meaning "to be small, child" (Everett and Kern 1997: 349).
9. See Everett (2005: 623–27) with comments from Berlin (2005: 635) and Levinson (2005: 637–38). See also Gordon (2004) and Frank et al. (2008).
10. For a generalization of the idea of numbers as cultural creations with a positive take on the possibility of communication between different systems, see Almeida (1999: 8) and Verran (2001).

indicated above. To begin with, the "few" ceases to be contextual and becomes a precise number, as occurs too with the different terms used to designate larger quantities. The most interesting aspect, however, resides in the problem of oneness. The translation for the Wari' term used for the number one is "alone." Whenever someone uses the Wari' term *xika'pe*, their primary intention is to announce a lack. A person alone evokes the absence of another, while dead game, when referred to using the term for one, indicates the absence of other game animals and thus suggests the hunter's hunger or ineptitude. In this sense, a more adequate numerical translation of the Wari' term for one would be any number from minus one to minus x.[11]

The attribution of a negative value to one is not exclusive to the Wari'. Mariana Kawall Leal Ferreira (2001), in a study of the numerical concepts of the Xavante of Central Brazil, relates oneness to solitude, contrasting it to the positive value attributed to two and to even numbers in general. In her words:

> By turning our attention to the mathematical philosophy of dialectical societies, what we learn, from the very beginning, is that unlike the Euclidian definition of a unit as "that by virtue of which each of the things that exist is called one," among dialectical societies I would suggest the following: each of the things that exist is called two—*maparané*—a couple because it is necessarily formed by a pair of ones—*mitsi*—a lonely self. (Ferreira 2001: 91)[12]

Pierre Clastres (1989) generalizes this contrast in a chapter of his famous book *Society against the state*, entitled "Of the one without the many," referring specifically to the Guarani. Clastres argues that the negative value of the one contrasts not with the many but with the two or double. In his words: "Evil is the One. Good is not the many, it is the dual, both the one and its other" (Clastres 1989: 173). Clastres attributes this valorization to the pregnancy of an anti-identificatory principle among the Guarani, echoing concepts developed by other Americanist

---

11. Anthony Pickles (pers. comm., 2017) suggested the following mathematical translation: $2 : 1 :: x : x - (x-n)$.

12. D'Ambrosio (2015), in a foreword to Ferreira's book, emphasizes precisely the solitary character of the unit. Amaral (pers. comm., 2017) and Fausto (pers. comm., 2017) observed the same association among the Ingarikó (Carib) of Roraima and the Parakanã (Tupi-Guarani) of Pará, respectively.

authors to describe the region's peoples, among them the idea of "dualism in perpetual disequilibrium" formulated by Claude Lévi-Strauss (1991).

Many years earlier, Lévy-Bruhl ([1926] 1985) had noted the inversion in values attributed to quantities in his analysis of differences between "modern" and Native peoples. He suggests that while many Native systems ignore one and begin their numerical system with the number two ([1926] 1985: 192), among the moderns, informed by their monotheistic religions and monistic philosophies, one is the principle of good, order, perfection, and happiness, while two acquires the negative character of imperfection, the principle of evil, and disorder, preserved in diverse languages when they refer to duplicity and the double life (209).[13]

While quantities may still appear imbued with values in the religious universe, it is at school that definitive steps are taken to externalize the world, fully objectifying it in the sciences.[14] As a nonIndigenous lecturer said in 2015 when presenting set theory to his Indigenous students at university, seeking to answer their numerous uncertainties concerning the criteria for set exclusion: "In the case of sets, the membership rule depends on the set type. In the case of numbers, there is no identity crisis."

Not only did floating quantities become precise numbers: myths too and so-called traditional knowledge are, in intercultural teaching, made equivalent to science, not in the perspectivist mode of difference but in the relativist mode of the continuity and complementarity of knowledge,

---

13. For an exception to the negativity of the one, see Mimica (1988: 46) on the valorisation of oneness among the Iqwaye, who see totality qua indivisibility as positive (1988: 47). In his words: "Two—or more accurately, the idea of twoness or dyad in opposition to oneness—is the marked and derived category, whereas oneness is the universal and original ontological category in the Iqwaye view of the cosmos." Lloyd (pers. comm., 2017) notes a duality in Greek thought: although for them the one is not an *arithmos* (numbers will begin with two, according to Euclid's definition of *arithmos* as a multitude composed of units), Greeks also held that one is the principle of good. Also see Lévi-Strauss (1968: 303, 309) on the association between twenty and the person (fingers and toes) in Mexico and Central America and its connotation of plenitude.

14. See Lowie (1947: 331) on the mystical value of determined numbers in Greek thought and elsewhere, and their perpetuation until the seventeenth century. According to Lloyd (pers. comm., 2017) there are also lots of analogous examples in China.

indissociable from naturalist universalism (Strathern 2009). In the relativist school approach, myth becomes something in which the individual may believe or not, suggesting an idea of truth and self previously entirely alien to the Amerindians. As one Wari' man said to me, in Portuguese, while we were talking about the animal spirits that cause diseases: "Perhaps I'm disrespecting my culture a little, but I don't believe so." Another example was a student from the Tupari Indigenous group during a science class on the intercultural teacher training course. Contrasting the course material on the heliocentric system with the geocentric system of his people, he observed: "When we enter the school system we begin to believe that these things are true. . . . In relation to the solar system, I'm more inclined to believe that the Earth moves around the sun."

Conclusion

To conclude, I wish to show that the transformation analyzed here does not occur solely in the linear form that, for expositional reasons, I have emphasized here. Although both Christianity and schooling lead to significant transformations, the Wari' perspective, despite some significant limitations, remains present, not in the form of a mixture, as in syncretic models, but in the form of the alternation typical of the relationship of Amazonian peoples with alterity, including the alternation between human, animal, or shamanic perspectives (Vilaça 2015b, 2016: 12–21).

In school and Christian translations alike, as missionaries are already well aware, use of the Indigenous language is an important anticonventional instrument (see Rafael 1993; Orta 2004; Durston 2007; Hanks 2010; Vilaça 2016) and thus an enabler of alternations in perspectives (Wagner 1975: 52) or of invisible communication between clashing ontologies (see Strathern, this volume). An interesting case is the translation, made by missionaries with the help of Indigenous translators, of the verb *to love* in Portuguese (*amar*), which was rendered as "not-dislike," the only equivalent Wari' term. While not-dislike is indeed the same as love, the Wari' term makes clear that the starting point of relations is enmity, related to dislike, with love as something to be constructed by human agency. Kin are made out of others. This registers an important difference between the Christian and Wari' given worlds, which through translation remains present in their lived world, actualized in determined contexts and alternating with the positive meaning of Christian love.

Similarly, the translation of the number one as alone has a two-way effect, maintaining the moral and negative character of oneness. This contrasts with the positive Christian value and the amorality learned at school. It is worth noting too that while the Wari' have adopted Portuguese numbers in their day-to-day life, they still use the word alone to designate the number one (Everett and Kern 1997: 347–48).

To the Wari' experience in the alternation of perspectives we can add the fact that Christianity, in all its different guises, offers the peoples that it colonizes the figure of the devil, analogous to mythological tricksters. The latter destroy the conventionalizing creative process of the demiurges, bringing back chaos, multiplicity, and disorder. For many Christianized Native peoples, the devil has become a central component of the Christian experience, encompassing diverse pre-Christian practices and ideas, even when these acquire a negative value (see Meyer 1996, 1999, 2008; Kopenawa and Albert 2010: 492; Mosko 2010: 230; T. Leite 2013: 87–88). Among the Wari', the devil at first would resubjectify animals by entering their bodies and making them act like humans and predators in the old way. As their Christian experience deepened and the missionaries were successfully able to pass on the divine perspective of creation, the devil shifted from the animal universe to the universe of relations among the Wari' themselves, who began to attribute to him behaviors deemed immoral. Although this shift is important, in both cases the devil acts as a figure of destabilization, initially of the condition of humanity and later of brotherhood, since his agency causes the reemergence of the internal differences attributed to affinity, which people seek to eliminate in the Christian community (Vilaça 2011, 2015a).

Science, as we know, has its own demons, called cyborgs (Haraway 1991) or hybrids (Latour 1993) by anthropologists. And although carefully purified, these are quickly recognized by Indigenous people. I recall a physics class for the intercultural teacher training course in 2015, when the lecturer was explaining the laws of action and reaction. Demonstrating with his body, he said, "if I punch a wall, it punches me back." Responding to the laughter of the students, who were probably surprised by the animist aspect of physics, he asked: "Can a wall punch someone? Yes, if I punch it, it punches me back." The students carried on laughing.[15]

---

15. See Latour (2004: 17) for an alternative proposal for science, which rather than proceeding to generalizations and unifications, aims to produce more connections, which in turn produce more divergences, which modify more and more the ingredients that make up the multiverse. Hence, this is not a

I would also note that, as a particle physics researcher from CERN (Bediaga, pers. comm., 2016) observed, physics as taught at high-schools derives from the eighteenth century, but quantum physics could enable a completely different dialogue with Indigenous ontologies. We can take, for example, the idea of antimatter, something that, according to scientists, was present in the creation of the early universe but exists in minute quantities today. Would the Amerindians find it difficult to relate anti-matter to the forces that existed in the mythic times but are not available on Earth today unless activated by shamans, who do the same kind of work as the particle accelerator in Switzerland?[16] According to Ignacio Bediaga, from a strictly scientific point of view, our ideas about the primordial era of the universe are as good as any Indigenous theory, since they cannot be testified or refuted. I should add that the Amerindians might not agree with that, at least with respect to their own images of the primordial world, widely confirmed by their shamans.

And it is not just shamanism that has the potential to make connections. Various studies of Indigenous schools in Brazil show the reintroduction of a relational perspective in mathematical calculations like those performed by the Suyá/Kisêdjê and Juruna/Yudjá of the Upper Xingu studied by Ferreira (1997). They may include past debts in calculating present sums, leading to unexpected mathematical results.[17] Moreover, mimetism and repetition as traditional forms of learning (Taussig 1993; Lattas 1998) flourish in the value attributed to copying school material on the chalkboard (Cohn 2004; Weber 2006), rather than simply reading the content in books, as well as in the faithful reproduction of school rituals by students (Collet 2006).

Nonetheless, the diverse possibilities for constructing bridges between ontologies (Almeida 1999; Lloyd 2011, 2012, 2016, this volume) are explored in very different ways by Indigenous peoples, on the one hand, and by missionaries and teachers, on the other. The latter, imposing

---

science that provides an accurate vision of the world, given that the multiverse is not the unified universe of the Christian Creation.

16. See the same kind of association made by Viveiros de Castro in Sztutman (2008: 45). On the relation between myth and quantum physics, see Lévi-Strauss (2016: 77–78; see also 1991: 12–13).

17. See Lévi-Strauss (1968: 277–78) on the relation between these kinds of calculations and myth, which he calls "aberrant [numerical] derivations," such as when 5 + 2 equals 8; see Vilaça (2018). See also Viveiros de Castro (2012) on the geometrical and mathematical complexities of Amerindian dualism.

their viewpoint as real and true—albeit with the distinct interpretative possibilities introduced by the lecturers—are rooted firmly in the naturalist Christian ontology. Thus, in searching for similarities, they end up treating Indigenous diversity simply as layers covering the one natural world. The Wari', on the other hand, seek, within limits, especially in their translations, to keep sight of some of the differences separating themselves from us, maintaining these differences as an important part of their relation with ourselves.[18]

Acknowledgments

I thank all the participants of the workshop "Science in the Forest, Science in the Past" for their comments on a draft of this essay. I especially thank Geoffrey Lloyd for the extensive discussions that gave origin to this essay and for his careful reading of its successive versions. Early versions of this paper were presented at the Fourth Mexican Congress of Social Anthropology and Ethnology and as a seminar at the Universidad Autonoma de México in October 2016. My thanks to colleagues and students present for their comments and special thanks to Roger Magazine and Carlo Bonfiglioli for the respective invitations. Field research among the Wari' was funded by the program Cientista do Nosso Estado (Scientist in Our State) of the Fundação de Amparo à Pesquisa do Estado do Rio de Janeiro (FAPERJ); the programs Edital Universal (Universal Notice) and Produtividade em Pesquisa (Productivity in Research) of the Conselho Nacional de Desenvolvimento Científico e Tecnológico (CNPq); the John Simon Guggenheim Foundation; and the Wenner-Gren Foundation. I am grateful for the support of the academic staff from the Department of Intercultural Education at the Universidade de Rondônia (UNIR) and the teams from the Secretaria da Educação, Juventude e Esportes (SEDUC) of Rondônia. I dedicate this essay to the memory of my Wari' father, Paletó, who died while I was writing it.

References

Alexiades, Miguel. 1999. "Ethnobotany of the Ese Eja: Plants, health, and change in an Amazonian society." PhD diss., City University of New York.

---

18. On this kind of equivocation or misunderstanding, see Viveiros de Castro (2004a: 18–19) and Wagner (1975: 20).

Almeida, Mauro. B. 1999. "Guerras culturais e relativismo cultural." *Revista Brasileira de Ciências Sociais* 14 (41): 5–14.

Berlin, Brent. 1992. *Ethnobiological classification: Principles of categorization of plants and animals in traditional societies.* Princeton, NJ: Princeton University Press.

———. 2005. "Comments on Daniel Everett, 'Cultural constraints on grammar and cognition in Pirahã: Another look at the design features of human language.'" *Current Anthropology* 46 (4): 635–36.

Berlin, Brent, and Elois Ann Berlin. 1977. "Ethnobiology, subsistence and nutrition in a tropical forest society: The Aguaruna Jivaro." In *Studies in Aguaruna Jivaro ethnobiology*, Report no. 1. Berkeley: University of California Language-Behavior Research Laboratory.

Biersack, Aletta. 1982. "The logic of misplaced concreteness: Paiela body counting and the nature of the primitive mind." *American Anthropologist*, n.s., 84 (4): 811–29.

Cao OroWaje, Wem Cacami. 2015. *Saberes matemáticos do povo Cao OroWaje.* Department of Intercultural Education, University of Rondônia (UNIR).

Carneiro da Cunha, Manuela. 2012. "Questões suscitadas pelo conhecimento tradicional." *Revista de Antropologia* 55 (1): 439–64.

Carrier, Achsah. 1981. "Counting and calculation on Ponam Island." *Journal of the Polynesian Society* 90 (4): 465–79.

Clastres, Pierre. 1989. *Society against the state.* Translated by Robert Hurley. New York: Zone Books.

Cohn, Clarice. 2004. "Os processos próprios de ensino e aprendizagem e a criança indígena." In *Cadernos de Educação Escolar Indígena*, 94–111. Barra do Bugres: UNEMAT.

Collet, Celia. 2006. "Rituais da civilização, rituais da cultura: a escola entre os Bakairi." PhD diss., PPGAS-Museu Nacional, Universidade Federal do Rio de Janeiro.

D'Ambrosio, Ubiratan. 2015. "Foreword." In *Mapping time, space and the body: Indigenous knowledge and mathematical thinking in Brazil*, by Mariana K. L. Ferreira, xi–xiv. Rotterdam: Sense Publishers.

Descola, Philippe. 1986. *La nature domestique: Symbolisme et praxis dans l'écologie des Achuar.* Paris: Maison des Sciences de L'Homme.

———. 2005. *Par delà nature et culture.* Paris: Gallimard.

Descola, Philippe, and Gísli Pálsson, eds. 1996. *Nature and society: Anthropological perspectives.* London: Routledge.

Dixon, Robert M. W. 2002. *Australian languages*. Cambridge: Cambridge University Press.

Durston, Alan. 2007. *Pastoral Quechua: The history of Christian translation in colonial Peru, 1550–1650.* Notre Dame, IN: University of Notre Dame Press.

Dwyer, Peter. 1996. "The invention of nature." In *Redefining nature: Ecology, culture and domestication,* edited by Roy Ellen and Katsuyoshi Fukui, 157–86. Oxford: Berg.

Ellen, Roy F. 1996. "The cognitive geometry of nature: A contextual approach." In *Nature and society: Anthropological perspectives,* edited by Philippe Descola and Gísli Pálsson, 103–23. London: Routledge.

Ellen, Roy, and Katsuyoshi Fukui, eds. 1996. "Introduction." *Redefining nature: Ecology, culture and domestication,* 1–36. Oxford: Berg.

Everett, Daniel. 2005. "Cultural constraints on grammar and cognition in Pirahã: Another look at the design features of human language." *Current Anthropology* 46 (4): 621–46.

Everett, Daniel L., and Barbara Kern. 1997. *Wari': The Pacaas Novos language of western Brazil.* New York: Routledge.

Ferreira, Mariana Kawall Leal. 1997. "When 1 + 1 ≠ 2. Making mathematics in central Brazil." *American Ethnologist* 24 (1): 132–47.

———. 2001. "People of my side, people of the other side: Socionumerical systems in central Brazil." *ZDM—International Reviews on Mathematical Education* 33 (3): 89–94.

———. 2015. *Mapping time, space and the body: Indigenous knowledge and mathematical thinking in Brazil.* Rotterdam: Sense Publishers.

Foucault, Michel. 1990. *The use of pleasure.* Translated by Robert Hurley. New York: Vintage Books.

———. 1997. *Ethics: Subjectivity and truth.* Vol. 1. New York: New Press.

Frank, Michael, Daniel Everett, Evelina Fedorenko, and Edward Gibson. 2008. "Number as a cognitive technology: Evidence from Pirahã language and cognition." *Cognition* 108: 819–24.

Gordon, Peter. 2004. "Numerical cognition without words: Evidence from Amazonia." *Science* 306 (5695): 496–99.

Haese, Érika. 2015. "Programa de filosofia para magistério indígena em Rondônia." *Projeto Açaí III. Módulo I.* Unpublished manuscript, January 12–February 14, 2015.

Hanks, William. 2010. *Converting words: Maya in the age of the cross.* Berkeley: University of California Press.

Haraway, Donna. 1991. "A cyborg manifesto: Science, technology, and socialist-feminism in the late twentieth century." In *Simians, cyborgs and women: The reinvention of nature,* 149–82. New York: Routledge.

Howell, Signe. 1996. "Nature in culture or culture in nature? Chewong ideas of 'humans' and other species." In *Nature and society: Anthropological perspectives,* edited by Philippe Descola and Gísli Pálsson, 127–44. London: Routledge.

Hugh-Jones, Stephen. 2012. "Escrita na pedra, escrita no papel." In *Rotas de criação e transformação: Narrativas de origem dos povos indígenas do rio Negro,* edited by Geraldo Andrello, 138–67. São Gabriel da Cachoeira: FOIRN/ISA. Translated as Hugh-Jones, Stephen. 2016. "Writing on stone; Writing on paper: Myth, history and memory in NW Amazonia." *History and Anthropology* 27 (2): 154–82.

Ingold, Tim. 2000. "Culture, nature, environment: Steps to an ecology of life." In *The perception of the environment: Essays on livelihood, dwelling and skill.* London: Routledge.

Jackson, Jean. 1995. "Preserving Indian culture: Shaman schools and ethno-education in the Vaupés, Colombia." *Cultural Anthropology* 10 (3): 302–29.

Kopenawa, Davi, and Bruce Albert. 2010. *La chute du ciel: Paroles d'un chaman yanomami.* Paris: Plon.

Lattas, Andrew. 1998. *Cultures of secrecy: Reinventing race in Bush Kaliai cargo cults.* Madison: University of Wisconsin Press.

Latour, Bruno. 1993. *We have never been modern.* Translated by Catherine Porter. Cambridge, MA: Harvard University Press.

———. 2004. "How to talk about the body? The normative dimension of science studies." *Body and Society* 10 (2–3): 205–29.

Latour, Bruno, and Steve Woolgar. 1979. *Laboratory life: The construction of scientific facts.* Beverly Hills, CA: Sage Publications.

———. 1997. *"A vida de laboratório: A produção dos fatos científicos."* Translated from the French edition by Angela R. Vianna. Rio de Janeiro: Relume-Dumará.

Lave, Jean. 1988. *Cognition in practice: Mind, mathematics and culture in everyday life.* Cambridge: Cambridge University Press.

Leite, Kécio, ed. 2013. *Teia de conhecimentos interculturais.* Departamento de Educação Intercultural, Campus de Ji-Paraná, Universidade Federal de Rondônia (UNIR).

Leite, Tainah. 2013. "Imagens da humanidade: Metamorfose e moralidade na mitologia Yanomami." *Mana: Estudos de Antropologia Social* 19 (1): 69–97.

Lenoble, Robert. 1969. *Esquisse d'une histoire de l'idée de nature.* Paris: Albin Michel.

Levinson, Stephen. 2005. "Comments on Daniel Everett, 'Cultural constraints on grammar and cognition in Pirahã: Another look at the design features of human language.'" *Current Anthropology* 46 (4): 637–38.

Lévi-Strauss, Claude. 1962. *La pensée sauvage.* Paris: Plon.

———. 1968. *Mythologiques: L'origine des manières de table.* Paris: Plon.

———. 1991. *Histoire de lynx.* Paris: Plon.

———. 2016. *We are all cannibals.* Translated by Jane Marie Todd. New York: Columbia University Press.

Lévi-Strauss, Claude, Barbara Glowczewski-Barker, Michel Izard, Elisabeth Copet-Rougier, Philippe Descola, and Bernard Saladin d'Anglure. 1991. "Débat: Les sociétés exotiques ont-elles des paysages?" *Études Rurales* (121–24): 151–58.

Lévy-Bruhl, Lucien. (1926) 1985. *How natives think.* Princeton, NJ: Princeton University Press.

———. 1952. "A letter to E. E. Evans-Pritchard." *British Journal of Sociology* 3 (2): 117–23.

Lloyd, G. E. R. 1966. *Polarity and analogy: Two types of argumentation in early Greek thought.* Cambridge: Cambridge University Press.

———. 2011. "Humanity between gods and beasts? Ontologies in question." *Journal of the Royal Anthropological Institute* 17 (4): 829–45.

———. 2012. *Being, humanity and understanding.* Oxford: Oxford University Press.

———. 2016. "Praying and preying: Book review." Review of *Praying and preying: Christianity in indigenous Amazonia* by Aparecida Vilaça. *Anthrocybib* (blog), University of Edinburgh, October 24, 2016. https://www.blogs.hss.ed.ac.uk/anthrocybib/2016/10/24/praying-preying-book-review/.

Lowie, Robert H. 1947. *An introduction to cultural anthropology.* New York: Rinehart & Company.

Luciano, Gersem José dos Santos. 2014. *Educação para manejo do mundo: Entre a escola ideal e a escola real no Alto Rio Negro*. Rio de Janeiro: Contracapa.

McIlwain, Trevor. 2003. *Alicerces Firmes: Da criação até Cristo*. 2nd ed. Translated by Adriana Lima Colaço Melgarejo. Anápolis: Missão Novas Tribos do Brasil.

Meyer, Birgit. 1996. "Modernity and enchantment: The image of the devil in popular African Christianity." In *Conversion to modernities: The globalization of Christianity*, edited by Peter van der Veer, 199–230. London and New York: Routledge.

———. 1999. *Translating the devil: Religion and modernity among the Ewe in Ghana*. London: Edinburgh University Press, for the International African Institute.

———. 2008. "Le diable." *Terrain* 50: 4–13.

Mimica, Jadran. 1988. *Intimations of infinity: The cultural meanings of the Iqwaye counting and number system*. Oxford: Berg.

Mosko, Mark. 2010. "Partible penitents: Dividual personhood and Christian practice in Melanesia and the West." *Journal of the Royal Anthropological Institute*, n.s., 16 (2): 215–40.

OroAt, Zebedeu. 2013. "Contagem do povo OroAt." In *Teia de conhecimentos interculturais*, edited by Kécio Leite, 171–72. Departamento de Educação Intercultural, Campus de Ji-Paraná, Universidade Federal de Rondônia (UNIR).

OroNao', Mauricio. 2013. "Forma tradicional de contagem do povo OroNao.'" In *Teia de conhecimentos interculturais*, edited by Kécio Leite, 119–20. Departamento de Educação Intercultural, Campus de Ji-Paraná, Universidade Federal de Rondônia (UNIR).

Orta, Andrew. 2004. *Catechizing culture: Missionaries, Aymara, and the "New Evangelization."* New York: Columbia University Press.

Pawley, Anderson. 2005. "Comments on Daniel Everett, 'Cultural constraints on grammar and cognition in Pirahã: Another look at the design features of human language.'" *Current Anthropology* 46 (4): 638–39.

Pica, Pierre, Cathy Lemer, Véronique Izard, Stanislas Dehaene. 2004. "Exact and approximate arithmetic in an Amazonian Indigene group." *Science* 306 (5695): 499–503.

Pouillon, Jean. 1993. *Le cru et le su*. Paris: Seuil.

Rafael, Vicente. 1993. *Contracting colonialism: Translation and Christian conversion in Tagalog society under early Spanish rule.* Durham, NC: Duke University Press.

Robbins, Joel. 2004. *Becoming sinners: Christianity and moral torment in a Papua New Guinea Society.* Berkeley: University of California Press.

Robbins, Joel, Bambi Schieffelin, and Aparecida Vilaça. 2014. "Evangelical conversion and the transformation of the self in Amazonia and Melanesia: Christianity and new forms of anthropological comparison." *Comparative Studies in Society and History* 56 (3): 1–32.

Rossi, Paolo. 2001. *The birth of modern science (making of Europe).* Translated by Cynthia De Nava Ipsen. Oxford: Blackwell.

Seeger, Anthony. 1981. *Nature and society in central Brazil: The Suya Indians of Mato Grosso.* Cambridge, MA: Harvard University Press.

Strathern, Marilyn. 1980. "No nature, no culture: The Hagen case." In *Nature, culture and gender,* edited by Carol MacCormack and Marilyn Strathern, 174–222. Cambridge: Cambridge University Press.

———. 2009. "Using bodies to communicate." In *Social bodies,* edited by Helen Lambert and Maryon McDonald, 148–70. New York: Berghahn.

Sztutman, Renato, ed. 2008. *Eduardo Viveiros de Castro—Encontros.* Rio de Janeiro: Azougue Editorial.

Taussig, Michael. 1993. *Mimesis and alterity: A particular history of the senses.* New York: Routledge.

Urton, Gary. 1997. *The social life of numbers: A Quechua ontology of numbers and philosophy of arithmetic.* Austin: University of Texas Press.

Vernant, Jean-Pierre. 1983. *Myth and thought among the Greeks.* London: Routledge and Kegan Paul.

Verran, Helen. 2001. *Science and an African logic.* Chicago: University of Chicago Press.

Vilaça, Aparecida. (1992) 2017. *Comendo como gente. Formas do canibalismo wari'.* 2nd ed. Rio de Janeiro: Mauad.

———. 1996. "Cristãos sem fé: Alguns aspectos da conversão dos Wari' (Pakaa Nova)." *Mana: Estudos de Antropologia Social* 2 (1): 109–37.

———. 1997. "Christians without faith: Some aspects of the conversion of the Wari' (Pakaa Nova)." *Ethnos* 62 (1–2): 91–115.

———. 1999. "Devenir Autre: Chamanisme et contact interethnique en Amazonie brésilienne." *Journal de la Société des Américanistes* 85: 239–60.

————. 2000. "O que significa tornar-se Outro? Xamanismo e contato interétnico na Amazônia." *Revista Brasileira de Ciências Sociais* 15 (44): 56–72.

————. 2006. *Quem somos nós: Os Wari' encontram os brancos.* Rio de Janeiro: Editora da UFRJ.

————. 2009. "Conversion, predation and perspective." In *Native Christians: Modes and effects of Christianity among indigenous peoples of the Americas,* edited by Aparecida Vilaça and Robin Wright, 147–66. Burlington, UK: Ashgate.

————. 2010. *Strange enemies: Indigenous agency and scenes of encounter in Amazonia.* Durham, NC: Duke University Press.

————. 2011. "Dividuality in Amazonia: God, the devil and the constitution of personhood in Wari' Christianity." *Journal of the Royal Anthropological Institute,* n.s., 17 (2): 243–62.

————. 2013. "Reconfiguring humanity in Amazonia: Christianity and change." In *Companion to the anthropology of religion,* edited by Michael Lambek and Janice Boddy, 363–86. Oxford: Wiley/Blackwell.

————. 2014. "Culture and self: The different 'gifts' Amerindians receive from Catholics and Evangelicals." *Current Anthropology* 55 (S10): S322–32.

————. 2015a. "Dividualism and individualism in Indigenous Christianity: A debate seen from Amazonia." *HAU: Journal of Ethnographic Theory* 5 (1): 45–73.

————. 2015b. "Do animists become naturalists when converting to Christianity? Discussing an ontological turn." *Cambridge Journal of Anthropology* 33 (2): 3–19.

————. 2016. *Praying and preying: Christianity in indigenous Amazonia.* Berkeley: University of California Press.

————. 2018. "'The devil and the secret life of numbers': Translations and transformation in Amazonia." *HAU: Journal of Ethnographic Theory* 8 (1–2): 6–19.

Viveiros de Castro, Eduardo. 1998. "Cosmological deixis and Amerindian perspectivism." *Journal of the Royal Anthropological Institute* 4 (3): 469–88.

————. 2004a. "Perspectival anthropology and the method of controlled equivocation." *Tipití: Journal of the Society for the Anthropology of Lowland South America* 2 (1): 3–22.

———. 2004b. "Exchanging perspectives: The transformation of objects into subjects in Amerindian ontologies." *Common Knowledge* 10 (3): 463–84.

———. 2012. "Radical dualism: A meta-phantasy on the square root of dual organizations; or, A savage homage to Lévi-Strauss." *Documenta* (13), *100 Notes—100 Thoughts / 100 Notizen—100 Gedanken*, no. 056. Berlin: Hatje Cantz. Published in conjunction with the *Documenta (13)* exhibition in Kassel, Germany.

Wagner, Roy. 1975. *The invention of culture.* Englewood Cliffs, NJ: Prentice-Hall.

———. 1977. "Scientific and Indigenous Papuan conceptualizations of the innate: A semiotic critique of the ecological perspective." In *Subsistence and survival: Rural ecology in the Pacific*, edited by Timothy P. Bayliss-Smith and Richard G. Feachem, 385–410. London: Academic Press.

Weber, Ingrid. 2006. *Um copo de cultura: Os Huni Kuin (Kaxinawá) do rio Humaitá e a escola.* Rio Branco: Edufac.

Wierzbicka, Anna. 2005. "Comments on Daniel Everett, 'Cultural constraints on grammar and cognition in Pirahã: Another look at the design features of human language.'" *Current Anthropology* 46 (4): 641.

CHAPTER THREE

A Clash of Ontologies? Time, Law, and Science in Papua New Guinea

Marilyn Strathern

Whether in Europe or the Pacific, the present imagined in terms of future becomings has recently engaged anthropologists interested in time. In Papua New Guinea (PNG) we encounter this in the aspirations of present-day legal scholars hoping to revitalize the future that was imagined at the time of independence in 1975, more than forty years ago. Forty years prior to that, the first Australian prospectors walked into the PNG Highlands, little knowing they were going to bring with them a "new time" and a "new law" for everyone. In fact, the locals probably knew it before the prospectors did. As development and educational projects were rolled out, enabled by official and unofficial elements of what seemed a self-evident judicial system, futures were promised and futures were imagined. From one point of view, in terms of their ideas about the future, the aspirations of colonizers and colonized alike could be construed as mutual. From another point of view, they could be construed as a veritable clash of ontologies. The period following pacification has led to many questions about intelligibility and translation; it also puts forward some less obvious questions about the recurrence of other new times before and since then. The crucial question is in what kind of "present" are people living? Thus, one of the temporalities at issue in "new" and "old" times concerns the evolution or regeneration of life and lives, and affects the ways in which societal transformation is conceived. An avenue of exploration encouraged by the editors prompts a further question about the extent to which natural science—that is, certain scientific precepts of naturalism—were embedded in the colonizer's law. The question enlarges the cosmological fields we might wish to consider, concluding with some highly speculative remarks on this score.

*　　*　　*

In 2010, PNG's Constitutional and Law Reform Commission (CLRC), set up at about the time of the country's independence in 1975, reopened an initiative begun ten years earlier with the passing of the Underlying Law Act (2000). That, in turn, had been a response to an aspiration of PNG's founding constitution. In addition to statute law, English common law had been a principal source of judicial reasoning; Indigenous customs were recognized, but as points of fact, pleaded as evidence to inform judgments, not as justiciable points of law. The founders of the constitution envisaged a future where custom would itself be regarded as just such a source. It was twenty-five years, however, before legislation was on the statute books to encourage the courts to have recourse to "customary law," as the Act called it, with precedence over common law. The lapse in time—1975 to 2000—meant that the courts had years of established protocols to overcome and, although they did not ignore the encouragement, they made little headway. The further lapse—between 2000 and 2010—compelled the CLRC to reopen debate, through a conference, journal, and seminar series. Debate was still active in 2015, one of the perspectives from which I write.

There seems nothing of particular remark here. The relationship between law and custom dogged "the imposition of law" (Burman and Harrell-Bond 1979) and its aftermath in many newly independent countries of the twentieth century, and delays occur for many reasons. More positively, one might interpret the reluctance of the courts as their wanting to look forward from—rather than back into—the country's traditional past. Yet this was not the impression that a number of elite trainee lawyers gave the anthropologist Melissa Demian (2015: 95–97) about their own lack of interest in customary law. She describes them harboring a chronic disinclination to think about custom as part of their work. The cause seems to have been that, far from custom being part of a past to be left behind, they had a very lively sense of its contemporary force.[1] The vernacular concept of custom (Neo-Melanesian [NM] *kastom*), known rather misleadingly by an adopted English term for past traditions, connotes the way people's distinctive practices are grounded in specific places, with an emphasis on their present salience and openness to innovation. As one lawyer expostulated, "it's just people's lives" (Demian 2015: 98). Above all, *kastom* can acquire resonance as a vehicle for power, drawn from that attachment to place; the law students were not going to meddle in other people's sources of power.

If invoking *kastom* is not about conserving past practices for the sake of tradition, no more, may we suspect, is recourse to the foundational constitution necessarily a backward look. What, then, makes a backward look? It is a certain kind of time that keeps the past behind one, and keeps it in place that way. So was something else happening in the Papua New Guinea in 2015? I raise some questions about "models of time" (Robbins 2001) in order to ask whether, of all the clashes that accompanied the colonization of PNG, it is helpful to recognize a clash of ontologies.[2] It may then be apposite to consider the role of scientific thinking in the form the clash took. Recent discussion within anthropology provides some guidance.

Presentism

Unpredictability, indeterminacy, a heterogeneous multiplicity of temporal relations: these are features that Felix Ringel (2016) sees in the way residents of an East German city deal with the postindustrial, postsocialist decay all around them. Finding the concept of culture too mired in its connotations of an identifiable moment that can be pinned down and therefore already in the past, he seeks another approach to

---

1. This is not the place to engage with anthropological debate over Pacific Island custom in the form of *kastom* (Demian [2015: 93–94] offers a brief introduction), but one might remark that differentiations between "custom" and *kastom* often chime with Carneiro da Cunha's (2009) distinction of "culture" and culture.

2. One cannot touch on the topic without some remark as to the vastness of the anthropological literature (e.g., Munn 1992; Scaglion 1999: 211). It should be clear, however, that this is not an essay "about" time; rather, it inquires into the making of time for the insights that they may or may not yield into the "clash of ontologies."

their predicaments. To "substitute, for the perspective from the past, that of the future" is to follow "informants' strategy for dealing with the changes at hand" (2016: 401). This allows the ethnographer to attend to relations as they exist in a field site's present, which will hold a multiplicity of temporal references. "I echo my informants' surprise," Ringel (2016: 392) says, "about situations in which 'objects'. . . take on unexpected temporal existence." He declares his approach to time to be nonontological: temporality is defined not as a metaphysical property of an epoch or a people; rather, temporal matters are a question of knowledge and politics—that is, epistemic and social phenomena.

> A presentist approach thus scrutinizes how far we get analytically when *not* reading the present and its relations to the future through their presumed links to the past, but in their own right. . . [and] since rhythms can be disturbed, houses unexpectedly demolished and social relations dissolved, it is the work that goes into upholding certain temporal orders, structures, rhythms and endurances that should catch our attention. (Ringel 2016: 392–93)

He thus wishes to derive a methodological stance ("presentism") from the need to take people as they are, always in the present, including the past that is part of it, and the future as it is imagined. Itself nonontological, as an approach it presumably can deal with any ontology.

Ringel singles out another work that criticizes past-fixated analyses: a collection of essays also steered by an analytical objection to the concept of culture, with a similar plea that anthropologists should attend to people's futures and thus to the horizon of their present. This would make the ethnographic reference point current aspirations and imaginings. So while he is not uninterested in the instituted modes by which people act (culture in a weak sense), Will Rollason (2014b) argues that anthropologists create problems for themselves by making culture their principal reference point (in a strong sense), and thus inevitably evaluating present circumstances with reference to the past. Revealing apparently innovative action to be transformations of cultural tradition can get us only so far; even Indigenous accounts of time and futurity are of little help because they will simply index the culture from which they come. After Hirokazu Miyazaki (2004), he defines the future "as a stance towards the world" (Rollason 2014b: 10), and primarily a methodological one on the anthropologist's part.

His own essay concerns a mid-twentieth-century millenarianist, Buliga (from the Louisiade Archipelago), who had prophesized that once the colonialists had been killed, Whites would become Black and the Blacks would become White.[3] This was exactly what Buliga accomplished after he had been captured; sentenced to death by the Australian administration, he used the White man's method of punishment to kill himself by hanging. Rollason (2014a) suggests that this was a co-option of White state power, and constituted an enactment of the future. It was a future that drew on Indigenous ideas about shame and personhood, which understood hanging in a cell as a public act, as well as on what hanging as a colonial practice conveyed to people: Buliga's actions were coherent in terms of local culture in a weak sense. However, Rollason argues that anthropologists have to transcend cultural interpretation, and to make that the core of analysis would be to ignore what Buliga was doing—acting as someone other than himself (an imaginary White self that was enacting the state's sovereign violence on his Black body). "While the terms on which this action might be. . . comprehensible can be drawn from a cultural tradition, it is clear that the form of the past is wholly inadequate to account for this act": there is a conflict between "the backwards prospecting of anthropological interpretation and the forward impetus of the sense of the act" (2014a: 62). Buliga's own interest, he surmises, was in self-transformation.

So might we conclude that it is not the concept of culture that is the problem so much as anthropology's familiar habit of using cultural reasoning—which can only be derived from the past—to attach to people's own visions? To put it another way, there is something about the conceptions of *culture* and *the past* in these accounts that themselves need explaining. Ringel and Rollason both object to an anthropological propensity to find culture in the past, despite the fact that anthropologists often pitch themselves against other scholars in insisting on culture as primarily a matter of what people do, an echo of all the objections raised to the English language connotation of custom as past tradition. Nonetheless, the general propensity endures. Arguably, it entails or reveals something of a disposition toward time, or rather a way of making time; we might even consider it of ontological import. That question is open at this point.

---

3. All place names in this essay refer to locations in Papua New Guinea, unless otherwise noted.

After Pacification

It was some forty years before independence when the first Australian patrols entered the Mount Hagen area of the PNG Highlands. Administrative development was interrupted by the Second World War; *kiaps* (NM for patrol officers and representatives of the administration) reestablished control afterwards, not least through embarking on development projects. By the early 1960s, people were familiar with cash cropping, medical services, and (then newly established) elected local government councils. Their present was full of many new things, the things of "now" as opposed to those of "before." Especially in the mouths of local dignitaries, or big men as the vernacular has it, a significant marker of "now" was pacification.

A corollary of pacification was law (NM *lo*). The term was understood to cover specific rules (such as procedures of dispute settlement); the kind of peaceable conduct that made someone a "man of *lo*" ("I was a fighting man but now I am old—you are all new men here, and a good *lo* has come up and now we sit down on top of it"); and a way of life that had transformed everything ("White men have come, *lo* has come up and the kiap shows us the road to business") (quotations from M. Strathern 1972: 130–34). However, the implicit contrasts are not simply with ancestral practices. The term also discriminated between more recent temporal horizons ("*Luluai* and *tultul* were strong, and the kiap told them to beat people, but now *lo* has come up we can't do this and people humbug")[4] with the expectation of new *lo* to come ("When *lo* [the future] finally comes up and our children are all at school, we shall be ruined. . . . [For] what will happen when *lo* comes and we have to buy everything with money?") (1972: 134).

With what seemed a remarkable degree of accord, Hagen people had by the 1960s endorsed the message of the kiaps. Indeed, the superior killing capacity of the kiaps and their armed constabulary aside, pacification would have had a much rougher passage had there not been general

---

4. *Luluai* and *tultul* were headmen appointed by the administration. I use "headman" (more appropriate to colonial Africa) to refer generally to *luluai* and *tultul*, as well as their predecessors called *bosboi*. One such headman, Ongka, recording how he was given orders to stop fighting, said, "So I began settling cases and if anyone refused [to attend], the kiap put him in jail" (A. Strathern 1979: 12). Reactions to the introduced legal system may have been very different elsewhere in PNG (see, for example, Scaglion 1985 on the Abelam).

acceptance of kiap law, the recognition that a "new time" had arrived. Across PNG, local men, often aspiring big men, were appointed to keep order, also translated as *lo*. However, remarkable in the Hagen case and elsewhere in the Highlands was the speed with which men seemingly assisted the process of pacification by moving into the position of dispute-settlers. Just as kiaps on patrol would act as magistrates, such men held what they also called courts (*kot*). With nothing less than enthusiasm, people took their grievances to such courts, attended them, turned up as witnesses, and so forth. The dispute-settlers borrowed protocols from official proceedings, regarded themselves as part of the judicial system, and above all spoke of the new *lo* that had come with the Australians.

The imitation of Whites that is so widely reported of "first contact" situations, Aparecida Vilaça (2016: 71–73) arrestingly turns into an understanding of translation through embodiment for the Amazonian Wari'. Take Andrew Lattas's (1998) study of Kaliai cargo cults (New Britain) and their transformative potential; what was copied from the Whites, Vilaça notes, was both their body postures and etiquette and their bureaucratic structures. True also of Hagen, I focus on the apparent accord that sustained the peace for many years, despite—or because of—the imaginative ferocity with which some appointed headmen initially meted out punishments. Here translation was, we might say, through modes of action that demonstrated effectiveness, the capacity for drawing power to oneself.[5]

Dispute-settlers did not have at their disposal the sanctions of the official judicial system, apart from appealing to that system itself, and so drew on already existing practices, notably compensation for injury. It would seem that the administration's message had gone home. *Lo* captured a general sense that a new time had arrived, or was on its way, so that one could speak of cash cropping (coffee) as following the law of business.[6] The kiaps' explicit vision for the future, instigated through people listening to them and obeying the law, embraced commerce, business,

---

5. I keep the term "translation" although, in the spirit of Vilaça's analysis of missionary attempts to translate the words of the Bible, for the circumstances relevant here it might be appropriate to introduce a substantive such as "re-enactment" or "remediation."

6. On the present being seen as the "time of law," see, for example, Hirsch (2004) on the Fuyuge-speakers of highlands Papua, who were clear that White men had put law into their heads—a matter of how to behave and what assets to command.

roads, hospitals, schools, and so forth. You could see what they meant in the trade stores cropping up along the roads on which locals labored one day a week. It was a promissory horizon, full of aspirations that Whites and indigenes alike seemed to share.

It is hard to believe now, but in that present the promises made no mention of independence. In the mid-1960s some kiaps even said such a prospect was a hundred years away. So much had to be done in terms of education, instilling proper practices, introducing economic goals, and so forth—trade stores with corrugated iron roofs were just the beginnings. In this context we might understand the official reaction to the unofficial courts. It was inconceivable to regard either the *kot* or the headmen as part of the judicial system. Justice was what the kiaps dispensed on their patrols and they often stressed the technical illegality of the courts (*kot*). A political education talk broadcast over Hagen radio in 1970 was explicit: "We can't take the law into our own hands."[7] More benignly, the courts so-called were at best informal arenas for mediation, tolerated as vehicles for keeping the local peace, dealing with minor conflicts, while major issues—such as homicide—would automatically go to the official courts. In the administration's view, Papua New Guineans were still at a very simple stage in their unfolding progress and much had to change. Hence one had to urge them on and talk about development. Above all, there could be no return to the past that was not a reversion to savagery—that would be turning their backs on the future.

Where did Hageners' enthusiasm for the law come from? The Australians could envisage what was ahead—orderly classrooms, effective hospitals, commercial plantations. This was hardly on the Hagen horizon. But what evidently loomed large in the Hagen present, and it has been reported time and again from Papua New Guineans' perceptions of Whites, was the power the kiaps dispensed, including the effectiveness of their punishments. This power was a particular challenge for competitively minded big men (how to access it). What the kiaps saw as people taking the law into their own hands, the dispute-settlers—and no locals really challenged them—saw as forging direct links with the official system, or rather with its embodiment in the persons of patrol

---

7. The speech was in NM, where "we" is literally "you and I" (plural) (*yumi*). But as a former headman observed, "the kiap hears courts, has words to say, lays down laws, instructs people, and that is exactly what I used to do." (This is not to overlook the stories of the fear that the appointed headmen initially instilled in the local population through their brutal methods.)

officers, district officers, and when they had heard of them, magistrates and judges. Person to person. Dispute-settlers translated their mandate as a chain of command; they had explicitly been told by the kiaps to hear courts.[8] The new time did not just happen—it had to be made, which is what they and the kiaps were (both) doing.

Enthusiasm dissolved somewhat in the 1970s. Major confrontations erupted into violence, with episodes of all-out war. Two features of this overt violence, which in Hagen lasted for a couple of decades before and after independence, are germane. First, many incipient conflicts were throughout this period kept in check by the still flourishing *kot*, replaced after independence by the introduction of official Village Courts. Second, those conflicts now leading to war were in large part an outcome of the expansion of regional horizons, through unaccustomed coalitions of groups into administrative units or the inadvertent homicides of vehicular traffic, encouraged by the amount of cash in the area and spectacular prospects of huge compensation payments.[9] Needless to say, the administration—and growing urban elite—regarded warfare as "tribal fighting," a reversion to a traditional past. One view in Hagen was that the resumption of warfare sprang from growing unrest over the official courts. Disappointingly, in their dealings with homicide, judges appeared to attend to petty issues (such as who dealt this or that blow), bypassing the crucial political implications of the causes or reasons behind particular actions. In these respects, the new law had failed to bring what it promised.

What are we to make of that initial accord, then, when people enthusiastically "tried out" the law, agreeing to be pacified to see what law would bring? And what do we make of the very different perceptions of the judicial system, Australian and Hagen, on which it seemed to

8. Kiaps would no doubt have regarded them as words put into their mouths; while some Hagen men appeared to be recalling specific conversations, a general exhortation to keep the law interpreted as a special message for dispute-settlers could well be rendered linguistically in terms of direct speech.

9. Maclean (1998) suggests that pacification failed through the kiaps' misreading of the convertibility of warfare, talk, and gift exchange (see below), and thus of the convertibility of offences into peaceful compensation procedures; quoted in Demian (2016: 25). Demian gives an accomplished reprise of this situation, and underlines the kiaps' own mimetic experiment in encouraging compensation, "doing what they thought Highlanders were doing" (2016: 26).

be based? We can understand these different perceptions as a clash of cultures or a clash of social systems, except that that the encounters that took place in Hagen at pacification did not simply contain many accommodations, they also generated seemingly mutual aspirations for peace and prosperity. And for all the violence that followed, and the subtler forms of attack at district or (later) provincial level through bribery, misinformation, and so forth, there was no resistance to the government as such.[10] Nor was *kastom* objectified as an entity around which to take forceful action (as in some parts of Papua New Guinea). Yet we witness a divergence: where the kiaps thought the dispute-settlers were usurping the law, the latter thought they were following it. When Hageners did indeed take the law into their own hands, bypassing the official courts through violent reprisals for violent acts, kiaps saw a reversion to primitive custom.

This could be taken as an obvious example of cultures being mixed bags of diverse possibilities or of social systems endorsing values differentially played out. Some things clash, and some things don't, a conclusion similar to one that, from the perspective of 2015, has been long voiced by the PNG judiciary: dealing with customary law is a matter of deciding which customs are suitable for a modern legal system and which are not. In any event, people are bound to see past one another. Meanwhile, life goes on. But suppose we were as interested in the mutual understandings as the misunderstandings. Can we in this case account for the accord as well as the disruption of it? I think we can, provided we see the apparent *similarities* as well as the differences as the outcomes of a deep divergence. In many respects the divergence was simply too radical to articulate.

A Clash of Ontologies?

It is no surprise that in the context of this volume, one might want to ask whether such a divergence had ontological import. Perhaps what

10. People tried out alternative routes to power—for example, sporadic cargo cult–like activity—but that did not involve attacks on government installations, though the Australians might see them as attacks on their institutions. "Power" here is not an analytic: it refers to an Indigenous notion entailing both strength and the capacity to have influence or effect on all kinds of others.

differentiates an ontological clash from a cultural clash lies in the nature of the evidence for it. It is not necessarily visible (Vilaça 2016: 118–20), either to those involved or to the anthropologist, whose account of ontological mismatch is likely to be at a tangent to overt perceptions of conflict. Or at least ontology cannot be visible in the way culture is (or else it is "culture"!). Here, I recall Manuela Carneiro da Cunha's (2009) description of how anthropologists move between two senses of culture. While they might think they are talking about culture as the coherence of an internal logic (Rollason's culture in a weak sense), to imagine a clash of cultures is to endorse an externalized, interethnic logic (invoking marked "cultures"). Ontological divergence is not going to look like a cultural—or indeed social—clash, where the clash is obvious. It may not even look like a "clash" at all.

Consider the agreements and disagreements of the 1960s. Taking the vantage point of people—Hageners and Australians alike—acting from the horizon of the present, I suggest that their presentism, so to speak, implies different approaches to the sequencing of events. The kiaps, for example, seem to have been acting out some specific assumptions about time.

In Ringel's East German city, Hoyerswerda, anything can change (it is what endures that should catch our attention, he says). One way people deal with unpredictability lies in the idea that they have been living through successive epochs, and could do so again. Not far behind all the smaller untoward events that shake up the contours of the present horizon lie the upheavals of larger epochal changes, notably de-industrialization and the vanishing of socialism, veritable revolutions (not Ringel's word). By diverting change along new paths, revolutions are at once interruptions in the ever-changing flow of events and enhanced moments of them. Indeed, I would see such moments, registered as radical, catastrophic, or whatever, being precipitated by assumptions about time that have been typified as "evolutionary" (McDowell 1985: 28, after Gellner 1964). This is not quite the paradox it seems. In this typification, the "Western worldview" of history and change is a linear, ever-flowing progression from past to present. Every temporal horizon is an accumulation of moments that are nonrepeatable: the past is from where the present has come, and is kept in its place behind it. Revolutions redefine the course of events, but do not compromise that inexorable forward movement—in fact, they draw attention to it.

When kiaps first came into the PNG Highlands, they must have thought they were revolutionaries of a kind. That was not their language;

government officers, by contrast with missionaries and gold prospectors, might have said they were on a mission of modernization. Nonetheless, the Australians brought technical marvels with them—iconically, the gramophone—and it is hard to avoid the conclusion that they were showing these off as achievements. At the least they expected such things would be greeted with amazement or wonder. Of course the locals did not appreciate the long history of technical development that lay behind them, the evolution of civilization itself, which was part of their power in the Australians' eyes. But they may readily have ceded that a new time had come.

Such an "evolutionary" perception of time's flow was part of Ernest Gellner's (1964: 42) understanding of what he called a "neo-episodic" theory of change or progress. The latter allowed for abrupt transitions interspersed with relatively homogeneous periods, although I infer that time as such did not change direction. A strictly "episodic" theory of change, by contrast (and also my inference), was focused on the abruptness of a before/after transition that did not require a notion of time flowing forward. These contrasts are open to skepticism (see, for example, Munn 1992: 112; Robbins 2001: 547n3). In any event they are not to be confused with that drawn between linear and cyclical "time," which enjoys the status of a dichotomy in some anthropological accounts, even distinguishing whole societies (Munn 1992). If evolutionary or linear history encompasses the cyclical return of similar moments, as in the year's seasons or the recurrence of religious festivals, each commemoration proceeding cumulatively, an episodic present may also have cyclic rhythms (Iteanu 1999; Scaglion 1999). Like André Iteanu and Richard Scaglion, and without entering into a broader debate on ideas of change, I stay with Nancy McDowell's adoption of Gellner's nomenclature (but specifically not of his intentions) of the evolutionary and episodic to characterize distinctive ways of being in the present. What is at issue in episodic presentism is not so much a sequencing of events "in time," as we shall see, as the effect of people's actions upon one another.

Suppose time were not ever-flowing. McDowell could only make sense of what people at Bun in the East Sepik told her about the present through appreciating that past and present were radically cut off from each other. For a moment this emphasis on the instituting break seems to recall the revolutionary times just noted. However, either side of the Bun boundary between past and present things are changeless. They are as they are, or as they had been: steady states recovering their equilibrium after rupture by catastrophic events (Scaglion 1999: 212). Which forms of life are attributed to "now" or which to "then" is a matter of emphasis, but each has its own character. Change itself has to be "total, drastic and radical" (McDowell 1985: 33); this does not mean things cannot change again. At Bun, the division between before and after the arrival of the White Australians was taken up in other formulations—indeed, the then and now (before and after) paradigm could be repeated on any scale. McDowell had in mind stories about earlier ruptures between present ways of doing things and how people existed before that came into being. What this leaves is a question mark over the idea of a future. After all, if the past is radically cut off, does it even make sense to talk of a future? Where the present is not tethered to an earlier epoch, then is there nothing ahead but a flat horizon of the ever-present?

Episodic presentism implies that how we are now entails everything about ourselves that is now. Yet, as Joel Robbins (2001) has pointed out, an analytical emphasis on a radical cut between epochs fails to account for the fact that people may understand themselves as at once existing in an entirely different epoch yet carry on with their lives much as before. This applies particularly to millenarian movements, and here is one answer to how the future may be imagined—as another break. It too will be a break with the present. Concomitantly, that break may be anticipated, in which case the promise of the future may have already changed everything in the present. Robbins describes how the Urapmin (Telefomin) undergo episodes of intense activity, working to bring such a promise about, while in-between ordinary life proceeds as usual. This is not a paradox. In English parlance, ordinary life sounds like continuity rather than change, but here the point is that the incisive change (the new horizon of future promise) is already in place.

> Everyday life in Urapmin is marked by a millenarianism that forces Urapmin to keep one eye on the coming apocalypse and another on what they call "things of the ground." (Robbins 2001: 533)

Robbins's trenchant phrase "everyday millenarianism" captures this routinization of radical breaks as a part of life. Anthony Pickles (2014: 102–3) uses it to great effect, for example, in describing the serial or epochal nature of the anticipation put into small scale transactions in Highlands Goroka.

The administration's old-new / before-after exhortations will have seemed eminently familiar to a 1960s Hagen. The exhortations pointed to a radical change to come. Here kiaps, Hagen men and women, and the anthropologist with analytical interests at heart, can all concur: what had already radically changed was the horizon of *present* possibilities. In truth, a sense of cataclysmic change did not need to rest on a totalized image of a world new in every aspect. Change was evident in those aspects of the present day that seemed crucial diagnostics of the new time.[11] In the Louisiade Islands, Buliga took the crux to be an eventual reversal of Black and White power relations; in the Highlands, Hagen men (including dispute-settlers) saw new grounds for competition as well as new possibilities for wealth, transforming them in terms of the power they could exert over their compatriots.[12]

Without prejudging whether time or history is the common ground ("time" and "history" seem to me already implying an evolutionary model), I turn to the methodological concept of presentism.[13] Perhaps we can say that the Australians and Papua New Guineans were not living in the same present. Robbins's everyday millenarianism opens up a further possibility, as a point of method, for showing an ontological signification in the way people exist in the present, and the beginnings of another answer to the question of where the future is. The possibility lies in the fact that both kinds of presentism are necessarily supported by, or embedded in, the ordinary occurrences of everyday life.

---

11. Many so-called origin myths have no problem about imagining a world very like the present but before the present has in fact been made in this or that vital aspect—so an otherwise ordinary pre-world is marred by some not yet instituted practice (such as cooking food / having sexual intercourse via the genitals / not recognizing wealth objects).

12. Between the two cases one would remark on the much longer period of colonization of the Louisiades. Nonetheless, there are parallels. Apparently Buliga constructed a bureaucracy, with a hierarchy of officers from king to motor driver, to step into the vacuum when the White expatriate population fled at the incursion of the Japanese in January 1942 and "Government abruptly ceased" (Rollason 2014a: 49). Blacks took the place of Whites. Government resumed in November 1942; Whites regarded these activities as an "uprising," and the subsequent "murder" of a kiap and others [to bring the future more quickly forward?] a reversion to savagery.

13. Munn's (1992: 116) "notion of 'temporalization' views time as a symbolic process continually being produced in everyday practices." Her formula implies that some practices may be more emphatically temporalized—that is, more evidently "make time"—than others.

The Routinization of an Evolutionary Present

Divergence between evolutionary and episodic presents shows no more clearly than in their everyday supports, in those perceptions of the world that keep certain ideas in place. I remark briefly on where we might find such supports in the evolutionary case before dilating rather more fully apropos the episodic.

Evolutionary flow entails a world in development. The present dispatches the past insofar as particular events can never be repeated; yet, given that this is a continuous process, the effects of the past are also ever-present. They may provide a measure of distance from things to be forgotten and discarded, or recovered and cherished, but above all the past is precursor to the present. Everyday ideas that uphold an evolutionary view include the logic of cause and effect, the evidence of growth and decay, and people's need for training, socialization, and education, along with other institutional practices, all of which rely on the passage of time before things are mature, ready, offer a return on investment, and so forth. Such ideas support one another, and in this are as much a part of the legal system as it was introduced in PNG as are explicit theories about judicial process. Legal development entails the time-lapse of growth. So things had to be taken step by step—until, that is, independence suddenly became a possibility and in a handful of years all was abruptly changed. Then, after everything was changed, it slowed down again.

Indeed, from the outset in the Highlands, no sooner had the Australians arrived and set about reforming political and economic life, all parts of legal development, knowing nothing would ever be the same again, than they backtracked [my phrase]. They might still go on talking (as they were in the 1960s) about the benefits that planting cash crops or penning pigs or "hearing the law" would bring—but they did not mean immediately. It would take years to develop the place and decades before people were ready for independence. Time had to work in its own slow way. So much was required for societal transformation, and cash crops were only the beginning. The current urgency was simply about getting started—sowing the seed, one might say. It would take time before the fruits of this preparatory work would appear. Although the relevant know-how, equipment, and materials could be imported at one go, it would be long before returns were evident. Coffee trees, the main Highlands cash crop, had their own maturation cycle, requiring attention at every stage. Then there had to be an infrastructure to turn the crop into a commercial enterprise: labor, trucks, processing plants, export markets, all long before fertilizers or insecticides were on the horizon, or local consumers for that matter. This was another mode of evolutionary revolution: a small change with momentous consequences.

I am assuming that these supports entail a degree of scientific knowledge, even if it is not registered as such; in other words, popular understandings about the processes of growth and generation, about time and development, are tantamount to a kind of "embedded science." This is not to deny occasions when the popular and the scientific, marked as "scientific," appear to clash, but not to deny either the place of scientific thinking in the everyday.[14] As for science in the marked sense, I offer two observations about the way it constantly appears to break with the past.

First, McDowell compares Gellner's typology with Thomas Kuhn's argument (in her words) that scientists "view their own history in an evolutionary fashion, complete with progress, advancement, discovery-building-upon-discovery," whereas frequently "science changes radically and in revolutionary ways with the complete substitution of one paradigm or conceptual framework for another" (McDowell 1985: 29). There is no need to flag the controversy this generated. But perhaps we can take what McDowell calls Kuhn's neo-episodic view as an example of "everyday revolutionism." Science forever pushes at its own barriers: this is so ordinary and taken for granted that it is no wonder that Kuhn's seeming denial of a flow of events attracted criticism. The image of scientific development as discovery-building-upon-discovery implies the perpetual change to be found in evolutionary thinking, not stopped through revolutionary paradigms but diverted by them along new channels.

Second, an illuminating example of science's ability to mobilize the cause-and-effect sequences bound up in time's flow alongside discontinuous leaps into new frameworks comes from Sarah Franklin's (2013) history of embryo research. Practitioners are aware that each juncture in their research is but a staging post in a sequence constantly faced with an unknown future (often summoned through their unknown ethical implications). Thus, in vitro fertilization (IVF) in mice led to various applications, including human clinical ones; but the platform it provided

---

14. I take science in the English sense of natural science; the epithet natural is not inappropriate more generally, since science based on "the continuity of the physicality of the entities of the world" (Descola [2005] 2013: 173) is a diagnostic practice of naturalism as a "modern ontology."

in the 1980s became a different platform for 1990s developments (cell reprogramming), and a decade on emerged in further cellular tools (induced pluripotent stem cells). "IVF has continued to undergo a rapid evolution as a technological platform, yielding newer mechanisms to facilitate human reproduction. . . as well as new means of harnessing the regenerative properties of embryos" (2013: 37). This repeats the truism that every invention depends on previous inventions (human embryonic stem cell research would have been impossible without IVF). Routine! And that is the point: the everyday revolution of forever recapacitated innovation.

Indeed there is a local language for an important aspect of (re)capacitation—translational research.[15] If "new cellular models generate new applications, and vice versa" (Franklin 2013: 55), the ethos of translation works these up, substance and technique alike, to make them newly reproductive (translational all over again). This workaday temporalization creates evolutionary time: being in the present is a matter of witnessing the latest evolution of the IVF platform. Franklin observes how the language of future-oriented discovery co-opts historic frontier narratives of boundaries already crossed. Her account is significant insofar as this view of forward development is heightened by the material on which the scientists in question are working: embryonic cells with their intrinsic capacity for growth. Organic growth works as a reference point for other ways in which the findings of science might "grow" and thus become newly "reproductive" (her metaphor) through translation. Alongside all the new platforms developed for further innovation, in the light of recent advances it is possible to go back to the embryo itself with its own generative potential, to harness that all over again. We might say that it is a version of this ordinary, commonsensical going-back, accommodated as it is within a linear, evolutionary time frame, that we encounter in the episodic presentism of the Papuan New Guinean sort. But there it works as a cosmic driver.[16]

---

15. In medical jargon, translational refers to the process of "embodying" knowledge in a technical procedure—for example, through turning scientific findings into applications for clinical practice (not that this "linear" narrative captures the complexity of the issues [Latimer 2013: 47]).

16. There is no temporal contradiction here: new technologies create new values; for one account of the (re)capacitation of "resources," see Weszkalnys (2014).

The Routinization of an Episodic Present

There are many ways of being in an evolutionary present, and that is no less true of the episodic. I turn specific attention to what might count as a Melanesian counterpart to bioscience. One of the great innovations of all time was plant domestication, based as it must have been on experiment.[17] Needless to say, it is only with the development of "science" that Euro-Americans might retrospectively wish to fold domestication into that canon: an informal science, if you like, stretched over a long period, trial and error more likely than deliberate strategizing and not necessarily encapsulated as "knowledge." (Indeed there is every reason to think it was encapsulated into practices of procreative kinship.) Nonetheless, cultivation is a prime arena in which people continued until very recently to innovate (and many still do), above all in constantly looking for new plant varieties.[18] Despite the significance that the time-lapse of growth plays in an evolutionary present, I argue that in, say, mid-twentieth-century Papua New Guinea, cultivation practices have supported not an evolutionary but an episodic sense of the present.

One might recall Jared Diamond's rehearsal of a question posed to him in 1972 by Yali, a so-called cargo cult leader from the PNG Lowlands. "Why is it that you White people developed so much cargo and brought it to New Guinea, but we Black people had little cargo[19] of our

---

17. The "humanization" or "personification" of plants might be closer than "domestication" (Carneiro da Cunha, this volume). Across Papua New Guinea, relationships with plants are held to require devotion, care, and coaxing to grow (e.g., Scaglion 1999; Crook 2007; Coupaye 2013; Panoff 2018). Solicitude may be needed to keep plants straying from the gardener's plot.

18. To take up Carneiro da Cunha's concern about stepping outside the forest, over the centuries, cultivation would have variously taken place under forest cover and in the anthropogenic grassland that intensive cultivation created in certain areas. In the 1960s, Hageners made new gardens in both forest and fallow gardenland. Apart from planting quick-growing tree species for fallow cover in old gardens, elsewhere in PNG are reports of other forms of tree-planting to support the nourishment of crops (Damon 2017; Panoff 2018).

19. Goods and material things, in common Australian/European-American understanding, famously turned around by Wagner's (1975: 32–34) address to Yali's predicament, as an interpretive counterpart to the notion of "culture." In the quotation, one suspects "develop" was put into Yali's mouth through translation. [I use Lowlands as a literary gloss here; cargo cults

own" (Diamond [1997] 1999: 14)? Euro-Americans very quickly turn the question into an evolutionary one: "Why haven't other people developed like us?" Diamond's answer provides an evolutionary argument in another tenor; the differences Yali saw are not a matter of basic endowment (as implied in the first evolutionary response) but of contingencies of a historical or environmental kind that, through long chains of cause and effect, have bestowed advantages on which people have built.[20] In either case, "time"—it goes without saying—keeps flowing. Yali was also looking for the source of difference, although one conceived as a difference of power, and in these terms PNG millenarianists also frequently turned to the past. Crucially, however, this was a past on which they could draw, repossessing what their ancestors had owned or laid down but that had failed to make it into the present. There were numerous stories about some ancestral moment at which the destinies of Whites and Blacks had diverged or—a response widespread in the Highlands where overt millenarianism occurred only sporadically—reports of the first Whites being greeted as returned ancestors. I take these as signs of an episodic mode of presentism. Yet another way of being in an episodic present was evinced by the Hagen dispute-settlers.

Dispute-"settler" was always a bit of a misnomer. It was not just that disputes were never finished, or were part of the ups and downs of social life (Tuzin 1974: 318). Rather, specifically for Hagen, the more disputes were "settled," and especially through wealth transactions, the more they erupted (M. Strathern 1985). Before the Australian regime, I doubt that "social order" was a default position of people's interaction, or that they had an interest in nonviolent action for its own sake. People did indeed peaceably terminate conflicts, and one Indigenous mechanism by which this was accomplished, compensation payment, gives us a clue as to their assumptions. The prospect of payment, compensating an aggrieved person through gifting, was basically a tool of conversion insofar as it enabled people to move from one state to another, from one kind of act or value to another. From war to wealth exchange. But then violent reprisals were conversions too, switching someone's state of mind from a

---

were most active in coastal areas and their hinterlands colonized in the late nineteenth / early twentieth century.]

20. Errington and Gewertz (2004: 25) argue that Diamond failed to grasp the fact that Papua New Guinean questions about cargo were not questions about White men's things as such, but about the nature of colonial relationships between Whites and Blacks, and the manifest inequality they enacted.

sense of grievance or injury into the satisfaction of revenge; any interaction could carry the possibility of grievance, and wealth exchanges might lead to war. From wealth exchange to war. And every episode of value conversion reinforced the practice. We saw, over a long period, the social oscillation from the ever-present threat of war to an interim suspension of all hostilities after pacification to the warfare that broke out in some places in the 1970s.

This contributed to the routine rhythms of an episodic life. At its extreme, every act, regardless of scale, implies that a previous one is converted into something else. However, we need to account for the breaks that an episodic present assumes as well as for how both the past, and the break with the past, can be recalled. I suggest some ways in which these may be embedded in everyday apprehensions of existence.

Past acts are routinely brought into the present as the "root" (in Hagen idiom) of a current state of the affairs. In this sense we may speak of cause and effect. As I understand Hagen reasoning in the 1960s, such notions (of cause and effect) do not create time as an on-going flow where everything has an antecedent, and where continuity, including continuous change, is presumed "over time" until it is diverted. To the contrary, if time does not move continuously in the first place, there can be no discontinuity, and in the episodic view, no obsession with the static as opposed to the moving. A previous epoch is only changeless until it changes; indeed, we should presume that its present is similar to today's present, with its horizon open to innovation. If we wish to imagine the division between epochs or episodes as a division between "past" and "present," that division is there in the very idea that certain features of the past have forward or future effects. Conversely, present flourishing requires such recourse to the past. This will become clearer if we qualify the abstract concepts of past-present-future with the fact that what is invariably being recalled or anticipated are the actions of persons. There is nothing predictable about effects of actions. The spontaneous self-evidence of the natural, as Philippe Descola ([2005] 2013: 199) calls it, including the way in which the divisions of the world present themselves, has no place here. Rather, only someone's reenactment of a previous action, whether of themselves or someone else, can show an act's forward effects. This entails a constant need to work on what has happened, whether to encourage or avoid such outcomes (Munn 1990: 5; Hirsch 2004: 20). In old Hagen, this was true of episodic cult performances with their message of rejuvenation. What on an ordinary basis was hoped from the loyalty of their ancestors, who oversaw the fertility of people and their gardens, from time to time demanded the special attention of certain spirit beings. These beings would bring everything back to the state of plenitude that had been brought into existence by previous performances. The climax of such a dramatic intervention was invariably followed by a period of decline until the cult returned (for Orokaiva, see Iteanu 1999: 272).

Recovering a reproductive action in the past to create a new time in the present brings me to a central set of supports that arguably sustain an episodic tenor to life. These are specifically supports for thinking how the "new times"—that is, events with regenerative effects—are routinely recovered from the past. They are of a quintessentially everyday nature. Each demands someone's deliberate action.

Ira Bashkow's (2006) account of the "meaning" of Whitemen to the Papua New Guinean Orokaiva (coastal Binandere) has an extensive discourse on Orokaivan opinion about Whitemen's food by contrast with their own. Above all, for things to grow and increase in beauty, they must be hidden. This applies to people who undergo critical periods of seclusion as well as to plants. Growth takes place out of sight, and Bashkow (2006: 125) makes an explicit contrast between wheat, rice, and corn, which "ripen in the open air," and Orokaivans' taro, yam, and sweet potato, "which grow unseen underground." It is underground that crops grow full and plump, just as girls emerge from their seclusion fat and bright. What is brought into the open, then, is spectacular: the moment that people see the results of their work, both magical and otherwise.[21] Conversely, growth is a focus of concern, even anxiety, and huge attention may be paid to ensuring that the food will grow, checking the parts of the plant that are above ground for tell-tale signs. Nonetheless, the relationship between what is above ground and below is indeterminate; the gardener cannot check the ripening crop itself as the cereal farmer does.[22] For all the signs, nothing is known until the moment the tuber

---

21. For the Orokaiva (and elsewhere) food seems more a matter of visible form (its form, the form it will produce [in the eater]) than nourishment. We may suppose that people may be surprised by what they see, as with all revelations, but not by the event itself.

22. It depends a bit on the crop. Thus, the growth of yams is bipolar—first throwing out shoots that gather nutrients above ground and then storing the nutrients underground, in the tuber. There are indicators, then, of what is happening underground, but no direct witness. Although we may generalize the description across several crops, including the sweet potato that

(yam) or corm (taro) is dug out. Here we have, so to speak, a routine enactment of a before and after, then and now.

There is nothing predictable or natural about growth, no nature to assist through fertilizers, and no seed that will automatically develop as the child or fruit of a parent plant when provided with the right conditions.[23] But where does past action come into it? Let me speculate, with some aspects of PNG cultivation practices in mind, and turn the negative characterization into a positive one by enlarging the cosmological field.

The gardens that the Australian colonials encountered in Hagen were planted with similar root crops—taro, yam, sweet potato—along with sugar cane and banana. Except sweet potato, these were being cultivated there seven thousand years ago (Golson et al. 2017). The beginnings of this activity were not much later than the domestication of seed crops in China and the Middle East. Diamond's account of the first steps toward population intensity was focused on the advantages afforded by cereals. While agriculture arose in many parts of the world, he observed, European and Asian grains were easier to store, and richer in protein than tropical bananas or root crops, which require the repetitive (ever-present) propagation of plant material. The domestication of certain varieties appears to have originated in Papua New Guinea. What did domestication entail? Prehistoric plant selection encouraged starch content, which worked, for example, in favor of certain sterile cultivars (Denham 2017: 42). Whereas the conventional story about the origins of agriculture is based on the exploitation of grasses with seeds, among the domesticates found in Papua New Guinea, seeds were never the focus of propagation; in the case of bananas, it was seemingly bred out of them.

Although today Hagen people tie up bananas and sugarcane as they ripen, so they are covered in protective wrapping, unlike root crops, they do not grow underground. But they share with root crops the capacity

---

has long dominated horticulture in Hagen, I focus on yam and taro, and to a lesser extent on banana. In many areas of PNG, yam and taro are subject to considerable ritual attention, and in the 1960s Highlands they were often treated as luxury foods.

23. Needless to add, for cereal growers the conditions are important, and will be monitored and held responsible for variations in crop yield. But growth as such is not a problem in the evolutionary view, insofar as the outcome is a product of the original (whether for instance it is of "good" or "bad" stock). Growth is an overt and much remarked upon problem in episodic management.

for vegetative regeneration, which means that offshoots are the principal planting material. Shoots are cut from a parent plant. However, any easy metaphorization of what is "parent" and what is "child" does not exhaust the description of yam and taro regeneration. Because of their sexual models of reproduction, Euro-Americans regard various kinds of vegetative propagation as "asexual," a characterization that obscures the procreative process. Vegetative propagation requires separating generative matter from what is consumed, often from the very same body, although sometimes—as in the case of small yams—separating those tubers to be planted from those to be eaten. In any event, new potential for growth is detached from what in being harvested has stopped growing. This sequence challenges how Euro-Americans might think of parent and child as old and new life. It is when an individual taro or yam is cut that *the new parent* emerges: it begins as the severed or separated fragment. Only after it is cut does the replanted corm or piece of tuber yield up the substance that will feed the new shoots soon to be growing above ground, before it itself shrivels and dies.

Let us pause for a moment, then, on how people propagate these crops. Very frequently it involves them cutting a tuber into pieces or chopping the tops off tubers or corms that are then pushed into the ground. Abelam speak of yam fragments as "mother" or "placenta" that will give birth to and nurture new tubers—that is, the mother is the part broken off to be planted (Coupaye 2013).[24] Bananas and sugar cane are similarly cloned through cutting. It is necessary to slice through the old corm or base of a banana that has fruited in order to detach its already growing suckers; however, the sucker must be detached with its own growing point, a section of the corm, still intact.

---

24. Similarly, the Highlands Wola call the parent taro corm, from which suckers sprout, the "mother" (Sillitoe 1983: 37). Abelam yam setts, the material that is replanted, may come either from a fragment of yam (its head or base), or from a whole tuber. In the case of taro, when its head is planted, that and the attached stem die back to develop into a taro with newly growing stem and leaves; however, offshoots growing from the corm may, if they are not bitter, also be cut and planted (e.g., in Wola). In addition, established parent corms may grow lateral (rhizomic) cormels that send up their own leaves. A taro sett may thus be either a rhizomic offset or the bottom piece of a stem (the top of the corm), but in either case the stalk—and the planted material underground—rots away once new shoots emerge from its center; for Orokaiva, for example, see Iteanu (1999: 269, 273; 1990) and Bashkow (2006: 176).

Do we conclude that growth and nongrowth are not just held in a temporal relationship but that regeneration itself depends upon one generation being severed from another? For Trobriand Islanders, yams are killed when they are harvested (Mosko 2009: 687). The plant that was a source of growth now itself ceases to grow. Of course, cereal seeds replace their parent plant, we might say, just as a new yam replaces the old one that gives it substance before dying. But there is nothing in the developmental cereal cycle of the radical change that affects the mature tuber or corm. In the case of yam and taro, it is not just those that are eaten but those kept for replanting that are killed—precisely by being planted. An already grown taro corm is moved from a growing to nongrowing state, for pushed back into the ground is its own capacity for growth, which is then consumed by another: the taro that grows from it is a "new" taro. What is seen are shoots springing above ground; what emerges from the ground—into the present—is the *present* taro, as fully formed as its parent. Each fresh planting recapitulates that movement. And in the case of any particular plant, each fresh planting potentially recalls the regenerative capacity of the parent's parent, a rehearsal of what had previously produced the corm whose larger part is now eaten.

In this context, "killing" is stopping growth (in number, size). It is not the obliteration of the identity of the plant. On the contrary, it would seem that people stress what botanists and geneticists (classically, Haudricourt 1964) contrast with the reproduction of plants through seeds (where each is a new individual)—namely, that what comes out of the ground as a new tuber or corm is another piece of the same plant as the parental and grandparental one. Abelam gardeners are conscious of the generations of yams (that is, of yam-growing) that link them to their ancestors: "Yams replace yams, and people replace people" (Scaglion 1999: 222).

Where is the Future?

The apparent concord between some of the aspirations of colonizers and (some of the) colonized might be taken as showing a degree of understanding between them, a mutual intelligibility between their outlooks. On the other hand, one might wish to take more information into account and consider some of the entailments of presentism in each case. Perhaps an emphasis on the everyday routinization of people's outlooks has put a little information in our way. It does not rest on an argument about intelligibility.

A diagnostic of such entailments can be framed in terms of a question: Where is the future? Do we arrive at the same answer in each case? Hoyerswerda people make all kinds of plans to ensure that the forms of living they value in the present will endure "into" the future, or rather give future a form by "giving particular forms a future" (Ringel 2014: 67). This includes what they see as coming from the past, but the uncertainty of that future guarantees a distinctive place for it in the as-yet unrealized unknown. That unrealized unknown is not the past.[25] In old Hagen, to the contrary, one might say that the past can sometimes be exactly where the future is, noting that the answer makes sense of a future envisaged in generative terms—the regenerative success of the past can be drawn into the present, thus comprising moments to which one can return. But, as others have observed, referring to past and future in this way introduces the kind of abstractions pervasive in (not necessarily exclusive to) a naturalist cosmology that temporalizes relations between events.

If it is useful to conceive of a Hagen presentism, it is locally imagined as relations between persons. The horizon people are recovering is the horizon of their *ancestors*, present with *its* own future potential, which people's present-day lives embody. In other words, they are the cuttings or offshoots of that previous promise, and they bring that potential into their present so they, too, will be the regenerators of a new future. The taro that had grown before grows again. People's efforts are directed less to sustaining continuity, or embracing discontinuity, than to bringing about "new" presents. The affirmation of that possibility lies in the break or cut between previous (old) and present (new) acts. And if what is being recalled or anticipated are the actions of persons, it also seems that relations of cause and effect are not being temporalized, or at least not in an evolutionary mode as the inevitable outcome of sequence. Cause and effect inhere in what people do, and in effect, what they do to one another. That is, it is a matter of how people's actions will have turned out to bear on other people's actions in the (equally unrealized, unknown) future. Provoking or eliciting such reactions is perhaps tantamount to temporalization in an episodic mode.

---

25. In this view, the horizon of the unknown is always changing, the future continuously turning into the past, the past being (by contrast) what did actually happen. This past is conceived as a "natural" state of affairs upon which diverse "cultural" inscriptions are made, so the past is unknown only in the sense of being (selectively) forgotten contested, rewritten, and so forth.

My references to Papua New Guinea have been mainly focused on the period following pacification in the Highlands. I turn to that period again to bring from it something to today's present. Consider the appeals to the national constitution: Are those lawyers and legal scholars striving to activate underlying law not returning to the regenerative moment that has led to the present day? If so, we might be mistaken in reading the appeals as an attempt to recover the past either for its own sake ("tradition") or to legitimate present-day actions ("ideology"). Rather, that return surely renews the productive differentiation effected in the nation's self-definition vis-à-vis its colonial history: the need to encourage new formulations of the underlying law are more like an effort to separate once more the postcolonial legal system from that of its colonial predecessors. If we focus instead on the persons involved, the return is being made by the potential evidence of that action's success (its offshoots, today's people). The return is at once a validation of the generative power of their own sources of existence, the cut with colonization that made them anew, and holds out the possibility that in recovering the very separation that led to themselves, they will make Papua New Guinean independence work all over again.

A Clash of Ontologies?—Again

If there was a clash between those Australians and PNG Highlanders, what was the role of scientific thinking in its ontological import? An answer applicable to both is in terms of the science embedded in approaches to change, literally and metaphorically referring to the unfolding of life processes in which persons had a cultivating role.

The material on which I draw is far from the fine-grained analysis of verbal and exegetical translations that Vilaça (2016) provides, and what goes on in dedicated teaching contexts (missionization, schools). My address is to a broader "educational" milieu, where a colonial administration felt it had a development mission. Here, there were innumerable "first contact" misunderstandings, about what the new time meant and what it indicated of the future—about new wealth, institutions, opportunities, and so forth—and there was much frustration and disappointment. Yet it seems that there was enough in the way each party appeared to the other for misunderstandings to be accommodated, within what people seemingly agreed about, along the lines that Lloyd (2007, 2012) has suggested in terms of "good enough" comprehension. (Rapid pacification simply would not have happened otherwise.) However, the very similarity in the aspirations that seemingly drove Australians and Highlanders alike tells us something significant: they (the aspirations) did not have to rest on mutual intelligibility of outlook. Concomitantly, there may indeed have been a clash, deeply and radically so, but it did not necessarily show itself.

In a nutshell, I suggest that we do not require the idea of a "clash" as overt conflict or ethnic distance in order to talk of a clash of ontologies. Let me build on two of G. E. R. Lloyd's own observations in order to clarify this position. "If ontologies do indeed differ radically. . . how is any mutual understanding between them possible" (Lloyd 2007: 147; emphasis removed)? This was a remark addressed to the relation between ethnographer and informant, among others. Thus, "successful communication between ethnographer and informant even in the matter of ontologies is strong evidence against any conclusion to the effect that mutual incomprehensibility reigns across the board" (Lloyd 2012: 113). The implication is that ontological outlooks have to be similar in some degree, entailing some mutuality of comprehension, for there to be communication. But I derive another conclusion from them; namely, that the relationship of similarity and dissimilarity to the capacity to interact is, at the least, multidimensional. Degree of comprehension—and thus degree of divergence—is not a predictor of the success of interchanges.

To talk of similarity or dissimilarity "between" ontologies is to treat them as though they were cultures. (And especially cultures in the strong sense. There are as many usages of the concept among anthropologists as Lloyd would find in any ancient debate; however, for the sake of argument I keep with the term as it has been critiqued earlier in the essay.) I follow Bruce Kapferer's (2014) response to Descola, which emphases the multiplicity of different—meaning diverse—ontologies as they emerge under specific, situated social circumstances across numerous spaces of social activity.[26] The phrase I would use is that they are like *gathered fields*. I mean to suggest not a gathering of beings or entities but the manner in which a point of view gathers to itself all its supports, reasons, conditions of existence—its own ecology—regardless of the role such elements may play in other fields. This was illustrated through two distinct enactments

---

26. Thus he talks of "the situated nature of ontology [such] that the logics relative to the formation of the person or of being in practice are constituted through practice and are context dependent" (Kapferer 2014: 396).

of presentism: the distinctiveness of each is a property these fields have quite apart from the similarities and dissimilarities the observer sees. In other words, anthropologists might take back the delegation that Gildas Salmon (2017) finds in so much scholarly procedure (imputing a mode of enquiry to what is under study), and allow themselves to designate just such similarities and dissimilarities between ontological scenarios without imputing *to* those scenarios the idea that any such determination affects how they work.

The phrase "gathered field" only makes sense in the context of these arguments about culture and the clash of ontologies. Everything people see around them can be gathered together in a manner coherent within a specific situation, which relays back to them that this is the way the world is. That's all. It keeps its own scale, as always, the way things are. The point is that, at any given point, everything conspires to produce this gathering together. With the broad brush used here, if you think, feel, or act in evolutionary terms apropos events, processes of growth, or whatever, certain moments reinforce an evolutionary approach; if you think, feel, or act episodically, the same moments reinforce an episodic approach.

There is nothing static here, no impediment to change, no need to avoid contradiction, for the field simply exists in the supports that keep it there. Hence seemingly similar events can nonetheless be gathered into distinctive and specific fields. Equally, each may gather up things strange and bizarrely "different" from another's perspective, so much so they can stand out as contrasts. Yet it is not that difference that specifies its ontological import: that lies in the gathering up, the echo-chamber effect by which the world plays back to people what they apprehend about it through the supports it gives to their ideas.

Acknowledgments

First and foremost I must acknowledge the inspiration of Andrew Moutu, and his unpublished paper, "The tyranny of analogy in legal precedent," which he gave to the Underlying Law Seminar Series, Port Moresby, in 2014; in a different idiom it presages much of the discussion here. The workshop organizers were of course the prime movers of this account; I thank the participants for their comments and criticisms, and especially Joel Robbins for his discussion.

References

Bashkow, Ira. 2006. *The meaning of whitemen: Race and modernity in the Orokaiva cultural world*. Chicago: University of Chicago Press.

Burman, Sandra, and Barbara Harrell-Bond, eds. 1979. *The imposition of law*. New York: Academic Press.

Carneiro da Cunha, Manuela. 2009. *"Culture" and culture: Traditional knowledge and intellectual rights*. Chicago: Prickly Paradigm Press.

Coupaye, Ludovic. 2013. *Growing artifacts, displaying relationships: Yams, art and technology amongst the Nyamikum Abelam of Papua New Guinea*. Oxford: Berghahn.

Crook, Tony. 2007. *Exchanging skin: Anthropological knowledge, secrecy and Bolivip, Papua New Guinea*. Oxford: Oxford University Press for The British Academy.

Damon, Frederick. 2017. *Trees, knots and outriggers: Environmental knowledge in the Northeast Kula Ring*. Oxford: Berghahn.

Demian, Melissa. 2015. "Dislocating custom." In "Symposium on internationalizing custom and localizing law," edited by Melissa Demian, special issue, *PoLAR: Political and Legal Anthropology Review* 38 (1): 91–107.

———. 2016. "Court in between: The spaces of relational justice in Papua New Guinea." *Australian Feminist Law Journal* 42 (1): 13–30.

Denham, Tim. 2017. "Domesticatory relationships in the New Guinea Highlands." In *Ten thousand years of cultivation at Kuk swamp in the Highlands of Papua New Guinea (Terra Australis 62)*, edited by Jack Golson, Tim Denham, Philip Hughes, Pamela Swadling, and John Muke, 39–49. Canberra: Australian National University Press.

Descola, Philippe. (2005) 2013. *Beyond nature and culture*. Translated by Janet Lloyd. Chicago: University of Chicago Press.

Diamond, Jared. (1997) 1999. *Guns, germs, and steel: The fates of human societies*. New York: W. W. Norton and Company.

Errington, Frederick, and Deborah Gewertz. 2004. *Yali's question: Sugar, culture and history*. Chicago: University of Chicago Press.

Franklin, Sarah. 2013. *Biological relatives: IVF, stem cells, and the future of kinship*. Durham, NC: Duke University Press.

Gellner, Ernest. 1964. *Thought and change*. London: Weidenfeld and Nicolson.

Golson, Jack, Tim Denham, Philip Hughes, Pamela Swadling, and John Muke, eds. 2017. *Ten thousand years of cultivation at Kuk swamp in the*

Highlands of Papua New Guinea (Terra Australis 62). Canberra: Australian National University Press.

Haudricourt, André. 1964. "Nature et culture dans la civilisation de l'igname: L'origine des clones et des clans." *L'Homme* 4 (1): 93–104.

Hirsch, Eric. 2004. "Techniques of vision: Photography, disco and renderings of present perceptions in highland Papua." *Journal of the Royal Anthropological Institute* 10 (1): 19–39.

Iteanu, André. 1990. "The concept of the person and the ritual system: An Orokaivan view." *Man*, n.s., 25 (1): 35–53.

———. 1999. "Synchronisations among the Orokaiva." *Social Anthropology* 7 (3): 265–78.

Kapferer, Bruce. 2014. "Back to the future: Descola's neostructuralism." *HAU: Journal of Ethnographic Theory* 4 (3): 389–400.

Latimer, Joanna. 2013. *The gene, the clinic and the family*. London: Routledge.

Lattas, Andrew. 1998. *Cultures of secrecy: Reinventing race in Bush Kaliai cargo cults*. Madison: University of Wisconsin Press.

Lloyd, G. E. R. 2007. *Cognitive variations: Reflections on the unity and diversity of the human mind*. Oxford: Oxford University Press.

———. 2012. *Being, humanity, and understanding: Studies in ancient and modern societies*. Oxford: Oxford University Press.

Maclean, Neil. 1998. "Mimesis and pacification: The colonial legacy in Papua New Guinea." *History and Anthropology* 11 (1): 75–118.

McDowell, Nancy. 1985. "Past and future: The nature of episodic time in Bun." In *History and ethnohistory in Papua New Guinea*, edited by Deborah Gewertz and Edward Schieffelin, 26–39. Sydney: University of Sydney, Oceania Publications.

Miyazaki, Hirokazu. 2004. *The method of hope: Anthropology, philosophy and Fijian knowledge*. Stanford, CA: Stanford University Press.

Mosko, Mark. 2009. "The fractal yam: Botanical imagery and human agency in the Trobriands." *Journal of the Royal Anthropological Institute*, n.s., 15 (4): 679–700.

Munn, Nancy. 1990. "Constructing regional worlds in experience: Kula exchange, witchcraft and Gawan local events." *Man*, n.s., 25 (1): 1–17.

———. 1992. "The cultural anthropology of time: A critical essay." *Annual Review of Anthropology* 21: 93–123.

Panoff, Françoise. 2018. *Maenge gardens: A study of Maenge relationship to domesticates*, edited by Françoise Barbira-Freedman. Marseilles: pacific-cedo.

Pickles, Anthony. 2014. "Gambling futures: Playing the imminent in Highland Papua New Guinea." In *Pacific futures: Projects, politics and interests*, edited by Will Rollason, 96–113. Oxford: Berghahn.

Ringel, Felix. 2014. "Post-industrial times and the unexpected: Endurance and sustainability in Germany's fastest-shrinking city." In "Doubt, conflict, mediation: The anthropology of modern time," edited by Laura Bear, special issue, *Journal of the Royal Anthropological Institute*, n.s., 20 (S1): 52–70.

———. 2016. "Beyond temporality: Notes on the anthropology of time from a shrinking field site." *Anthropological Theory* 16 (4): 390–412.

Robbins, Joel. 2001. "Secrecy and the sense of an ending: Narrative time, and everyday millenarianism in Papua New Guinea and in Christian Fundamentalism." *Comparative Studies in Society and History* (CSSH) 43 (3): 525–51.

Rollason, Will. 2014a. "The hanging of Buliga: A history of the future in the Louisiade Archipelago, Papua New Guinea." *Pacific futures: Projects, politics and interests*, edited by Will Rollason, 28–70. Oxford: Berghahn.

———. 2014b. "Introduction: Pacific futures, methodological challenges." In *Pacific futures: Projects, politics and interests*, edited by Will Rollason, 1–27. Oxford: Berghahn.

Salmon, Gildas. 2017. "On ontological delegation: The birth of neoclassical anthropology." Translated by Nicolas Carter. In *Comparative metaphysics: Ontology after anthropology*, edited by Pierre Charbonnier, Gildas Salmon, and Peter Skafish, 41–60. London: Rowman and Littlefield International.

Scaglion, Richard. 1985. "Kiaps as kings: Abelam legal change in historical perspective." In *History and ethnohistory in Papua New Guinea*, edited by Deborah Gewertz and Edward Schieffelin, 77–99. Sydney: University of Sydney, Oceania Publications.

———. 1999. "Yam cycles and timeless time in Melanesia." *Ethnology* 38 (3): 211–25.

Sillitoe, Paul. 1983. *Roots of the earth: Crops in the Highlands of Papua New Guinea*. Manchester: Manchester University Press.

Strathern, Andrew. 1979. *Ongka: A self-account.*, London: Duckworth.

Strathern, Marilyn. 1972. *Official and unofficial courts. Legal assumptions and expectations in a Highlands community.* Canberra: New Guinea Research Bulletin No. 47.

———. 1985. "Discovering 'social control.'" *Journal of Law and Society* 12 (2): 111–34.

Tuzin, Donald. 1974. "Social control and the tambaran in the Sepik." In *Contention and dispute: Aspects of law and social control in Melanesia,* edited by A. L. Epstein, 317–44. Canberra: Australian National University Press.

Vilaça, Aparecida. 2016. *Praying and preying: Christianity in indigenous Amazonia.* Translated by David Rodgers. Berkeley: University of California Press.

Wagner, Roy. 1975. *The invention of culture.* Englewood Cliffs, NJ: Prentice-Hall.

Weszkalnys, Gisa. 2014. "Geology, potentiality, speculation: On the indeterminacy of first oil." *Cultural anthropology* 30 (4): 611–39.

CHAPTER FOUR

Mathematical Traditions in Ancient Greece and Rome

Serafina Cuomo

In his dialogue *Republic*, the fourth-century BCE Athenian philosopher Plato laid the foundations for the idea of two cultures in ancient Greek mathematics. While discussing how best to educate the future leaders of the ideal state, Socrates says:

> It would be appropriate. . . to legislate this subject for those who are going to share in the highest offices in the city and to persuade them to turn to calculation and take it up, *not as laymen do*, but staying with it until they reach the study of the natures of the numbers *by means of understanding itself, not like tradesmen and retailers*, for the sake of buying and selling, but for the sake of war and for ease in turning the soul around, away from becoming and towards truth and being. (Plato, *Republic* 525b–527a, Loeb trans.; italics mine)

Possibly drawing on Pythagorean ideas, Plato set up a contrast on more than one level. Different ways of doing mathematics corresponded to different expertise, purpose, and people. Indeed, in another dialogue, the *Philebus*, Plato has Socrates ask: "Are there not two kinds of arithmetic, that of the many (*oi polloi*) and that of philosophers" (Plato, *Philebus* 56d, modified Loeb trans.)?

The term *hoi polloi* used here implies that one of the essential features of the philosophers' arithmetic is its segregated, elitist character.

Fast forward a few centuries. Around 45 CE, the temporarily exiled Roman senator and translator of Plato's *Republic* Marcus Tullius Cicero wrote:

> With the Greeks, geometry was regarded with the utmost respect, and consequently none were held in greater honour than mathematicians, but we Romans have restricted this art to the practical purposes of measuring and reckoning. (Cicero, *Tusculanae Disputationes* I.2, Loeb trans.)[1]

Mathematics is only one of the ways in which Greeks and Romans differ, according to Cicero, but his characterization has remained especially influential, shifting Plato's dichotomy toward a distinction on the basis of "national" or "cultural" identity. To simplify a long and complicated story, Plato and Cicero are significant milestones in the genealogy of the idea that there were two mathematical cultures, or traditions, in classical antiquity: one theoretical, the other practical; one aimed at general truths, the other at solutions to specific problems; one achieving persuasion through rigorous logical proof, the other didactic and "algorithmic"; one interested only in knowledge, the other open to applications.

Prima facie, the idea of two mathematical traditions appears to be supported by the textual evidence. There is a relatively well-defined group of texts, explicitly and intertextually linked with each other, which has often been identified as "mainstream" Greek mathematics: Euclid's *Elements*, most of Archimedes's treatises, Apollonius's *Conics*, and so on. This tradition operates for the most part within an axiomatico-deductive demonstrative framework, which means that both its theorems and its problems are formulated in general and abstract terms. On the other hand, there is a sprawling tradition of texts in Greek, arguably sometimes intertextually linked with texts in cuneiform languages, in ancient Egyptian languages, in Latin, and possibly in Arabic, which has been identified as "folk" or "practical" mathematics, and consists of procedures for solutions carried out on specific instances of a problem. It bears no authenticated authorial identification, although some of it goes under the umbrella of pseudo-Heronian tradition (Høyrup 1997).

---

1.   Similar sentiments appear in Horace, *Epistulae* II 3.323–332.

Let us look at one example: the equivalence between the square on the hypotenuse of a right-angled triangle, and the sum of the squares on its cathetes. Today this equivalence (let's call it P) is known as the theorem of Pythagoras, even though the attribution to Pythagoras, alleged to have lived in the sixth century BCE, is not found in our sources until much later. Euclid's *Elements*, originally compiled around the early third century BCE, contains P in the following form:

In right-angled triangles the square on the side subtending the right angle is equal to the squares on the sides surrounding the right angle.

Let ABC be a right-angled triangle having the angle at BAC right. I say that the square on BC is equal to the squares on BA and AC.

For let a square, the BDEC, be described on BC; on BA and AC the squares GB and HC, and the AL have been drawn through A parallel to either BD or CE, and let AD and FC have been joined. And because each of the angles at BAC and BAG are right, two straight lines AC and AG, not lying on the same side, make the adjacent angles with a random straight line BA and a point A on it, equal to two right angles. Therefore CA is on a straight line with AG. Because of these things then also the BA is on a straight line with AH. And because the angle at DBC is equal to the angle at FBA, for both are right angles, let the angle at ABC be added in common. Therefore the whole angle at DBA is equal to the whole angle at FBC. And because DB is equal to BC, ZB to BA, and the two DB, BA to the two FB, BC, respectively, and the angle at DBA is equal to the angle at FBC, therefore the basis AD is equal to the basis FC, and the triangle ABD is equal to the triangle FBC. And the parallelogram BL is double the triangle ABD, for they have the same basis BD and are between the same parallels BD, AL. The square GB is double the triangle FBC, for again they have the same basis FB and are between the same parallels FB, GC. Therefore the parallelogram BL is also equal to the square GB. Similarly the AE, BK being joined, it will be proved that the parallelogram CL is also equal to the square HC. Therefore the whole square BDEC is equal to the two squares GB, HC. And the square BDEC is described on BC, while the squares GB, HC on BA, AC.

Therefore the square on the side BC is equal to the squares on the sides BA, AC. Therefore in right-angled triangles the square on the side subtending the right angle is equal to the squares on the sides surrounding the right angle. As it was necessary to prove. (Euclid, *Elements* I.47; my translation)

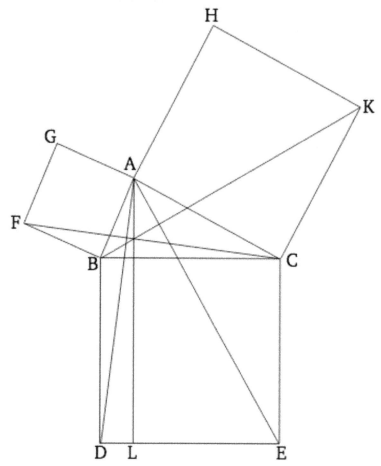

Figure 1. Diagram for Euclid, *Elements* I.47, the so-called theorem of Pythagoras.

Euclid's formulation can be taken as emblematic of the "theoretical" tradition: it is axiomatico-deductive in that it starts with a general statement, and then proceeds logically from undemonstrated premises and from statements that have been proved earlier in the *Elements*, to conclusions that, provided the reader has agreed with the initial premises and with the "rules of the game," are logically necessary. Characteristically, it deploys a lettered diagram.[2]

---

2. The *locus classicus* on lettered diagrams is Netz (1999). For the deductive structure of the *Elements*, see Mueller (1981).

Now consider the following text, dating to the second century CE:

> Let there be a right-angled triangle with the vertical side 3 feet long, the hypotenuse 5, find the basis.
> We will find it like this.
> The 5 multiplied by itself makes 25. And the 3 multiplied by itself makes 9. And from the 25 take away the 9, the remainder is 16. Its root is 4. It will be the basis: 4. Similarly too we will find with other numbers. (*P Geneva* III 124 *verso*; my translation)

This text also sets off from a(n implicit) statement of/that P, but is organized very differently from the passage in the *Elements*: P becomes a means to solving a problem rather than the focus of a proof; the text deals with a particular case and specific measurements; it appeals directly to the reader, taking them through a sequence of steps and calculations (a sequence sometimes referred to in modern scholarship as an "algorithm"), and it uses, as visible in Figure 1, a numbered diagram, where the key geometrical objects of the problem are marked by a number expressing their length or area.

These differences are what gives substance to the idea of two cultures of Greek mathematics. Most recently, Markus Asper has described them as follows:

1. General mathematical knowledge emerged from practical mathematical knowledge.[3] In Asper's words, "To think of [practical mathematics, *ndr*] as "subscientific" makes sense, as long as one remembers that *our* understanding of what science is has been heavily influenced by Greek *theoretical* mathematics. The "sub" here should be taken literally: ancient practical mathematical traditions were certainly all-pervasive in ancient Greece, on top of which theoretical mathematics suddenly emerged, like a float on a river's surface—brightly colored and highly visible, but tiny in size"(Asper 2009: 114; italics in original). This claim has some corollaries:
   a) There is a sense in which, even though "it is doubtful whether the notion of an abstract rule was present behind all the actual

---

3. Asper: "Manipulating pebbles on an abacus can lead to the discovery of general arithmetical knowledge" (2009: 108); "These two cases show how specialized, practical knowledge could become abstract and move beyond the circle of specialists" (2009: 109).

procedures" of practical mathematics (Asper 2009: 113), the re-iteration of procedures and the accumulation of cases led toward understanding at a general and abstract level;[4]

b) The emergence of the theoretical tradition from the substratum of the practical tradition is a case of Bourdieu-type social distinc-tion (Asper 2009: 123–25). The theoretical tradition was a sort of closed club, almost a "game" played by a small group, who set their way of doing mathematics, and consequently themselves, in con-trast to the larger groups engaged in practical mathematics. The crucial context for this Bourdieu-type social-distinction opera-tion is, in Asper's view, classical Athens (fifth and fourth centuries BCE). On this view, the Plato we have cited at the beginning is, as it were, channeling the *Zeitgeist*, rather than creating *ex novo* the notion of a mathematics of the *kaloi kagathoi* ("the fine and the good") and one of *hoi polloi*.

2. By contrast with the theoretical tradition, which thus has an inception point, the practical tradition is presented as essentially ahistorical: its roots go deep within Egyptian and Mesopotamian mathematics and, looking forward, it continues within Arabic mathematics. Despite some qualifications, the terminology used by Asper (and others) to refer to the persistence and stability of the practical tradition implies that it remained to a large extent unchanged.[5]

3. The people active within either culture were socially distinct (this as a result but also a precondition of 1b, above). In particular, math-ematicians within the practical tradition, and possibly including a

---

4. Asper: "The numbered diagram is meant to 'ensure that the reader un-derstands the actual procedure and, thereby, the abstract method" (2009: 119, 122; in particular 110); "Strangely, the method itself is never ex-plained in general terms, nor is its effectiveness proved. . . . Obviously, the reader is meant to understand the abstract method by repeatedly dealing with actual, varied cases. The leap, however, from the actual case to the abstract method is never mentioned in these texts. Learning a general method is achieved in these texts by repeatedly performing a procedure, understanding its effectiveness and memorizing the steps by repetition" (2009: 111).

5. Asper: "Long and remarkably stable tradition. . . (but, admittedly, may have changed along the way)," Babylonian scribes "must have used essentially the same accounting board," "the tradition resurfaces" (2009: 109; see also 112). Asper cites Høyrup, probably the most influential "continuist" regarding the practical tradition's expanse across time and space.

greater portion of "foreigners" or "migrants," "must have been of a rather low social level" (Asper 2009: 114), whereas the theoretical mathematicians were "at home in the upper circles of Athenian society" (123).

4. The language of both traditions was highly standardized and remote from oral discourse (Asper 2009: 119–20). Nonetheless, the texts of the practical tradition were accompanied by oral, personal explanation—they presupposed a teacher and a "live" situation. By contrast, the texts of the theoretical tradition are seen by Asper as autonomous—that is, constructed in such a way that they could, and still can, be understood on their own (Asper 2009: 126).

Asper's idea of distinction is an interesting twist on G. E. R. Lloyd's examination of competitive social practices in classical Athens and antiquity more generally (e.g., Lloyd 1987), but not everything in his picture, albeit sophisticated and nuanced, is equally convincing. He probably overemphasizes the extent to which the language of practical mathematics was standardized, and there are other issues that I shall raise below.[6] Let's assume for the moment, however, that Asper's two-cultures model is correct, and apply it to our example.

It would go something like this: At some point in the very remote past, somewhere or in more than one place, somehow—possibly through repeated experience on concrete cases—people became aware of P. Since then, they have been both applying P in everyday measurement situations, and teaching P through specific examples to the next generations, presumably so that they are equipped in their turn to solve measurement problems. At a certain point, possibly in classical Athens, having honed their demonstrative skills through the exercise of competitive rhetoric, a small group formulates P in a general form, and constructs a proof of it. A discourse is thus created for the purposes of social distinction, according to which the general formulation of P is the only true knowledge of P, and people who can participate in the language in which the proof is formulated are the only true mathematicians. The majority of mathematicians outside this small elite continue to do their thing, same as it ever

---

6. Linguistic analyses of this type are not unproblematic: for instance, they define "standardization" by contrast with what they refer to as "oral discourse," and yet in a context like that of the classical or Hellenistic Greek world, where our knowledge of oral discourse ultimately derives from written texts.

was, but find themselves operating within a practice that is now distinct from, and construed as incompatible with, the first one.

This could be described as a clash of ontologies, in line with the theme of this volume, but, crucially, Asper highlights the fact that despite social differences there was a shared cultural substratum, and that the clashing ontologies have been constructed rather than simply being there or "emerging." Even so, once the distinction has been made and become successful, thanks to favorable historical circumstances, such as the need of Hellenistic monarchs for cultural legitimation (which led, for instance, to the compilation of Euclid's *Elements*, and to the patronage of Archimedes by the kings of Syracuse), the two cultures appear, both to ancient observers and to future generations, hypostasized, clearly distinct in status and cultural capital. In other words, what were in origin epistemic constructs can become ontologies at a later stage, in a successful example of what Bruno Latour and Steve Woolgar described as an "inscription": a process whereby an epistemic construction becomes the scientific truth, and the scaffolding of its initial construction is dismantled and erased (Latour and Woolgar 1979).

Asper's picture is, as I said, sophisticated and, for several aspects, persuasive. Nonetheless, there are some threads left hanging.

I. Despite the recurrence and persistence of certain features, the practical tradition is arguably as subject to change and as context-dependent as any other cultural and mathematical practice. To adapt Angela Carter's (1990) words about fairy tales, "Who first invented meatballs? In what country? Is there a definitive recipe for potato soup? Think in terms of the domestic arts. 'This is how *I* make potato soup'"; there is no mathematical Potato Soup of the Folk, nor any solution to the problem of measuring a field that has simply been passed down the generations. Even if we encounter the same problem about right-angled triangles, with the same set of numbers, in different cultural contexts, that may be how a particular person or group "made potato soup"—we should question whether it is legitimate to erase its specificity and just label it as "yet another instantiation of potato soup." The latter of which is also a very Platonic thing to do.

II. Several of the authors in the theoretical tradition also contributed to the practical tradition by engaging—for instance, in the problem of measuring the circle and producing numerical values for the ratio between circumference and radius.[7] Indeed,

III. Some mathematical texts or authors from antiquity are hard to classify—for instance, Diophantus or Ptolemy, or Archimedes's *Sand-Reckoner*. In fact, many treatises on astronomy, optics, or harmonics may be difficult to unambiguously ascribe to one tradition to the exclusion of the other. This would seem to imply that some mathematicians—*most* mathematicians?—were active in both traditions, and that Asper's social differentiation as described at point 3 (above) needs revising. Arguably, this went both ways—not only were theoretical mathematicians occasionally "slumming it" in the practical tradition but also practical mathematicians may have been aware of the texts and practices of the theoretical tradition.

IV. While it is true that the practical tradition is mostly transmitted through papyrus and the theoretical tradition mostly through manuscript (Asper 2009: 109–10), there is theoretical mathematics on papyrus or ostrakon (specifically, material that has been identified as Euclidean).[8] Equally, there is practical mathematics transmitted through manuscripts—for instance, the *Corpus Agrimensorum Romanorum* or, as mentioned, the so-called pseudo-Heronian material. In the rare cases where such information is available, the archaeological context for "practical" mathematics (including arithmetical tables) does not seem significantly different from the archaeological context of material that one might expect to be associated with the culture or status of theoretical mathematics, such as classical Greek literature, or official documents denoting an elevated place in society.[9] Also, we find Greek and "Egyptian" material (meaning both material in demotic, and material pertaining to "Egyptian culture," such as temple texts) in the same archaeological context. In other words, the differentiation of theoretical mathematics and practical mathematics along lines of social status or cultural identity is not borne out by evidence external to our interpretation of the text.

V. There is the small matter of Hero of Alexandria's *Metrica*, to which we now turn.

---

7. For example, Archimedes, *Measurement of the circle* 3; see also other authors in Eutocius's commentary on Archimedes's treatise.

8. The most complete list is still in Fowler (1999).

9. See Cuomo (forthcoming) with further references.

Written around the second half of the first century CE, the *Metrica*'s potential to revolutionize our picture of ancient Greek and Roman mathematics has yet to be fully realized. Here is a representative passage:

> Let there be a right-angled triangle ABC, having the right angle in correspondence of B and let the AB be of 3 units, while BC is of 4 units. To find the area of the triangle and the hypotenuse.
>
> Let the ABCD be completed. Because the area of the rectangular parallelogram ABCD, as was proved above, is 12, the triangle ABC is half of the parallelogram ABCD, therefore the area of the triangle ABC will be six. And because the angle at ABC is right, and the squares on AB, BC are equal to the square on AC, and the squares on AB, BC are of 25 units, and the square on AC therefore will be of 25 units. Therefore that side, the AC, is of 5 units.
>
> The method is this. Having multiplied the 3 by the 4, take their half. It makes 6. Of these the area of the triangle. And the hypotenuse: having multiplied the 3 by themselves and similarly having multiplied the 4 by themselves, put them together. And they make 25. And having taken the root of these, have the hypotenuse of the triangle. (Hero, *Metrica* I.2; my translation)

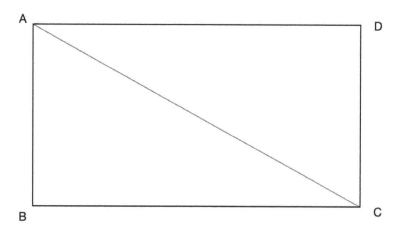

Figure 2. Diagram for Hero, *Metrica* I.2 (author's drawing).

The *Metrica*'s special position in the history of Greek mathematics lies in its approach: measurement is tackled *both* as a general problem, solved via a proof applicable to all geometrical objects of a certain type, *and* as a specific problem, solved by measuring a particular geometrical object of that type.

> Historians of mathematics used to be dismissive. Van der Waerden thought that it was a very childish little book. . . . Nothing but numerical examples, without proofs. Just like a cuneiform text. . . . There is no doubt in my mind that similar cookbooks have always existed. . . . Occasionally something is added, sometimes found by a real mathematician. . . but usually the source is anonymous. Some of the numerical examples in Heron are already found in cuneiform texts. . . . It is next to impossible to prove their dependence or to trace the road along which they were transmitted. And, after all, it is not very important. It is mankind's really great thoughts that are of importance, not their dilution in popularizations and in collections of problems with solutions. Let us rejoice in the masterworks of Archimedes and of Apollonius and not mourn the loss of numberless little arithmetic books after the manner of Heron. (van der Waerden 1954: 277–78)

The idea that the *Metrica* has something non-Greek ("cuneiform") about it was echoed by Otto Neugebauer in *The Exact Sciences in Antiquity*:

> As a particularly drastic example might be mentioned the elementary geometry represented in the Hellenistic period in writings which go under the name of Heron of Alexandria (second half of the first century AD). These treatises on geometry were sometimes considered to be signs of the decline of Greek mathematics, and this would indeed be the case if one had to consider them as the descendants of the works of Archimedes or Apollonius. But such a comparison is unjust. In view of our recently gained knowledge of Babylonian texts, Heron's geometry must be considered merely a Hellenistic form of a general oriental tradition. (Neugebauer 1957: 146)

More recently, the characterization has shifted to what we could call "hybridity": *Metrica* has been called a blend (Fowler 1999: 9), a combination of elements from several traditions (Tybjerg 2004: 31, 35), a mélange of subgenres, linked to an "algorithmic" approach.[10] Toward the conclusion

---

10. Acerbi and Vitrac (2014: 41, 58), are also careful to point out that the *Metrica* is not unique, but that it has obvious similarities with other

of a nuanced analysis of Hero's metrological work, which eschews strong commitment to the "hybridity" thesis, Vitrac nonetheless suggests:

> Quoi qu'il en soit, les *Métriques* ne relèvent d'aucun des deux registres que nous avons distingués, puisque leur finalité manifeste est précisément d'articuler les démarches métrologiques de type algorithmique et les résultats de la géométrie démonstrative pour valider les premières à l'aide des seconds, et ce, selon différentes modalités. (Vitrac 2011: 14)[11]

The implication here appears to be that demonstrative geometry is viewed as epistemologically superior to metrology, and thus able, in Hero's project, to validate it.[12] I find Karin Tybjerg's analysis to be better balanced: "In general, the techniques employed by Hero show that it is not possible to maintain the notion that Euclidean-Archimedean geometry was sealed off from the traditions of professional problems and calculation techniques" (Tybjerg 2004: 34–35).

The debate around the the role of Hero's *Metrica* vis-à-vis the "two cultures" of Greek mathematics is meaningful because it reveals underlying assumptions, not only in the use of labels like "Greek" or "Oriental" and the respective values they are made to carry but also in the attempt at a resolution of what is perceived as its singular cultural identity. The existence itself of Hero's *Metrica* is a potential threat to the idea of two cultures, because rather than bridging them (Asper 2009: 127), it may be taken to collapse them. Conversely, Hero's *Metrica* may demand a more complex vocabulary of identity, a model other than a binary one.

With that in mind, I would like to explore the potential fruitfulness of a couple of ideas borrowed from anthropology and linguistics: the notion of situation-specificity, or situated learning, as advanced by Jean Lave,

---

algorithmic—and specifically metrological—texts, both from the Graeco-Roman tradition and from other mathematical traditions. Their metrological tradition is basically congruent with what Asper terms the "practical tradition."

11. "Be that as it may, the Metrics do not belong to either of the two registers we have distinguished, since their obvious purpose is precisely to articulate metrological approaches of the algorithmic type and the results of demonstrative geometry in order to validate the former with the help of the latter, and this according to different modalities."

12. Similar criticism appears in Tybjerg (2004: 39).

both as sole author and in joint authorship with Etienne Wenger (Lave 1986, 1988; Lave and Wenger 1991); and the notion of code-switching, which is primarily a linguistic notion, but has fruitfully been applied to issues of cultural identity and imperialism, both metaphorically and more literally, given that language was crucial for the articulation of identity in ancient Greece and Rome.[13] I will also try to apply some insights about identity and free spaces articulated by Kostas Vlassopoulos (Vlassopoulos 2007, 2009, with references to earlier bibliography).

Let's start with situation-specificity. This is not an entirely new concept for historians of science, but in Lave's work it stems from observations about mathematical practice, which makes it particularly helpful, and arguably relevant, for our historical case.[14]

In observations of the mathematical behavior of late twentieth-century Californians, Lave found that people who appeared to be mathematically incompetent (or not very proficient) in a school context, proved to be mathematically proficient when asked to deploy the same mathematical knowledge (same in the sense that P is the same across our two previous examples) in a different, nonschool context, such as the supermarket or the home. Lave's supermarket "experiments" were in the vein of similar research conducted in different countries and situations, from tailors in Liberia to street kids selling goods at the market in Brazil.[15] In Lave's own words: "The same people differ in their arithmetic activities in different settings in ways that challenge theoretical boundaries between activity and its settings, between cognitive, bodily, and social forms of activity, between information and value, between problems and solutions" (Lave 1988: 3).

Given that school proficiency, or the lack thereof, can often be mapped onto class, gender, and race, and given that the observations about the situatedness of mathematical knowledge have almost always involved participants who are in some way disadvantaged in comparison to the stereotypically mathematically proficient White middle-class, college-educated man, situation-specificity can be deployed as a powerful

---

13. I have drawn extensively on the following: Heller (1995); Webster (2001); Cooley (2002); Adams (2003); Gardner-Chloros (2005); Wallace-Hadrill (2008).

14. For example, Chemla (2012) is very much in tune with it (without explicitly using the concept).

15. Examples include Ginsburg, Posner, and Russell (1981); Carraher, Carraher, and Schliemann (1985); Lave (1986).

political statement, even if Lave's account itself is not overtly political. Western-style school mathematics, or the "theoretical tradition," or "mental arithmetic" as opposed to, say, finger calculation, are only some among many possible mathematical "situations." They just happen, for historical reasons that are often as well known as they are ultimately ignored, to have become institutionalized, to the point where they stand in for "numeracy" or "mathematical knowledge" or "calculating skill" tout court, respectively (Harouni 2015).

The advantage, in my view, of using the notion of "situation" instead of "tradition," "culture," and even "ontology," is that "situations" are finer grained and more flexible, and also better suited to exploring use and practice, rather than "systems" (Johnstone 2011); action rather than theory. Moreover, "situations" make more room for unauthorized agency and interaction, can be similar across time and space, but are also historically localized, and they can be characterized in terms of issues of access and power (which suits both Lloyd's competitive context, and Asper's context of social distinction).

Next, consider the idea of code-switching, or a speaker's ability to alternate between two or more languages, depending on situation and context. It has long been recognized that language was key to articulating cultural identity in antiquity. At the same time, bilingualism and code-switching have become useful metaphors to talk about cultural identities in antiquity. A passage in the *Dissoi Logoi*, in the context of debating the question whether one can teach and learn wisdom and virtue, states:

> And if someone is not convinced that we learn our words, but rather that we are born knowing them, let him gain knowledge from this: if someone sends a child to Persia as soon as the child is born and has it brought up there without ever hearing Greek sounds, the child will speak Persian. If someone brings the child from Persia to Greece, the child will speak Greek. That is how we learn words, and we do not know who it was who taught us. (*Dissoi Logoi* 6.12, Loeb trans.)

The facts that language crops up in the discussion, and that a discussion about virtue implicates the difference between Greek and barbarian, are significant here. Examples could multiply: the notion of *paideia*, literary education, often seen as the dominant cultural paradigm of the elite in the Roman period, rested on strong competence in the Greek language, and is a very good example of the fact that, in Lave and Wenger's words, "learning involves the construction of identities" (Lave and Wenger 1991: 53). It is also well known that code-switching in antiquity could be about "the expression of different types of identity" (Adams 2003: 302; cf. also 356–82, 413–15).

All this suits *Metrica* rather well. The text has been seen as an instantiation of hybridity, but the problem with that term is its passivity. To talk in terms of code-switching, which is a more agent-centered concept, does more justice to Hero's very deliberate ("marked," in linguistic terms) combination of the reference frame of axiomatico-deductive mathematics, and of calculations.[16] The ability to speak more than one language may still leave space for a distinction between "mother tongue" and others, including pidgin languages, which are recognizably "acquired," and creolization (which could be another way to describe *Metrica*), but the main point is not competence—rather, it is the fact that agents switch linguistic codes and indeed cultural identities, according to the context of performance and communication (the situation).[17]

Situation-specificity thus creates a plausible framework for the switching of codes, and supports the possibility that *Metrica* may not have been such a rare beast—perhaps multilingualism, mathematically speaking, was not as exotic as we might think. Together, these two notions approximate a better model than the two cultures, for understanding mathematicians who "crossed boundaries" in either direction. Rather, the new model dissolves the idea of crossing boundaries, thus making sense of the fact that, as I mentioned above, whenever we are able to reconstruct a more localized context for mathematical knowledge, we are faced with "multilingualism."

---

16. See Tybjerg (2004) for a nuanced analysis.

17. I do not find the notion of linguistic incompetence as a reason for code-switching (see Adams 2003: 305–8) useful in this context, for two reasons. First, code-switching is here a way of talking about cultural identity, so that the equivalent of incompetence would be the lack of authority in self-definition, which I reject. Second, I take Lave and Wenger's (1991) notion of legitimate peripheral participation as a useful model of learning. On that model, and particularly if code-switching is a way of talking about knowledge practices, participation is *always* legitimate, and competence or lack of competence are therefore not useful concepts. As well put by Gardner-Chloros (2005: 18): "Code-switchers upset the notion of performance errors by contravening and rewriting the expected rules."

Similarly to situation-specificity, there are underlying political connotations to code-switching. For a long time, this way of "mixing things up"
was associated with incompetence, displacement, and subordination—a
linguistic phenomenon associated with the immigrant, the insufficiently
educated, and the geographically marginal. And yet, the prime example
of code-switching in classical antiquity is the member of the elite but
also *homo novus* Cicero, whose usage of Greek represents very complex
code-switching (Adams 2003: passim). Even today, according to Penelope Gardner-Chloros, the perception of code-switching, even on the
part of many of the code-switchers themselves, can be one of laziness,
surprise, and embarrassment, although she notes that "approval of CS
tends to coincide with a laid-back attitude towards authority" (Gardner-
Chloros 2005: 14–15).

Moreover, and briefly, the idea of cultural identity has been problematized by Vlassopoulos in a way that is relevant to our purposes. While
acknowledging the existence of discourses advocating strong cultural
identity differences (Greek v. barbarian, Athenian v. non-Athenian, slave
v. free), Vlassopoulos draws on abundant ancient evidence to make the
point, specific to classical Athens in his work but in my view easily ex-
tendable to other ancient contexts, that identities were confused, confus-
ing, and subject to continuous negotiation and renegotiation. He points
out that, despite a rhetoric of separation and distinction, there were
many communal "free spaces" (the *agora*, the *ergasterion* [workshop, *ndr*],
the household, the harbor, the ship) where people from across alleged
cultural boundaries met, interacted, and communicated. As Vlassopoulos points out, at least in some cases those free spaces must have involved
literal as well as metaphorical multilingualism and code-switching
(Vlassopoulos 2007, 2009).

Thus, the notion of "tradition" or "culture" seems compatible with
a scenario where cultural identity is relatively unproblematic, and as
such susceptible to relatively easy identification (e.g., a certain piece
of mathematics looks unmistakably Greek or, conversely, non-Greek),
subject to, at most, "mixing." However, more recent and self-reflective
discourses, such as Vlassopoulos's, take it that cultural identity is *always* a construct, and therefore always problematic; that identification
could be, and was, contested, thus raising the question of whom should
be qualified to assign or deny a certain cultural identity attribution or
label, particularly if we accept that it is possible for an individual to

activate or switch different identities at will, without asking for external authorization.[18]

In conclusion, what are the consequences of applying situation-specificity, code-switching, and "free-space" cultural identity—in preference to "tradition" or "culture," in the sense in which they have been used in the relevant literature—to the study of mathematical practices in ancient Greek and Roman world? First of all, "theoretical" and "practical" turn out to be not different cultures or different traditions but different situations. It is no longer enough to populate mathematical practices with just minds at work, seen through the lens of texts. Situated learning requires that we get a better sense of the "nexus of relations between the mind at work and the world in which it works."[19] That is compatible with Asper's idea of a shared original substratum, but it also allows for people unproblematically to participate in more than one situation, and it does not map social status or institutional status onto a certain way of doing mathematics, while leaving open the possibility of mapping social or institutional status in terms of the specific situation to which that person would have had access. It leaves us open to the possibility of situations that mix things up a little, or a lot.

Situation-specificity is conducive to greater symmetry. The situation-specificity of theoretical mathematics is not essentially different from the situation-specificity of practical mathematics. Consequently, they both have a history, and the abstract, general quality of theoretical mathematics does not rest on ontological grounds. Ontologies are a feature of situations, but not the only feature. Indeed,

> a theory of situated activity challenges the very meaning of abstraction and/or generalization. . . . An important point about such sequestering when it is institutionalized is that it encourages a folk epistemology of dichotomies, for instance, between "abstract" and "concrete" knowledge. These categories do not reside in the world as

---

18. For a modern but relevant parallel, witness the recent discussions around LGBT, trans- and cis-gender, and gender identity.

19. Lave: "These studies converge towards a view that math 'activity' (to propose a term for a distributed form of cognition) takes form differently in different situations. The specificity of arithmetic practice wthin a situation, and discontinuities between situations, constitute a provisional basis for pursuing explanations of cognition as a nexus of relations between the mind at work and the world in which it works" (1988: 1).

distinct forms of *knowledge*, nor do they reflect some putative hierarchy of forms of knowledge among practitioners. Rather, they derive from the nature of the new practice generated by sequestration. *Abstraction* in this sense stems from the disconnectedness of a particular cultural practice. Participation in that practice is neither more nor less abstract or concrete, experiential or cerebral, than in any other. (Lave and Wenger 1991: 37; see also 33–34, 104)

Second, even though the practices we are discussing are largely textual, shifting the focus to situation-specificity and to code-switching

emphasizes the inherently socially negotiated character of meaning and the interested, concerned character of the thought and action of persons-in-activity. This view also claims that learning, thinking, and knowing are relations among people in activity in, with, and arising from the socially and culturally structured world. (Lave and Wenger 1991: 50–51)

I think we should recognize the inevitability of personal, tacit knowledge even when all we have are texts, and cast doubt over the possibility of truly autonomous texts—even Archimedes first learned mathematics from some other person. Basic numeracy skills, which are situation-specific and include a component of tacit, interpersonal knowledge, are the sine qua non of mathematical knowledge. In this sense, again, Asper is right.

Third, especially when marked, code-switching emphasizes self-determination and situation-specific agency. The authority to ascribe identity thus shifts from an external classification of people and mathematical activities (including at the hands of modern historians), to self-definition or, in the absence of explicit statements, the presumption of self-definition. The mathematicians active both within the theoretical tradition and the practical tradition, the big authors and the anonymous ones, and others involved in mathematical practices who may have not produced any texts, under this model ought to be all recognized as agents. The idea that we can separate out "real" mathematicians from those who never wrote a text, and specifically a text proving a theorem, is, in my view, unacceptably arbitrary (*pace* Netz 2002). You could see this as an extreme version of preferring actors' to observers' categories, which is again very much one of Lloyd's seminal contributions to the history of ancient science.

A perspective that frames things in terms of situation-specificity rather than culture or tradition recognizes that there are power relationships to do with mathematical practices and mathematical knowledge, but does not attribute power exclusively to the group or tradition that happen to be more similar to modern mathematics, or to modern scholars. Monica Heller has drawn on (again) Pierre Bourdieu to argue that code-switching can be used to gain entry to groups with cultural capital. Using the metaphor of a game with rules,

> specific groups set the rules of the game by which resources can be distributed. . . . It is necessary to display appropriate linguistic and cultural knowledge in order to gain access to the game, and playing it well requires in turn mastery of the kinds of linguistic and cultural knowledge which constitute its rules. Buying into the game means buying into the rules, it means accepting them as routine, as normal, indeed as universal, rather than as conventions set up by dominant groups in order to place themselves in the privileged position of regulating access to the resources they control. (Heller 1995: 160)

And yet, Heller does not allow for participants to change the game, deliberately in an act of subversion, or less deliberately by not playing the game well. She surrenders control of the game to the already-established participants, not simply in terms of setting or abiding by the rules but also in terms of who should access the game, and how well they are playing. Transferring this to cultural identity, if both situated learning and code-switching are ways to reclaim and construct—to own—cultural identities, then Lave and Wenger, compared to Heller, reaffirm the significance of self-definition over authorization by other parties. Transferred to Hero, this means that we, historians, ought to take seriously his claim to belong to the same tradition as Eudoxus and Archimedes, while recognizing it as an operation of code-switching. Transferred to wider discourses about cultural capital and learning in the ancient Greek and Roman worlds, this creates an alternative, and possibly a subversion, to the concept of *paideia*, which can be easily recognized as a Bourdieu-type social-distinction linguistic and cultural game. This would seem to work particularly well for ancient Greece and Rome because, while there were political, social, and economic hierarchies and inequalities, culture was not deeply institutionalized, and for many forms of knowledge there was, as Lloyd has repeatedly demonstrated, a marketplace.

References

Acerbi, Fabio, and Bernard Vitrac, eds. 2014. *Héron d'Alexandrie: Metrica*. Pisa: Fabrizio Serra.

Adams, James Noel. 2003. *Bilingualism and the Latin language*. Cambridge: Cambridge University Press.

Asper, Markus. 2009. "The two cultures of mathematics in ancient Greece." In *The Oxford handbook of the history of mathematics*, edited by Eleanor Robson and Jackie Stedall, 107–32. Oxford: Oxford University Press.

Carter, Angela. 1990. *The virago book of fairy tales*. London: Virago Press.

Chemla, Karine. 2012. "Historiography and history of mathematical proof: A research programme." In *The history of mathematical proof in ancient traditions*, edited by Karine Chemla, 1–68. Cambridge: Cambridge University Press.

Cooley, Alison, ed. 2002. *Becoming Roman, writing Latin? Literacy and epigraphy in the Roman West*. Portsmouth, RI: Journal of Roman Archaeology Supplementary Series.

Cuomo, Serafina. Forthcoming. *Ancient numeracy*. Cambridge, MA: Harvard University Press.

Fowler, David H. 1999. *The mathematics of Plato's Academy: A new reconstruction*. Rev. ed. Oxford: Clarendon Press.

Gardner-Chloros, Penelope. 2005. *Code-switching*. Cambridge: Cambridge University Press.

Ginsburg, Herbert P., Jill K. Posner, and Robert L. Russell. 1981. "The development of mental addition as a function of schooling and culture." *Journal of Cross-Cultural Psychology* 12 (2): 163–78.

Harouni, Houman. 2015. "Toward a political economy of mathematics education." *Harvard Educational Review* 85 (1): 50–74.

Heller, Monica. 1995. "Code-switching and the politics of language." In *One speaker, two languages: Cross-disciplinary perspectives on code-switching*, edited by Lesley Milroy and Pieter Muysken, 158–74. Cambridge: Cambridge University Press.

Høyrup, Jens. 1997. "Hero, Ps.-Hero, and Near Eastern practical geometry: An investigation of *Metrica*, *Geometrica*, and other treatises." In *Third International Conference on Ancient Mathematics: Proceedings of the Third International Meeting, Delphi, Greece, July 30–August 3, 1996*, edited by John Lennart Berggren, 93–116. Burnaby, BC: Simon Fraser University Press.

Johnstone, Steven. 2011. *A history of trust in ancient Greece*. Chicago: University of Chicago Press.

Latour, Bruno, and Steve Woolgar. 1979. *Laboratory life: The construction of scientific facts*. Beverly Hills, CA: Sage Publications.

Lave, Jean. 1986. "The values of quantification." In *Power, action and belief: A new sociology of knowledge*, edited by John Law, 88–111. London: Routledge.

———. 1988. *Cognition in practice: Mind, mathematics and culture in everyday life*. Cambridge: Cambridge University Press.

Lave, Jean, and Etienne Wenger. 1991. *Situated learning: Legitimate peripheral participation*. Cambridge: Cambridge University Press.

Lloyd, G. E. R. 1987. *The revolutions of wisdom*. Berkeley: University of California Press.

Mueller, Ian. 1981. *Philosophy of mathematics and deductive structure in Euclid's* Elements. Cambridge, MA: MIT Press.

Netz, Reviel. 1999. *The shaping of deduction in Greek mathematics*. Cambridge: Cambridge University Press.

———. 2002. "Greek mathematicians: A group picture." In *Science and mathematics in ancient Greek culture*, edited by Christopher J. Tuplin and Tracey E. Rihll, 196–216. Oxford: Oxford University Press.

Neugebauer, Otto. 1957. *The exact sciences in antiquity*. 2nd ed. Providence, RI: Brown University Press.

Carraher, Terezinha Nunes, David William Carraher, and Analúcia Dias Schliemann. 1985. "Mathematics in the streets and in schools." *British Journal of Developmental Psychology* 3 (1): 21–29.

Tybjerg, Karin. 2004. "Hero of Alexandria's mechanical geometry." *Apeiron* 37 (4): 29–56.

Vitrac, Bernard. 2011. "Faut-il réhabiliter Héron d'Alexandrie?" In *Faut-il réhabiliter Héron d'Alexandrie?*, 281–96. Montpellier: Les Belles Lettres. https://hal.archives-ouvertes.fr/hal-00454027.

Vlassopoulos, Kostas. 2007. "Free spaces: Identity, experience and democracy in classical Athens." *Classical Quarterly* 57 (1): 33–52.

———. 2009. "Beyond and below the *polis*: Networks, associations, and the writing of Greek history." In *Greek and Roman networks in the Mediterranean*, edited by Irad Malkin, Christy Constantakopoulou, and Katerina Panagopoulou, 12–23. London: Routledge.

van der Waerden, Bartel. 1954. *Science awakening*. Translated by Arnold Dresden. Groningen: Noordhoff.

Wallace-Hadrill, Andrew. 2008. *Rome's cultural revolution*. Cambridge: Cambridge University Press.

Webster, Jane. 2001. "Creolizing the Roman provinces." *American Journal of Archaeology* 105 (2): 209–25.

CHAPTER FIVE

Is There Mathematics in the Forest?

Mauro W. B. de Almeida

Is it possible to translate forest mathematics into modern language? The immediate answer is yes, because otherwise there could be no ethnography—not to mention history—of mathematics, a bleak conclusion that would deprive of meaning many works on counting systems among illiterate people and on their worldviews.

This argument, of course, begs the point, which is precisely whether or not there *is* mathematics among nonliterate, Indigenous cultures in the first place—that is to say, whether we are talking about the same thing when we include finger-counting among Indigenous societies and theorem-proving in axiomatic style as comparable instances of mathematics. Are we not, in so doing, committing another act of charitable translation, by redressing other people's acts and assertions so as to make them look better in our modern garb? And, granted that there is, so to speak, mathematics in the forest, is it the same as Western mathematics, and can it be translated without distorting the peculiarities of Indigenous ontologies in which it is embedded?

Ethnographies as well histories of mathematics that deal with different cultures suggest strongly that we can actually engage in meaningful conversations with people in other cultures, in the sense of talking significantly to each other, and not merely just misunderstanding each other. Thus it is that a contemporary introduction to the Theory of Numbers invokes the "sophisticated means" employed by Babylonian clerks to generate Pythagorean triples, uses the "Chinese remainder theorem" in proofs, and places Euclid's "division algorithm" as the foundation stone of the whole subject.[1] Anachronistic as these references may seem to the eyes of the modern scholar, and notwithstanding the deep differences between the worldviews of ancients and moderns, there remains the fact that Euclid's division algorithm survives a variety of translations from bad to excellent. The reason for this fact is what is at stake. I am aware that while mathematical agreement in the pragmatic and structural sense may be consistent with ontological pluralism, it can also be the case that this sense of familiarity of moderns when reading ancient mathematical texts lies in the fact that our own mathematics belongs to the Greek tradition, and has developed along successive rewritings of Euclid's as well as of Archimedes's and Diophantus's works.[2] But there is more to it than that, because we also understand intuitively the use of Roman and Greek calculating boards as well as of Chinese and Japanese sorobans and African counting systems (Cuomo 2001, 2007; Zaslavsky 1973; Lloyd 1990, 1996; Lockhart 2017). When it comes to nonliterate Amerindian societies, these issues are the subject of controversy. Anthropologists argue that there is indeed mathematics among Indigenous people, involving counting with the body, with actions, with beads, and embodied in social life. They look for mathematics embedded in social practices and institutions as well as in kinship, cosmology, and religion (Mimica 1988; Crump 1990; Urton 1997; Verran 2001; Passes 2006; Ferreira 2015), and also "in the stones" (Hugh-Jones 2016) as well as in "in everyday life" and "in the street" (Lave 1988; Nunes, Schliemann, and Carraher 1993; Mesquita, Restivo, and D'Ambrosio 2011).

Ethnographic studies tend to conclude that "forest mathematics" is incommensurable with modern mathematics, and oppose the ontological content of Indigenous numeral systems—for instance, with the supposedly abstract, disembodied, ontology-free arithmetic of modern times.

---

1. On Babylonian mathematics, the Chinese Remainder Theorem, and Euclid's Division Algorithm, see Stillwell (2003: 12–13, 66, 158, 171–76); see also Lloyd (1996, 2004) and Cuomo (2001).
2. An authoritative author argues that Gauss "not only did see that Euclid was right . . . he also saw that [the parallel axiom] implied the existence of a geometry different from that of Euclid" (Kelly and Matthews 1981: 12). Archimedes is described as the forerunner of the Integral Calculus (Pólya 1973: 155).

Against this stance, mathematicians such as Ubiratan D'Ambrosio, Marcia Ascher, and Hervé Bazin have argued that there are common mathematical ideas expressed by different means in different cultures and times, and look for Indigenous "mathematical ideas" that overlap modern mathematical themes (Ascher and Ascher 1981; Ascher 1991, 2002a; D'Ambrosio 2001; Bazin and Tamez 2002).[3] Concurrent with the second interpretation, mathematicians have in the last century illustrated abstruse areas of pure mathematics, such as crystallographic groups, knot theory, and permutation groups, by means of such concrete subjects as Egyptian decorative patterns (Tietze 1942), Polynesian navigation charts and quipus (Speiser [1922] 1937) and Australian kinship systems (Weil [1949] 1967). These examples suggest that the "unreasonable effectiveness of mathematics" in the natural sciences (Wigner 1960) may have a counterpart in the human sciences, where mathematics appears to play a role similar to that of music as a means of communication between different cultures, although with different meanings. The latter view can of course be dismissed as charitable at best, and Eurocentric at worst, or, in other words, as yet another variant of a Whig view in which all previous modes of knowledge converge toward contemporary science. Should then anthropologists counter this supposed scientific ethnocentrism with the thesis of radical noncommensurability? Against this dismal epistemic posture, I think that a defense of mathematical translatability across time and space is compatible with the acknowledgement of the unlimited varieties of mathematical activity in different cultures and epochs.[4] A plurality of mathematical ontologies and the consequent ambiguity and indeterminacy of mathematical translation are not an impediment to transcultural mathematical understanding. More specifically, I argue that the pragmatic effects of mathematics, as well as its relational and iconic character, account for its interculturality, despite the multiplicity of ontologies associated with mathematical activities in the same or in different cultures.[5] The thesis, of course, is far from new. It is

---

3. Cf. Sahlins's proposal that there is a common core of "kinship ideas" recognizable across all known cultural forms (Sahlins 2013).

4. This point may perhaps be taken as a special case of Lloyd's argument against the incommensurability thesis and the homogeneity of mentalities (Lloyd 1990).

5. For these points I am indebted to Da Costa's pluralistic philosophy of science (Da Costa, Bueno, and French 1998; Da Costa and French 2003), and from his reading of Peirce's pragmatism (Peirce 1932, 1965).

a reinstatement of a view pioneered by Wilhelm von Humboldt early in the nineteenth century, the point being that all languages are capable of expressing any human thoughts, although with different grammatical means and carrying, accordingly, distinct connotations.[6] To use an analogy employed by Edward Sapir, translating between languages is like changing the coordinate system when representing a geometrical figure. The representation will come across in both frames of reference, but some reference systems allow an elegant representation, while others lead to a cumbrous formulation, as becomes evident when we look for an equation representing a circumference in the Cartesian plane (Sapir [1924] 1949).[7] The important point in Sapir's analogy is that the completeness of all human languages is not the same as semantical equivalence.[8]

One could advance the argument a bit further to suggest that modern mathematics is well equipped for conveying the ontological variety of non-Western cultures, sharing somehow the similar claim of anthropological and historical disciplines. For contemporary mathematics is a multicultural continent where Platonists, formalists, and constructivists live together while disagreeing on basic issues of existence and method (Connes, Lichnerowicz, and Schützenberger 2001; D'Espagnat and Zwirn 2017). Mathematics is ultimately "what mathematicians do." Incidentally, this is not a unique feature of modern culture, for a similar plurality of views and methods flourished in ancient Greece and China (Lloyd 1996). Platonic realism, represented by some of the most eminent

---

6. "No language has ever been found that lies outside the boundaries of complete grammatical organization . . . even the so-called rude and barbaric language families already possess everything that is needed to a complete usage." Humboldt's most noteworthy example is "a literature flourishing since millennia in a language nearly devoid of any grammar in the usual sense of the word," that is, Chinese (Humboldt [1820] 1994:1ff.; [1822] 1994).

7. Jerrold Katz stated the point as the "principle of effability" (Katz 1978). The creator of the "Sapir-Whorf" hypothesis was neither Sapir nor Whorf, but the editor of the posthumous works of Whorf (Whorf [1941] 1956:134ff.).

8. While asserting that the "Eskimo" have linguistic means to express the notion of causality and to translate Kant's work, Sapir calls attention to how grammatical schemata have ontological implications: "Stone falls is good enough for Lenin, as it was good enough for Cicero . . . [the] Chinese . . . content themselves with a frugal 'stone fall,' and in Nootka no stone is assumed at all, and 'the stone falls' may be reassembled into something like 'It stones down'" (Sapir [1924] 1949: 124, 158–59, 160–66).

modern mathematicians, maintains that sets exist in a realm of their own that is independent of human thought and inaccessible to senses.[9] It also holds that mathematicians have an intuitive perception of such suprasensible beings.[10] Kurt Gödel's ontological and epistemological position is diametrically opposed to the views that mathematics is the result of human activity. But in this camp, there is no consensus either, because there are those who say that only mathematics objects exist that can constructed by well-defined rules (Bridges and Richman 1987), and those for whom mathematics is the free creation of human mind—not to mention the naturalistic attitude that sees mathematics as an empirical science dealing with properties of the physical world (Maddy 1997).[11] In short, just as Indigenous and ancient mathematics are laden with multiple metaphysical worlds, contemporary mathematics overbrims with ontological and epistemological varieties ranging from idealism to constructivism and formalism, just as anthropology has its own corresponding epistemic strategies—namely, looking for metaphysical systems, describing how things are actually constructed, searching for rules and algorithms.[12]

---

9. "The objects of transfinite set theory . . . clearly do not belong to the physical world, and even their indirect connection with physical experience is very loose (owing primarily to the fact that set-theoretical concepts play only a minor role in the physical theories of today)" (Gödel (1964) 1990: 267–68).

10. "I don't see any reason why we should have less confidence in this kind of perception, i.e., in mathematical intuition, than in sense perception, which induces us to build up physical theories and to expect that future sense perceptions will agree with them" (Gödel (1964) 1990: 268). Meinong's ontology, which allows for the existence of "impossible objects" such as square circles (Meinong (1904) 1999) and Da Costa's "paraconsistent logic," which allows inconsistent propositions (Da Costa 1974) are examples of contemporary ontological anarchism (Almeida 2013).

11. It is perhaps of interest to anthropologists who struggle with "neopositivism" to mention that Quine deconstructed a long time ago the "two dogmas of empiricism"—that is to say, the separation between "logical truths" (independent from experience) and "synthetical truths" (relying on experience), and between theory and observation (Quine 1953).

12. These three broad branches are not the whole story. There are radical constructivism (cf. Bridges and Richman 1987), naturalism (Maddy 1997), and structuralist mathematics (Bourbaki 1994), among other varieties.

Do the Amerindians have Numbers?

The thesis of the universal existence of mathematics across cultures would seem to have been refuted by Daniel Everett's thesis, according to which the alleged absence of "recursiveness" in the Pirahã language explains why the Pirahã people lack "numbers of any kind or a concept of counting" (Everett 2005: 621). Everett empirically supported his argument with the absence of words for numbers among the Pirahã (Everett 2005: 621).[13] In his 2005 article, Everett relied heavily on Peter Gordon's counting experiments among the Pirahã, from which Gordon concluded that Pirahã were unable to count large "numerosities" with exactness, attributing this failure to the lack of number-words (Gordon 2004).[14] The same issue of *Science* that features Gordon's report includes another experiment on Indigenous counting abilities, this time with the Mundurucu, whose language lacks words for "numbers beyond 5," but who "are able to compare and add large approximate numbers that are far beyond their naming range," although "failing in exact arithmetic with numbers larger than 4 or 5" (Pica et al. 2004); the point being that there is a distinction between a system of approximate counting without numerals and a language-based system for counting that consists in a routine for pairing in a one-to-one way objects with numerals (Pica et al. 2004: 499, 503). We can conclude from the latter statement that the "no-number, no counting" thesis is based on the mistaken identification of the number concept with the use of numerals, and of the counting concept with "counting with numerals" (Gelman and Butterworth 2005). In fact, that is not all there is to it. In a later paper, contra Gordon (2004) and contra Everett (2005), Michael Frank (2008) and collaborators (including Everett) recognize after new experiments—this time using a more culturally friendly setting—that Pirahã speakers, although they have "no linguistic method of expressing any exact quantity, even 'one,'" are, after

---

13. A large section of Everett's 2005 essay is dedicated to the "absence of number concept," giving as corroborating evidence the absence of numerals or number-words among the Pirahã (Everett 2005: 623-24, 626). We are also told that the Pirahã do not have "ordinal numbers" either, although they order generations as above and below Ego (Everett 2005: 633).

14. Everett's central thesis is that, pace Chomsky and collaborators (Hauser, Chomsky, and Fitch 2002), recursiveness is not a universal feature of human languages, the Pirahã being a counterexample (Everett 2005). Everett gives this thesis as the explanation for the "the absence of numbers of any kind or a concept of counting" among the Pirahã (Everett 2005: 621).

all, able "to perform exact matching tasks with large numbers of objects when these tasks do not require memory," the conclusion being now that the Pirahã lack "words for numbers," which are a "technology" indispensable for memorizing and comparing "large quantities" (Frank et al. 2008: 820). Notwithstanding, the Pirahã proved in these experiments to be able to pair quantities one-to-one and thus compare quantities as larger and smaller: "performance on the one-to-one matching task was nearly perfect, and performance on the uneven match task was close to ceiling as well" (Frank et al. 2008: 822). The authors conclude: "a total lack of exact quantity *language* did not prevent the Pirahã from accurately performing a task which relied on the exact numerical equivalence of large sets" (Frank et al. 2008: 823; my emphasis). Facing this evidence, the remaining argument is that, although the Pirahã can check the "numerical equivalence of large sets," they lack "memory" devices for numbers, which are supposed dependent on *words*.

How about the "absence of a number concept" and of a "counting concept"? Let us recall the main empirical facts revealed by a second counting experiment, which differed from the one performed by Gordon in that "matching" was done with objects familiar to Pirahã: first, Pirahã can distinguish a collection with n from another having $n+1$ objects, and can compare cardinally two collections, as larger and smaller.

In fact, in Peano's axioms, natural numbers are constructed from a sign for one, and by the act of adding one to a number already constructed—that is, from 1 and from the operation designated as $n+1$, or, even more basically: starting from $|$, juxtaposing $|$ successively, so as to obtain $|, ||, |||$, and so on.[15] Therefore, the Pirahã, having the ability to make these distinctions, already have all that is needed for doing Peano's arithmetic—without the use of numerals. Also, in Cantor's set theory, *infinitely large* numbers are *compared* by means of one-to-one matching of two collections, an act that can be performed with bundles of sticks.[16] And this is precisely the method used by another Amazonian Indigenous

---

15. This is Hilbert's basic characterization of the number system (Hilbert (1904) 1967).

16. In the manual of arithmetic in Tukuya language (Bazin and Tamez 2002; Cabalzar 2012), Tukuya's finger-based counting system is represented as bundles of sticks, with the addition of a Mayan symbol for positional zero (to allow the construction of big numbers). Calculation with an abacus or a soroban is essentially another way of "counting with fingers," without using number-words at all.

group. As for memorizing quantities, the Palikur of northwestern Amazonia, when inviting a neighbor for a party, used a "day-counting" device consisting in "a number of finger-sized sticks," "richly decorated with cotton and feathers." Curt Nimuendaju, the German ethnographer, continues: "After receiving the Iyen-ti, the invited person kinks off daily the ends of two sticks. If at the end there is still one stick left, then the party starts at noon of this day, but if there is none left, then the party starts at night" (Nimuendaju 1926: 94, quoted in Vidal 2007: 23, my translation).

There seems to be no doubt left about the presence of a modern *concept* of counting and of number even among the Pirahã, not to mention of the actual ability to *count large numbers* by means of the matching method. If there is any conceptual shortcoming here it is not on the Pirahã's side. As for the "memory" role of numerals, one should recall, besides the *Iyen-ti* technique quoted above, the method of *quipus* and of the Christian rosaries as efficient techniques for storing large numbers without words (Almeida 2015).

Mathematics in the Forest

This is our cue to go back to the comparative ethnography of mathematics, which was the starting point of my argument. Studies of Indigenous mathematics have focused on number systems (Zaslavsky 1973; Closs 1986; Gilsdorf 2012; Ferreira 2015; Lockhart 2017) and on related pedagogical issues (Verran 2001; Bazin and Tamez 2002; Cabalzar and Bazin 2004). How to go beyond the focus on the metaphysics of numbers in the Tylorian tradition ([1871] 1920), toward a wider view of mathematics?

I go back to Gary Urton's thesis: that Quechua number ontology has a relevant contribution to make to contemporary philosophy of numbers (Urton 1997). While agreeing with the point, I suggest that contemporary mathematics has also a relevant contribution to make to anthropology, by offering a wider view of what mathematics is about. This wider perspective is illustrated by the cooperative work of mathematicians and anthropologists, which has thrown light on nonnumerical, non-measure-oriented "mathematical ideas" embedded in human life. One of the best examples is Marcia and Robert Ascher's *Mathematics of the Incas: Code of the Quipu* (Ascher and Ascher 1981), a deep analysis of the many uses and possible meanings of *quipu*. In subsequent books, Marcia Ascher drew attention to the interesting and nontrivial mathematics implied in "sand drawings" by Angolan children and in "tracing graphs around rice grains" by Tamil Nadu women (Ascher 1991: 30; 2002a: 162; 2002b; on children's drawing, see also Gerdes 2007). Other areas where Ascher revealed subtle "mathematical ideas" are "the logic of kin relations" and other "systems of relationships" (1991: 67–83; 2002a: 128–59), a point to which I will return. The "symmetric patterns" (1991: 154ff.) and "models and maps" (2002a: 89; 2002b: 122) are other domains where "mathematical ideas" are found. Other examples of cooperative work by anthropologists and mathematicians include the catalogue of plane patterns found in Indigenous designs by Dorothy Washburn and Donald Crowe (1988, 2004), based on the theory of groups. This is the approach that I will use in the next section, as a tentative example of how mathematics can be found in social systems.

The Point of Incommensurability: "My Father is My Son"

I now turn to an example of translation from another modern mathematical theory into a Native idiom of kinship, emphasizing the point that the translation does make ontologies commensurable, for what is being translated are ideas about *relations*, not about *things* related by them. I take as an instance the Cashinahua kinship language.[17] First, I argue that ontological translation is unavoidably ambiguous in this case.

Epan is the Cashinahua vocative translated as *pai* in Portuguese and as "father" in English. This is clearly a case of equivocation both in the extensional sense and in the intensional sense, since in standard usage, Brazilian *pai* refers to a single individual at the next ascending generation, while a Cashinahua can address as *epan* not only his "father" in the English sense but also all his "father's brothers" and also his "sons" together with his "brother's sons"—keeping in mind that English kinship terms within quotation marks are not meant as translations of Cashinahua terms. Thus, terminologically, "father" and "son" could refer in different contexts to individuals that a Cashinahua speaker would address as

---

17. The Cashinahua are an Indigenous people inhabiting the course of the upper Jurua River. They belong to the Panoan linguistic family, which encompasses several Indigenous groups distributed along the Jurua River and the Ucayali River. My main sources are the monographs by Kensinger (1995) and McCallum (2001), as well as Capistrano de Abreu (1941) and Camargo (2002), in addition to conversations with Sian Caxinauá.

epan, as well as all his "father's brothers" and his "brother's sons."[18] As an example, Sian, a Cashinahua of Jordão River, explained in Portuguese to an undergraduate class, *"Eu respeito meu filho porque meu filho é meu pai"* ("I respect my son because my son is my father").

To understand this, it is necessary to know that Cashinahua people are divided not only by gender and moiety but also in groups of people who are namesakes (*chuta*) to each other. Sian addresses both his "son" and "father" as *epan*. Similarly, a male speaker addresses both his "grandsons" and "grandparents" in the male line as *huchi*, the same term used for "elder brothers."[19] The consequence of this is that all generations are collapsed into two alternating sets of "brothers" or "namesakes": INU AWA and INU KANA, and DUA YAWA and DUA DUNU. There are therefore two INU sections (represented by the jaguar) in alternating generations, and two DUA sections (represented by the puma) in alternating generations, which result in four male namesake sections (see Kensinger 1995; McCallum 2001). For each male namesake section, there is a female namesake section, resulting in a female set of four namesake sections, parallel to the four male sections. For the sake of convenience, I will focus on male namesake sections in Figure 3, which represents the kinship terminology used between moieties and namesake sections.

A Mathematical Translation

I now proceed to a mathematical translation of the above fragment of the Cashinahua's rules for combining kinship terms. These rules express the way the Cashinahua relationship words are combined to produce new ones.[20] The formal version of the relationships shown above are depicted in Figure 4.

---

18. Anthropologists will be familiar with the terminological identification of "father" with "father's brothers," and of "sons" with "brothers' sons"; on the other hand, the terminological identification of "father" with "son" is a rare feature of systems with "alternating generations."
19. For instance, Sian is a DUA YAWA member and his son is a DUA DUNU. The latter's son will again be named Sian and be a DUA YAWA.
20. For reasons of space and of simplicity, the full set of relational words and their possible combinations will not be shown here.

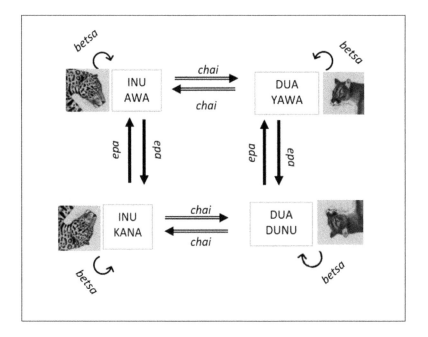

Figure 3. The symmetries inherent in the kinship terminology are illustrated as symmetries in the Jaguar and Puma images representing the INU and DUA moieties, respectively. These two moieties are connected by the marriage alliance term *chai* (shown by hollow arrows). The *epa* term (thick arrows) connects men in the two namesake sections INU AWA and INU KANA (alternating generations of the INU moiety) in a reciprocal manner, just as it does for the two namesake sections DUA YAWA and DUA DUNU. The relationship between two *epa* is called *betsa* ("my other me"), a term also used between same-sex siblings. It has the role of the identity in mathematics.

Rule I. *Betsa* is a neutral term, which, when combined with any other term, produces that other term. Here is how it operates with the term *epa*:

$$epa * betsa = epa$$

The term for same-sex parent is *epa*, and the term for same-sex sibling is *betsa*. We can also translate the above equation as:

same-sex parent * same-sex sibling = same-sex parent,

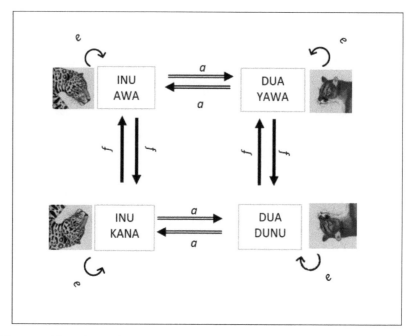

Figure 4. The relationships between moieties and namesake sections are shown in formal terms: the relationship between *epa* is shown formally as *ff*, while that between *chai* is represented by *aa*, and the neutral term *betsa* is shown as *e*. Two *epa* may call each other *betsa*, which can be expressed algebraically as *epa / epa = betsa*, or in its formal version as *ff* = *e*. The two moieties INU and DUA, connected by the operator *chai*, also follow the rule of *chai / chai* = *betsa*, represented in its formal version as *aa* = *e*. All these equations are versions of the familiar multiplication rule $p \times p^{-1} = 1$.

which can be mistranslated as:

<blockquote>a father's brother = a father,</blockquote>

and formally, as:

$$f^* e = f.$$

The above reasoning holds good when the order of terms is reversed, which means that (in the English mistranslation) "a brother's father is a father."

By putting all this together, we obtain the following formal representation:

$$f * e = f = e * f$$

And this is familiar algebraic property, with which we are familiar in the form

$$a \times 1 = a = 1 \times a,$$

where a is any rational number (this holds also for integers). This holds true not only for *epa* but also for all Cashinahua kinship terms. This means that the term *betsa*, formally represented as e, behaves syntactically as the number 1 in multiplication. This is the algebraic version of Lewis Morgan's diagnostic trait for "classificatory systems of relationships," by which he meant systems that mix linear and collateral relatives (Almeida 2018).

Rule II. Every term has an inverse. Again focusing on relations among men and using the descriptive form *epa* as an example, without a loss of generality:

$$epa * epa = betsa,$$

or "a father's father is a brother," and, in the algebraic translation,

$$f * f = e$$

This rule means that the inverse of f is f itself, that is to say:

$$f = f^{-1}$$

Rule II says that there is an inverse for every kinship term. This parallels the fact that, for any rational number a, there is a multiplicative inverse a^{-1} such that $a \times a^{-1} = 1$. Recall also that in Boolean algebra, $1 + 1 = 0$, where 0 is the neutral element, so that here 1 plays the role of its own additive inverse. It should be noted that $ff^{-1} = e$, or in the additive version, $1 + 1 = 0$, is the algebraic version of Sian's assertion that "my father is my son," since it is equivalent to say that "my father's father is my brother" in one of many possible mistranslations.

Extending this analysis would demand a separate essay, so I will stop here, having already probably abused the patience of the reader with what Bronisław Malinowski called depreciatively the "mock-algebra of kinship." The point is that there is here a legitimate isomorphism between the Cashinahua calculus of kinship relationships and a particular mathematical structure. This structure occurs in many contexts.[21]

Let me return to the analogy traced above between Cashinahua's kinship relational calculus and a mathematical structure. My point is that there is more than an analogy: for the Cashinahua kinship rules are a way of calculating with words, just as the abstract symbols of algebra are a way of calculating with another class of words, and to say that these calculi have a common structure—or, in other words, that there is an isomorphism connecting one system into the other, where by "isomorphism" is meant a dictionary that translates the symbols of one system into symbols of the other system so as to preserve the structure.[22]

The existence of such an isomorphism has the following pragmatic consequence. Suppose one wishes to calculate a product of f and a in a mathematical system (Fig. 4). One way to perform the calculation is as follows: first translate f and a (Fig. 4) into Cashinahua kinship terms (Fig. 3) and ask a Cashinahua speaker for the term that results from combining them; finally, translate the resulting kinship terms back into the formal symbols (Fig. 4). The results should agree. This intriguing idea was suggested to me by the Tamil anthropologist Ruth Manimekalai Vaz (2014).[23]

---

21. The specific structure is not trivial at all. For we face here the task of generating *eight* relations (corresponding to the eight *xutabaibu* classes, divided in moieties, generations, and gender) by means of just *two* relations corresponding to filiation and gender-change. The key to this effect is combination of alternating generations and noncommutativity (see diagrams in Almeida 2014: 4–6).

22. Lévi-Strauss once asked the eminent Henri Hadammard for help with a complicated problem in "Australian kinship," being told that "mathematics deals with the four operations and kinship could not be assimilated to anyone of them"; he then met younger André Weil, who told him that "only the relations among marriages mattered" (Lévi-Strauss and Eribon 1988: 79). Hadammard was a renowned but aging mathematician, while the young Weil was one of the founders of the Bourbaki structuralist reconstruction of mathematics.

23. I gave a precise formulation for Vaz's conjecture on Dravidian kinship calculation by means of a calculating method borrowed from quantum physics—that is, Pauli matrices (Almeida 2014).

The Issue of Reverse Translation

The above example is a particular case of a more general fact. I think that, as a matter of fact, every translation of ancient/forest mathematics in the language of modern mathematics is automatically a candidate for a reverse translation of modern mathematics in Indigenous terms.

Keeping the focus on kinship issues, I will suggest a case of a concept in modern mathematics that was originally expressed in the language of kinship. The theory of relations, created independently by Richard Dedekind and by Gottlob Frege as a foundation for mathematical induction, was expressed by Alfred Whitehead and Bertrand Russell in *Principia Mathematica* (following the lead of Frege) in the idiom of descent, ancestrality, heredity, succession, and generation (Whitehead and Russell 1910: 570). This is how the principle of mathematical induction works: given that number 1 has the property *P*, and granted that, if a number *n* has a property *P*, its *successor* n + 1 *inherits* the property *P*, then all *descendants* of 1 have the property *P*, and the property *P* is shared by all *ancestors* of *n*. This means that the property is *hereditary*, as Whitehead and Russell put in a nice way: "If *m* is the Peerage, *m* is hereditary with respect to the relation of father to surviving eldest son" (Whitehead and Russell 1910: 570).

The authors of *Principia Mathematica* were using—in the first really mathematical chapter of the book—the fact that the ordering of positive integers is isomorphic to the ordering of *peers*, a fact that justifies the use of the language of British peerage to define the concept of an inductive relation as equivalent to that of a hereditary relation.

Could Euclid Prove √2 x √3 = √6?

Dedekind claimed that his construction of irrational numbers afforded for the first time a proof that √2 x √3 = √6 (Dedekind 1963: 40). The mathematician and historian of mathematics John Stillwell countered Dedekind's claim with a proof that √2 x √3 = √6 in purely Euclidean terms (Stillwell 2016: 156–57). The mechanism of the proof is essentially the same as Euclid's proof of Pythagoras's theorem, since in both cases the point is to show that successive transformations of an initial figure preserve their areas. The beautiful geometrical proof requires, however, as an initial step the translation of the product √2 x √3 of irrational numbers (as constructed by Dedekind) into a geometrical figure—namely a rectangle having irrational sides that are the geometrical translations of √2 and √3. This geometrical object is then successively transformed by means of purely Euclidean constructions, all of them justified in Book I of the *Elements*, resulting in a final rectangle equal to the initial rectangle—in modern language, having the same area. And the final rectangle has sides that are the unit and the Euclidean version of √6. Translating the Euclidean result into Dedekind's language, one obtains √2 x √3 = √6 (see Figure 5).

One has again an isomorphism between two proofs. However, there is a catch. While Euclid's geometrical √2 is constructed by means of rule and compass—being the diagonal of a square with unit side—Dedekind's √2 is defined as a couple of infinite sets of rational numbers: those the square of which is less than 2, and those the square of which is bigger than 2. Dedekind's "cut," composed by two *infinite sets* of rational numbers—in the actual sense, not the potential sense—looks very much like two Zeno tortoises approaching one another without ever meeting because there is no rational number for them to meet at—the whole point being that the races themselves define a new kind of number.[24] And notwithstanding this ontological chasm separating Euclid's and Dedekind's mathematical universes, there is a bridge connecting them. For not only does the translation between the two languages preserve the structure of the proof, but Archimedes and Dedekind would agree on the following: given an arbitrarily small quantity, it is possible to produce a rational number that, when squared, differs from 2 by less than this quantity by excess or by default. Another case in point, and more relevant, is Euclid's proof that, given any list of prime numbers, one can show that there is a prime number not in it (*Elements* IX: 20). Not a single word needs to be changed in Euclid's proof by today's standards, but modern versions of it are often phrased as stating that "the set of primes is infinite," while Euclid's subtle statement avoids any reference to "infinite" altogether. (The Cambridge mathematician Godfrey Hardy, who praised Euclid's proof as an example of immortal beauty in mathematics, did not participate in this ontological mistranslation.)

Mathematical Translation and Ontological Bridgeheads

As a final note, I am aware that mathematical agreement in the pragmatic and structural sense may be consistent with ontological pluralism, but

---

24. "I still regard the statement . . . that the theorem √2 √3 = √6 has nowhere yet been strictly demonstrated" (Dedekind 1963: 40).

Step 0. Translate the product √2 x √3 (Dedekind's irrational numbers) into a Euclidean object—namely, an object constructed by means of unmarked rule and compass. This is a rectangle with irrational sides that we can interpret as √2 and √3 (Stillwell 2016: 156).

Step 1. Transform the initial rectangle into a rectangle with sides that we interpret as 2√3 and √2/2. This transformation conserves the area.

Step 2. Transform the resulting rectangle into a parallelogram, cutting at left and adding at right half a square. This again conserves the area (*Elements* I). The diagonal of the square is 1 by Pythagoras's theorem.

Step 3. Left: Rotate the resulting parallelogram, transforming it into a parallelogram with base equal to the unit and height equal to the side h of a square with diagonal equal to 2√3. Right: Transform the resulting parallelogram into a rectangle with unit base and height equal to h. As it happens, $h^2 + h^2 = (2√3)^2 = 4 \times 3 = 12$ by Pythagoras's theorem, so $h^2 = 6$ and $h = √6$. The area of the last rectangle is therefore $1 \times √6 = √6$.

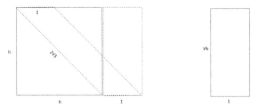

And since all the figures are equal in area, the initial rectangle with sides √2 and √3 is equivalent in area to the final rectangle with sides equal to the unit and to √6. Translating this back in Dedekind's irrational numbers, this can be interpreted as meaning √2 x √3 = √6.

Figure 5. A Euclidean proof of a theorem that Dedekind claimed Euclid could not prove (Stillwell 2016: 156–57).

it can also be a means for ontological cleansing and active evangelization (Vilaça 2018), a point also exemplified by Gottfried Leibniz's proposal of using his binary mathematics as a bridgehead for religious conversion in Chinese (Leibniz 2006: 305–16). Against these ontological invasions and under the disguise of mathematical pedagogy, there remains the alternative of struggles for ontological autonomy also in the domain of mathematics (Viveiros de Castro 2003).

References

Almeida, Mauro W. B. 2013. "Caipora e outros conflitos ontológicos." *R@U: Revista de Antropologia da Universidade Federal de São Carlos* (5) 1: 7–28.

———. 2014. "Comment on Vaz's 'Relatives, molecules and particles.'" *Mathematical Anthropology and Cultural Theory: An International Journal* 7 (3): 1–8. www.mathematicalanthropology.org.

———. 2015. "Matemática concreta." *Sociologia & Antropologia* (5) 3: 725–44.

———. 2018. "Almeida's comment on D. Read 'Generative Crow-Omaha terminologies.'" *Mathematical Anthropology and Cultural Theory* (12) 7: 1–23. www.mathematicalanthropology.org.

Ascher, Marcia, and Robert Ascher. 1981. *Mathematics of the Incas: Code of the quipu.* New York: Dover.

Ascher, Marcia. 1991. *Ethnomathematics: A multicultural view of mathematical ideas.* Boca Raton, FL: Chapman & Hall.

———. 2002a. *Mathematics elsewhere: An exploration of ideas across cultures.* Princeton, NJ: Princeton University Press.

———. 2002b. "The Kolam tradition: A tradition of figure-drawing in southern India expresses mathematical ideas and has attracted the attention of computer science." *American Scientist* (90) 1: 56–63.

Bazin, Maurice, and Modesto Tamez. 2002. *Math and science across cultures.* New York: New York Press.

Bourbaki, Nicolas. 1994. *Elements of the history of mathematics.* New York: Springer.

Bridges, Douglas, and Fred Richman. 1987. *Varieties of constructive mathematics.* Cambridge: Cambridge University Press.

Cabalzar, Flora, ed. 2012. *Educação Escolar Indígena do Rio Negro 1998–2011.* São Paulo and São Gabriel da Cachoeira: Instituto Socioambiental and Federação das Organizações Indígenas do Alto Rio Negro.

Cabalzar, Flora, and Maurice Bazin, eds. 2004. *Utapinopona Saina hoa Bauaneriputi: Keore.* Santa Isabel and São Paulo: Federation of Indigenous Organizations of Rio Negro and Instituto Socioambiental.

Camargo, Eliane. 2002. "Narrativas e o modo de apreendê-las: A experiência entre os caxinauás." *Cadernos de Campo* 10 (10): 11–25.

Capistrano de Abreu, João. 1941. *Rã-txa Hu-ni-ku-ĩ: Grammatica, textos e vocabulário caxinauás.* 2nd ed. Rio de Janeiro: Sociedade Capistrano de Abreu.

Closs, Michael P., ed. 1986. *Native American mathematics.* Austin: University of Texas Press.

Connes, Alain, André Lichnerowicz, and Marcel P. Schützenberger. 2001. *Triangle of thoughts.* Providence, RI: American Mathematical Society.

Crump, Thomas. 1990. *The anthropology of numbers.* Cambridge: Cambridge University Press.

Cuomo, Seraphina. 2001. *Ancient mathematics.* London: Routledge.

———. 2007. *Technology and culture in Greek and Roman antiquity.* Cambridge: Cambridge University Press.

D'Ambrosio, Ubiratan. 2001. *Ethnomathematics: Link between traditions and modernity.* Rotterdam: Sense Publishers.

D'Espagnat, Bernard, and Hervé Zwirn, eds. 2017. *The quantum world: Philosophical debates on quantum physics.* New York: Springer.

Da Costa, Newton. 1974. "On the theory of inconsistent formal systems." *Notre Dame Journal of Formal Logic* 15 (4): 497–510. doi:10.1305/ndjfl/1093891487.

Da Costa, Newton, Octavio Bueno, and Steven French. 1998. "Is there a Zande logic?" *History and Philosophy of Logic* 19 (1): 41–54.

Da Costa, Newton, and Steven French. 2003. *Science and partial truth.* Oxford: Oxford University Press.

Dedekind, Richard. 1963. *Essays in the theory of numbers.* New York: Dover.

Everett, Daniel. 2005. "Cultural constraints on grammar and cognition in Pirahã: Another look at the design features of human language." *Current Anthropology* 46 (4): 621–46.

Ferreira, Mariana K. L. 2015. *Mapping time, space and the body: Indigenous knowledge and mathematical thinking in Brazil.* Rotterdam: Sense Publishers.

Frank, Michael C., Daniel L. Everett, Evelina Fedorenko, and Edward Gibson. 2008. "Number as a cognitive technology: Evidence from Pirahã language and cognition." *Cognition* 108: 819–24.

Gelman, Rochel, and Brian Butterworth. 2005. "Number and language: How are they related?" *Trends in Cognitive Sciences* 9 (1): 6–10.

Gerdes, Paulus. 2007. *Drawings from Angola: Living mathematics.* Morrisville, NC: Lulu Enterprises.

Gilsdorf, Thomas. 2012. *Introduction to cultural mathematics, with case studies in the Otomies and Incas.* New Jersey: Wiley.

Gödel, Kurt. (1964) 1990. "What is Cantor's continuum problem?" In *Collected works*, vol. 2, edited by Salomon Feferman, John W. Dawson, Jr., Stephen C. Kleene, Gregory H. Moore, Robert M. Solovay, and Jean van Heijenoort, 176–78. Oxford: Oxford University Press.

Gordon, Peter. 2004. "Numerical cognition without words: Evidence from Amazonia." *Science* 306 (5695): 496–69. doi: 10.1126/science.1094492.

Hardy, Godfrey Harold. 1940. *A mathematician's apology.* Cambridge: Cambridge University Press.

———. 1952. *A course of pure mathematics.* 10th ed. Cambridge: Cambridge University Press.

Hauser, Marc D., Noam Chomsky, and W. Tecumseh Fitch. 2002. "The faculty of language: What is it, who has it, and how did it evolve?" *Science* 298 (5598): 1568–69.

Hilbert, David. (1904) 1967. "On the foundations of logic and arithmetic." In *From Frege to Gödel: A source book in mathematical logic, 1879–1931*, edited by Jean Heijenoort, 130–38. Cambridge, MA: Harvard University Press.

Hugh-Jones, Stephen. 2016. "Writing on stone; writing on paper: Myth, history and memory in NW Amazonia." *History and Anthropology* 27 (2): 154–82. http://dx.doi.org/10.1080/02757206.2016.1138291.

Humboldt, Wilhelm von. (1820) 1994. "Über das Vergleichende Sprachstudium in Beziehung auf die Verschiedenen Epochen der Sprachentwicklung." In Über die Sprache, edited by Jürgen Trabant, 11–32. Tübingen: UTB für Wissenschaft.

———. (1822) 1994. "Über das Entstehen der Grammatischen Formen, und ihren Einfluss auf die Ideenentwicklung." In Über die Sprache, edited by Jürgen Trabant, 53–81. Tübingen: UTB für Wissenschaft.

Katz, Jerrold. 1978. "Effability and translation." In *Meaning and translation: Philosophical and linguistic approaches*, edited by Franz Guenthner and M. Guenthner-Reutter, 191–234. London: Duckworth.

Kelly, Paul, and Gordon Matthews. 1981. *The non-Euclidean, hyperbolic plane: Its structure and consistency*. New York: Springer.

Kensinger, Kenneth M. 1995. *How real people ought to live: The Cashinahua of eastern Peru*. Illinois: Waveland Press.

Lave, Jean. 1988. *Cognition in practice: Mind, mathematics and culture in everyday life*. Cambridge: Cambridge University Press.

Leibniz, Gottfried W. 2006. *Der Briefwechsel mit den Jesuiten in China (1689–1714)*. Edited and with an introduction by Rita Widmaier. Translated by Malte-Ludolf Babin. Hamburg: Felix Meiner.

Lévi-Strauss, Claude, and Didier Eribon. 1988. *De près et de loin*. Paris: Odile Jacob.

Lloyd, G. E. R. 1990. *Demystifying mentalities*. Cambridge: Cambridge University Press.

———. 1996. *Adversaries and authorities: Investigations into Greek and Chinese science*. Cambridge: Cambridge University Press.

———. 2004. *Ancient worlds, modern reflections: Philosophical perspectives on Greek and Chinese science and culture*. Oxford: Oxford University Press.

Lockhart, Paul. 2017. *Arithmetic*. Cambridge, MA: The Belknap Press.

Maddy, Penelope. 1997. *Naturalism in mathematics*. Oxford: Oxford University Press.

McCallum, Cecilia. 2001. *Gender and sociality in Amazonia: How real people are made*. Oxford: Berg.

Meinong, Alexius. (1904) 1999. *Théorie de l'objet et présentation personnelle*. Paris: Vrin.

Mesquita, Monica, Sal Restivo, and Ubiratan D'Ambrosio. 2011. *Asphalt children and city children: A life, a city and a case study of history, culture, and ethnomathematics in São Paulo*. Rotterdam: Sense Publishers.

Mimica, Jadran. 1988. *Intimations of infinity: The cultural meanings of the Iqwaye numbers*. Oxford: Berg.

Nimuendaju, Curt. 1926. *Die Palikur-Indianer und ihre Nachbarn*. Göteborg: Elanders Boktryckeri Aktiebolag. http://www.etnolinguistica.org/biblio:nimuendaju-1926-palikur.

Nunes, Terezinha, Analucia D. Schliemann, and David W. Carraher. 1993. *Street mathematics and school mathematics.* Cambridge: Cambridge University Press.

Passes, Alan. 2006. "From one to metaphor: Toward an understanding of Pa'ikwené (Palikur) mathematics." *Tipití: Journal of the Society for the Anthropology of Lowland South America* 4 (1): 153–76.

Peirce, Charles S. 1932. *Collected papers of Charles Sanders Peirce.* Vol. 2. Cambridge, MA: Harvard University Press.

———. 1965. *Collected papers of Charles Sanders Peirce.* Vol. 5. Cambridge, MA: Harvard University Press.

Pica, Pierre, Cathy Lemer, Véronique Izard, and Stanislas Dehaene. 2004. "Exact and approximate arithmetic in an Amazonian Indigenous group." *Science* 306 (15): 499.

Pólya, George. 1973. *Mathematics and plausible reasoning.* Vol. 1, *Induction and analogy in mathematics.* Princeton, NJ: Princeton University Press.

Quine, Willard O. 1953. *From a logical point of view.* New York: Harper Torchbooks.

Sahlins, Marshall. 2013. *What kinship is . . . and is not.* Chicago: University of Chicago Press.

Sapir, Edward. (1924) 1949. "The grammarian and his language." In *Selected Writings in Language Culture, and Personality*, 150–59. Berkeley: University of California Press.

Speiser, Andreas. (1922) 1937. *Die Theorie der Gruppen von Endlicher Ordnung: Mit Anwendung auf Algebraische Zahlen und Gleichungen sowie auf die Krystallographie.* 3rd ed. Berlin: Julius Springer.

Stillwell, John. 2003. *Elements of number theory.* New York: Springer.

———. 2016. *Elements of mathematics: From Euclid to Gödel.* Princeton, NJ: Princeton University Press.

Tietze, Heinrich. 1942. *Ein Kapitel Topologie: Zur Einführung in die Lehre von den Verknoteten Linie.* Leipzig: B. G. Teubner.

Tylor, Edward. (1871) 1920. *Primitive culture.* Vol. 2. London: John Murray.

Urton, Gary. 1997. *The social life of numbers: A Quechua ontology of numbers and philosophy of arithmetic.* With the collaboration of Primitivo Nina Llanos. Austin: University of Texas Press.

Vaz, Ruth M. 2014. "Relatives, molecules and particles." *Mathematical Anthropology and Cultural Theory* 7 (1): 1–57. http://mathematicalanthropology.org/toc.html.

Verran, Helen. 2001. *Science and an African logic.* Chicago: University of Chicago Press.

Vidal, Lux B. 2007. *Povos Indígenas do Baixo Oiapoque. O Encontro das Águas, o Encruzo dos Saberes e a Arte de Viver.* Rio de Janeiro: Museu do Índio and Iepé.

Vilaça, Aparecida. 2018. "The devil and the hidden life of numbers: Translations and transformations in Amazonia." *HAU: Journal of Ethnographic Theory* 8 (1–2): 6–19.

Viveiros de Castro, Eduardo. 2003. "(anthropology) AND (science)." Manchester Papers in Social Anthropology 7. Manchester: Department of Social Anthropology, University of Manchester.

———. 2004. "Perspectival anthropology and the method of controlled equivocation." *Tipití: Journal of the Society for the Anthropology of Lowland South America* 2 (1): 3–22.

Washburn, Dorothy K., and Donald W. Crowe, eds. 1988. *Symmetries of culture: Theory and practice of plane pattern analysis.* Seattle: University of Washington Press.

———. 2004. *Symmetry comes of age: The role of pattern in culture.* Seattle: University of Washington Press.

Weil, André. (1949) 1967. "Sur l'étude algébrique de certains types de lois de mariage (système murgin)." In *Les structures élémentaires de la parenté*, by Claude Lévi-Strauss, 257–63. Paris, Mouton.

Whitehead, Alfred N., and Bertrand Russell. 1910. *Principia mathematica.* Cambridge: Cambridge University Press.

Whorf, Benjamin L. (1941) 1956. "Science and linguistics." In *Language, thought, and reality: Selected writings of Benjamin Lee Whorf*, edited by John B. Carroll, 207–19. Cambridge, MA: The MIT Press.

Wigner, Eugene. 1960. "The unreasonable effectiveness of mathematics in the natural sciences." *Communications in Pure and Applied Mathematics* (13) 1: 1–14.

Zaslavsky, Claudia. 1973. *Africa counts: Number and pattern in African cultures.* 3rd ed. Chicago: Lawrence Hill Books.

CHAPTER SIX

Different Clusters of Text from Ancient China, Different Mathematical Ontologies

Karine Chemla

Dedicated to the memory of Michel Kerszberg,
whose mind faded away all too early.

In the different contexts in which mathematics has been practiced, we can observe a certain diversity in the types of entities actors' work has actually brought into play. So far as numbers are concerned, we note that some groups of actors in the ancient world worked only with integers as such (this is notably the case in Euclid's *Elements* [1956]), while others, as we shall see, took into consideration quantities composed with integers and fractions, and also sometimes measurement units.

Moreover, when *we* might think that different actors are dealing with the same kind of entity, that may well not be the case for *them*. For instance, we can recognize that the circle figures in all extant mathematical corpora but only in some contexts did its center play a prominent role. Further, the geometrical constructions carried out on circles, and also the statements considered, differ depending on the contexts.

So the *nature* of the entities that actors deal with in the context of a given mathematical activity cannot be taken for granted. This statement holds true in general and for the ancient world in particular, though

there the scarcity of sources makes the nature of the mathematical entities considered especially difficult to address. This will be the main focus
of this study.

The issue is even trickier when we ask what the actors' own ontological ideas and assumptions were, for our texts are seldom explicit on that
topic. In Euclid's *Elements*, for instance, we have definitions, postulates,
and axioms, followed by theorems and problems with proofs, yet no
second-order statements addressing ontological issues. Tackling Euclid's
own views on that subject raises a methodological problem. This was
already a point of contention in antiquity.

In the framework of this volume, we can certainly not afford to project
our observers' assumptions on the texts, for that would erase the diversity
within and among them. We should also refrain from seeking answers in
ancient Greek writings that seem to *us* to belong to the same context as
Euclid's *Elements* and that yield evidence on the issue of the ontology of
mathematical entities. Such a hermeneutical practice is doomed to shape
Greek antiquity as more uniform than it actually was. I shall argue that
this, too, would be anachronistic since, after all, *we* are those who shape
the writings as pertaining to the same context and then interpret some of
them in the light of the others. Is it surprising that as the result of such a
practice, we end up speaking of "the Greeks," or elsewhere, of "the Chinese"? Perhaps our method puts the rabbit in the hat in which, as if by
magic, we find it at the end of the operation. What other method can we
use? I shall suggest that to address ontological questions, we should (and
actually can) rely on corpora shaped by groups of actors themselves. This
element of method is correlated with an assumption that holds that the
answers to our ontological questions should be sought not in general but
rather only in specific contexts. This principle will turn out to be justified
by the facts that it will enable us to perceive.

But when corpora shaped by actors do not explicitly discuss the ontological questions that interest us, how should we proceed? One of the
goals of this essay is to suggest a possible way ahead.

I shall use a case study to show how actors' ontological positions are
reflected in their technical language and their material practices insofar
as they can be reconstructed. This case study will rely on the corpus of
Chinese mathematical canons and commentaries that, from 656 CE on,
were used as textbooks in one of the two curricula taught in the Imperial
"School of Mathematics," established in the first decades of the Tang
Dynasty (618–907). Some of the commentaries that had been selected
and edited in this context include terse ontological statements. I will

show how we can suggest an interpretation for these statements, relying on an observation of the technical language and material practices shaped to carry out mathematical activity in this framework. The interpretation that I will offer will thus reveal a correlation between ontological statements on the one hand, and features of the technical languages and material practices on the other hand. Hence, this suggests that we can rely on a close study of technical languages and practices to grasp at least some aspects of actors' ontological views.

I will then apply the same method to another cluster of Chinese mathematical texts—that is, mathematical manuscripts dating from early imperial China, some of which were recently found in tombs sealed in the last centuries BCE and others bought on the antiquities market. Again, these manuscripts do not contain any statement that makes explicit aspects of the scribes' ontological ideas. However, both the technical language these documents use and the features of the material practices to which they attest do not appear to reflect ontological assumptions similar to those to which the first corpus of writings testifies. The same conclusion holds true for another corpus of mathematical writings in Chinese that Zhu Yiwen recently uncovered (I return to a more precise description of my clusters of writings below).

This set of facts invites a first general conclusion; that is, that actors' ontological ideas in mathematics are not determined by the language they speak and write, and even do not necessarily depend on it. Indeed, in ancient China, we have different clusters of writings whose authors seem to have embraced different ontological positions even though they probably spoke the same language. More generally, I will suggest that in any given context, actors' ontological ideas, technical language, and material practices in mathematics are correlated with one another, since they were all shaped by actors while carrying out mathematical activity and they were thus produced in intimate relation to one another. My case study further invites the second (more speculative) conclusion that, in the same way as technical language and material practices change while mathematical work is carried out, ontological ideas also change accordingly.

A First Cluster of Mathematical Texts: Canons and Commentaries

Let me outline the context in which actors put together the corpus of texts on which I will rely for my main case study, since this will highlight how I suggest using it.

In 656, Li Chunfeng 李淳風 (?602–670) presented to the Tang throne an anthology of mathematical writings entitled *The Ten Canons of mathematics* (*Suanjing shi shu*, 算經十書; hereafter, *The Ten Canons*).[1] This anthology was the result of a task that Li Chunfeng had fulfilled upon imperial request, together with a group of scholars who had been convened for this purpose. Li and the colleagues working under his supervision had selected ten Chinese mathematical canons, with—for some of them—ancient commentaries. They had prepared new editions for all these writings and had composed annotations on them.[2] Immediately after the anthology had been completed and presented to the throne—that is, from 656 on—its canons and commentaries, together with two additional writings, were used as textbooks in the newly established Imperial "School of Mathematics," which trained students in mathematics with a view to securing a career in the bureaucracy for those who had passed the examinations.[3] The study of eight among these canons, with their commentaries, formed the core of an elementary curriculum, while the other two canons defined a more advanced program. My argument only requires that I focus on the elementary curriculum.

This curriculum began with the study of *Mathematical Canon by Master Sun* (*Sunzi suanjing* 孫子算經), a book completed in circa 400 CE and whose ancient commentaries are lost. The third book that was taught, *The Nine Chapters on Mathematical Procedures* (*Jiuzhang suanshu* 九章算術; hereafter, *The Nine Chapters*), was the major piece of the curriculum, in the sense that its study, together with that of the fourth book (a short tract that had been composed as a complement to the last of the nine chapters), required three years and was thus by far the longest. In fact, the title *The Nine Chapters* referred not only to the canon bearing that title, which had been completed in the first century CE, but also to the commentary on it that Liu Hui 劉徽 completed in 263, and finally to Li Chunfeng et al.'s subcommentary. The curriculum concluded with the study of two books with commentaries and subcommentaries: *The Gnomon of the Zhou* (*Zhoubi* 周髀), a canon, the most recent layers of

---

1. In the last decades, two critical editions of the anthology have been published: Qian Baocong 錢寶琮 (1963) and Guo Shuchun 郭書春 and Liu Dun 劉鈍 (1998). They organize the canons in chronological order.
2. I have examined the evidence we have about the editorial work carried out by Li Chunfeng's team in Chemla (2013a).
3. For details about the school, its official organization, its curricula and modes of examination, see Volkov (2014), on which I rely here.

124

which (commentaries aside) dated to the first century CE, and which was devoted to mathematics required for the calendar, and a sixth-century compilation, *Mathematical Procedures for the Five Canons*, which gave mathematical procedures accounting for numerical values stated in historical commentaries on Confucian Canons and other related classical texts.[4]

I interpret the fact that these canons, composed during different periods, were taught in the same curriculum at the time as evidence that for seventh-century actors they could be considered as delivering a coherent body of mathematical knowledge and practices, even if one can find minor differences between them. This is a key hypothesis for my argument. It implies that before the seventh century, the specific body of mathematical knowledge and practices to which these canons testify and that will be at the center of my argument had been handed down in some milieus for centuries. Moreover, evidence shows that these ten canons were regularly re-edited upon imperial order, and were used for teaching in subsequent centuries in China. These last remarks thus additionally imply that these elements of mathematical knowledge and practice continued to be handed down later.

For the sake of my argument, a second type of evidence will prove useful. The first six canons taught in the first curriculum were mainly composed of problems and mathematical procedures. In addition, their texts all refer to the use of counting rods to write down numbers on a calculating surface, which was separate from the text and on which computations were carried out. By contrast, this type of content is only part of what we find in the commentaries and subcommentaries on these canons that have survived until today—that is, only a fraction of those that Li Chunfeng et al. had selected or else further composed for the 656 edition. This holds true, in particular, for Liu Hui's commentary and

---

4. About the order of study, which is an important point in my argument here, see Volkov (2012: 515–18; 2014: 61). This order differs from the one adopted in modern critical editions of *The Ten Canons*. The status of the critical editions is in fact not clear. Since they both include one of the additional texts studied at the School of Mathematics, it seems that they give a critical edition of the writings studied in this school. However, the order of the writings that they adopt is chronological, and hence is not related to the order of the curricula. On the specific canons just mentioned, one can consult, respectively, Lam and Ang (2004); Chemla and Guo Shuchun (2004); Cullen (1996); Zhu Yiwen 朱一文 (2016).

Li Chunfeng et al.'s subcommentary on *The Nine Chapters*. These commentaries include, among other things, discussions about mathematics, and explicit references to mathematical practice. They also provide evidence on how the earliest readers we can observe read and interpreted the canons. Of particular importance for us in this study is the fact that commentaries further formulate the terse ontological statements that I mentioned above and whose interpretation we will discuss below.

For these reasons, commentaries, and the features of the canons to which they can be related, play a central role in my argument, which accordingly, grants pride of place to *The Nine Chapters* and its commentaries. However, another canon will also give us essential elements of information—that is, *Mathematical Canon by Master Sun*, with which the elementary curriculum began.

Restoring Material Practices to Which All Canons and Commentaries Refer

Indeed, the fact that *Mathematical Canon by Master Sun* was the first textbook taught in the elementary curriculum has important implications for us. The assumption that the corpus taught delivered a globally coherent body of mathematics entails that the elementary pieces of knowledge and practices presented in the first pages of this canon can be considered as valid for the whole corpus (but, as I will show later, not for all mathematical writings from ancient China).[5] Let us outline them.

Mathematical Canon by Master Sun began with basic knowledge about measurement units and key constants, before explaining how to use counting rods to represent numbers. This material representation of numbers was formed on a surface, on which we do not have precise information, apart from the fact that canons and commentaries regularly prescribe to "put *zhi* 置" numbers on it (sometimes making explicit how to arrange them in specific positions) in order to execute computations.[6] Computations could, and did, rely on the numbers thus represented and

---

5. This strategy was used in Proust (2007), in which knowledge taught to scribes in schools is used to interpret more advanced tablets.

6. Martzloff ([1997] 2006: 188) notes that we have no evidence that "counting boards" existed, by contrast with counting rods, which are mentioned explicitly in texts, and samples of which have been found in several excavations. See also Volkov (2001).

arrayed to proceed. The way in which computations were conducted shows that they also made use of the facts that numbers written with rods could be moved on the surface, and the value of the numbers placed in a given position of the surface could likewise be changed. We will shortly see an example of this, with the first calculations presented in *Mathematical Canon by Master Sun* immediately after the description of the number system.

As a consequence, in the practice of mathematics to which our corpus of texts attests, computations were carried out wholly outside the texts, and only materially (if we set aside the possibility of mental computation, which, however, our corpus never evokes). Further, when numbers were mentioned within mathematical writings, they were written using the Chinese language. It was for computations, and only for computations, that the number system using rods that *Mathematical Canon by Master Sun* described was employed. Before the tenth century, we know of no graphic illustration that would have been included in a text to show how numbers were represented with rods, or how computations were actually conducted.[7]

Features of the practice of computations taught in the elementary curriculum (the practice with respect to which our corpus makes sense) are pivotal for my goal in this essay. However, the argument requires that we restore (at least part of) this practice, on the basis of the references that writings make to numbers and computations. The first pages of *Mathematical Canon by Master Sun* yield precious evidence for this.

Let us examine what these pages tell us about the number system using rods. To represent numbers, *Mathematical Canon by Master Sun* prescribed to "first determine the positions," which correspond to successive decimal components of the numbers, and then, to place rods for the subsequent digits, from right to left, first the units, vertically, then

---

7. The earliest known documents showing illustrations of the number system to which *Mathematical canon by Master Sun* refers are Dunhuang manuscripts. Manuscript *Pelliot chinois 3349*, which bears the title *Suan jing* 筭經 (Mathematical canon), and seems to date from the second half of the tenth century, features both a description of the number system close to that in *Mathematical canon by Master Sun* and illustrations for it inserted into the writing. The same number system is recorded in the Dunhuang manuscript *Or. 8210/S.930*, with captions similar to that of *Mathematical canon by Master Sun*.

the tens, horizontally, and then, alternatively, vertically (for even powers of ten) and horizontally (for the odd powers) (Qian Baocong 錢寶琮 1963, 2: 282). Let us leave aside the specific way of using rods to write digits (Lam and Ang 2004: 33ff., 191ff.). In what follows, to represent computations that I restore using the descriptions given in the text, I replace rods with Hindu-Arabic numerals. What the canon describes here is indeed a place-value decimal system, in the sense that, up to the change of orientation, the same set of digits is used to write down decimal components of numbers in successive positions, and the position where a digit is placed determines the order of magnitude (the power of ten) with which it must be understood, in the same way as in the inscription 123, 1 means a hundred in relation to its position in the sequence of digits.[8] With our assumption of the coherence of the corpus, we can assume that this number system described in the *Mathematical Canon by Master Sun* was the one to which all the other canons taught in the same curricula refer.

In the absence of any illustration of the number system in our corpus, we find evidence for our assertions about it in clues collected from computations of our corpus that rely on it. In particular, the two procedures that follow in *Mathematical Canon by Master Sun* and outline the processes to multiply (*cheng*) and divide (*chu*) with this number system on the calculating surface, confirm the place-value decimal features of the number system. These procedures will play a central role in my argument (see Figures 6a–6b for how the executions of multiplication and division, respectively, are commonly restored relying on *Mathematical Canon by Master Sun*). The key fact for us is that the text for the division algorithm begins *not* with a prescription but with a statement. It asserts that the algorithm for division is "exactly opposed" to that of multiplication (Qian Baocong 錢寶琮 1963, 2: 282). This assertion yields a clue though its precise meaning is not immediately clear. Interpreting this statement will highlight an important feature of the practice with counting rods on the surface.

---

8. This is what Dunhuang manuscripts show. The fact that the orientation of the rods alternates from one position to the next has no impact on this conclusion. This point is confirmed by the nature of the arithmetic. I have dealt with this issue elsewhere, and since it is of minor importance here, I do not return to it.

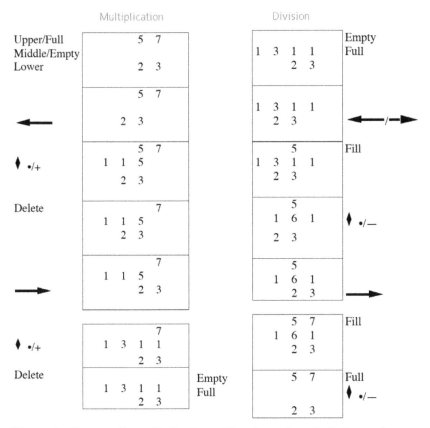

Figure 6a. Process of a multiplication with rods on the calculating surface, according to *Mathematical Canon by Master Sun*, circa 400 (the example chosen is mine).

Figure 6b. Process of a division with rods on the calculating surface, according to *Mathematical Canon by Master Sun*, circa 400 (the example chosen is mine).

According to the texts recorded in *Mathematical Canon by Master Sun*, the algorithms for multiplication and division combine two types of "positions (*wei*)." First, numbers are written as a horizontal sequence of digits placed in successive (decimal) "positions." These positions echo a characteristic feature of the algorithms—that is, that the algorithms iterate the same subprocedure along the sequence of digits to execute the operations, exactly like in present-day practices of place-value decimal notation in multiplication and division (I use the plural, since they present variations worldwide).

Second, the execution of each operation uses three positions (upper, middle, and lower). In the lower position, the multiplier (Figure 6a) and the divisor (*fa* 法, Figure 6b) are respectively placed. In the context of the execution of the two operations, both the multiplier and the divisor are similarly moved leftward (multiplied by a power of ten) at the beginning of the process and, then, progressively moved rightward during the execution. The Chinese text uses a classical pair of opposed operations for this: "moving forward" 進 *jin* versus "moving backward" 退 *tui*. We return to this point below. The significant digits of the numbers placed in these lower positions thus similarly do not change, whereas their decimal position is constantly modified in their respective rows. Note that in this, the algorithms rely on the place-value number system.[9] This illustrates why, more generally, operations reveal features of the number system to which they are applied. This remark explains how operations in *Mathematical Canon by Master Sun* give clues to material inscriptions with rods, which left no trace in the writings.

How Mathematical Practices Make Statements About Mathematical Entities

For both multiplication and division, the type of change occurring in the lower rows stands in contrast with those undergone by the numbers placed in the two rows above: the decimal position of the latter will not be shifted, whereas their numerical value will change along the process of computation. In these two rows, the starting configurations of multiplication and division both have an empty row and a full row, but which is which depends on the operation (what follows constantly refers to Figure 6a–6b). The starting configurations for multiplication and division are thus opposed to one another, exactly like the final ones will be. Indeed, for both multiplication and division, the execution will proceed through emptying the full row while filling up the empty row. Again, here, the Chinese text evokes a classical pair of opposed processes for this: 得 *de* "yield" versus 失 *shi* "lose," when it states that the

---

9. The text of the algorithms in *Mathematical canon by Master Sun* makes clear that the positions writing down the numbers are decimal and these motions of the counting rods representing the numbers correspond to multiplications by powers of ten. They thereby yield key clues indicating the place-value decimal features of the number system underlying these procedures.

multiplication yields the result in the middle row, while the division yields it in the upper row. We also return to this pair below.

In the process of multiplying, the leftmost digit of the multiplicand, in the upper row, will be multiplied by the multiplier, and the product is *added* to the middle row. Once the subprocedure is over, the leftmost digit of the multiplicand is *deleted*, the multiplier is moved one position rightward, and the subprocedure is applied again with the next leftmost digit in the upper position. By contrast, in the upper row of a division, the successive digits of the "quotient" are *inserted* at each stage, and each digit is multiplied by the divisor, in the corresponding position, the product being *subtracted* from the middle row (the "dividend" *shi* 實). We thus see that the two rows (upper and middle) in the processes of multiplication and division behave in ways exactly opposed to each other.

As a result, these executions of multiplication and division are globally devised in such a way that the processes of computation on the calculating surface, as they can be restored using the text, display a network of oppositions and similarities. In particular, the relationship of opposition between the operations translates into a row-to-row dynamic opposition between the processes of computation. Vertical positions (upper/middle/lower) and their arrangement are essential for this, since if we compare the two processes, we see rows are involved in either identical or opposed operations, and thus present identical or opposed behaviors. It is by reference to this property of the flows of computation that I suggest interpreting the statement inserted in *Mathematical Canon by Master Sun* that the algorithm for division is "exactly opposed" to that of multiplication. The statement implies a more general conclusion, essential for us: processes of computations on the calculating surface are not merely means to yield a result, but they are also designed to *assert* something about the relationship between the operations thereby executed. Positions (*wei*), with the type and sequence of elementary operations applied to them, provided actors with tools that analyzed these processes. In other words, the practice with positions was used for mathematical theory.

In this case, the algorithms and the rows have one more property. Suppose we were dividing not 1,311, but 1,312, by 23. The computation would yield in the three rows, respectively, 57, 1, 23, which would be read as the exact result 57 + 1/23. The process of multiplication, applied to these three rows, would restore the original values and configuration of the division. The succession of multiplication and division on the calculating surface cyclically restores the original configuration of the previous operation. In addition, multiplication and division are operations for the execution of which algorithms are given. They are also operations that occur in other algorithms executing other operations. The property of canceling each other out holds for the operations as well as for the configurations (since results are given as exact). In conclusion, multiplication and division are both opposed to each other and cancel each other out when applied in succession.

This example illustrates an unexpected practice of computation with the calculating surface, which is specific to the mathematical culture to which our corpus of text attests. The practice is exemplified by two processes, whose relationship with each other conveys meanings that *Mathematical Canon by Master Sun* makes explicit.[10] Without restoring this material practice, we would miss meanings stated in ways that are different from common modes of expression today. Moreover, we would not be able to interpret accurately the statement made about the processes of computation in *Mathematical Canon by Master Sun*. What is essential for us is that the interpretation of the statement reveals how actors in this context observed processes of computation on the surface.

Remember that these algorithms and this book were learned at the beginning of the elementary curriculum. This suggests that the practice was taught at the time, including a specific way of reading material processes of computation in relation with one another and analyzing the relation of opposition between them on this basis. In fact, several other canons, taught in the same curriculum, testify to the use of a similar way of working with dynamic processes of computation on the calculating surface. I will only evoke them briefly here, to shape the background on the basis of which I will offer an interpretation of some ontological statements, and also draw a contrast between this first corpus and other corpora of mathematical texts from ancient China.

The Nine Chapters already contains texts for all the processes of computation for which I could identify the same practice on the calculating surface. It must be noted that this canon does not describe algorithms for multiplication and division. However, the way in which *The Nine Chapters* refers to multiplication *cheng* and division *chu* supports the hypothesis of the coherence of the corpus; that is, that the algorithms learned with *Mathematical Canon by Master Sun* were also those on which *The Nine Chapters* relied, and in particular, those with respect to

---

10. In this chapter, space precludes further worked examples. They can be found in Chemla (2000, 2017).

which processes of computation described in *The Nine Chapters* likewise stated relations of similarity or opposition.

For instance, in this latter canon, we find texts for algorithms executing square root and cube root extractions.[11] Like multiplication *cheng* and division *chu*, they rely on the positions of the decimal expansion of the number, whose root is extracted. Moreover, likewise, these algorithms bring into play three main positions (upper/middle/lower), called respectively "quotient," "dividend," "divisor."[12] In the same way as the names for the positions borrow the terms used for division in *Mathematical Canon by Master Sun*, the elementary operations used to execute both square and cube root extractions derive for the most part from the process of division. As a result, the elementary operations applied to each of the positions "quotient," "dividend," and "divisor" present a strong similarity with those featuring in the process of a division. The use of the same name thus echoes the fact that the positions undergo correlated changes in the process of execution. As a result, the material processes of computation on the surface, as they can be restored, appear to state a similarity between division and root extraction in exactly the same way as in *Mathematical Canon by Master Sun* the related processes stated the relation of opposition between multiplication *cheng* and division *chu*. In addition, the same practice of writing processes on the calculating surface indicates that likewise, a relation of similarity between square and cube root extraction is asserted.

Other canons in our corpus contain texts for algorithms executing square and cube root extractions, which present slight variations by comparison with those in *The Nine Chapters*. Interestingly, these texts of algorithms appear to use exactly the same practice of stating relationships between operations using the processes of computation on the calculating surface. However, the way in which they shape similarities differs. This suggests that these processes of computation were a tool with which actors explored how one could understand the relationships between operations (Chemla 1994). Again, without reading these processes as we have seen above actors read them, we would miss part of the mathematical work carried out using these means.

---

11. Chemla (1994) deals with these algorithms, and the others executing the same operations that occur in *The Ten Canons*. I do not repeat the details, and only state the conclusions here.

12. By contrast, fleeting positions are sometimes inserted below these three, and they receive no name.

To return to *The Nine Chapters*, we could highlight other phenomena on the basis of restoring material processes of computation and reading them in the same way as was described above. Interestingly, these phenomena correspond to phenomena affecting the terminology. We have an example of this in the two expressions "dividing this by extraction of the square root *kai fang chu zhi* 開方除之" and "dividing this by extraction of the cube root *kai lifang chu zhi* 開立方除之," which are used to prescribe square and cube root extractions, respectively. The terminology thus shows a structure in the set of three operations that is strictly parallel to what the processes of computation state.

The Nine Chapters introduces a fourth operation in a similar way. For us, it is a quadratic equation. In the canon, it appears as an arithmetical operation. The process of its execution is extracted from the process of computation of a square root extraction, using the latter execution from a given point onward.[13] Accordingly, on the calculating surface, the process of computation of the former is a part of the latter. The operands to which the quadratic equation as an operation is applied are precisely those featuring on the calculating surface at the point where the part of the process of square root extraction that is kept begins. In this case, positions on the calculating surface serve to introduce a new operation that builds upon one that is already known. These operands are referred to as "dividend" and "joined divisor," which evoke the names given to these positions in the context of the execution of a square root extraction. Finally, the new operation is prescribed using the expression "dividing by extraction of the square root." So, again, the relationship of similarity between the processes of computation of the quadratic equation and the square root extraction echoes the relationship expressed using the terminology.

Positions are again central in a fifth algorithm described in *The Nine Chapters* to solve what for us corresponds to systems of linear equations.[14] The text of the algorithm prescribes to lay out the data corresponding to each equation in a column in such a way that all the data corresponding to the same unknown in different equations are placed in the same

---

13. On the argumentation supporting the claims about the quadratic equation that follow, and the transformations of the operation in the next centuries, see Chemla (2017), which contains a more complete bibliography on the topic.
14. What follows relies on Chemla (2000), where a more detailed argument and references are given.

row. Accordingly, *The Nine Chapters* again uses a place-value scheme. The data of each problem form a rectangle, in which the data associated to unknowns are arranged in a square, whereas the constant terms of the equation form a row under this square. The algorithm solving the problems will rely on this rectangular layout to determine the unknowns.

What is remarkable is that the algorithm combines essentially two main operations that are repeated, one between columns, and the other between positions in the upper square and the lower row. The former operation, which (relying on the physical properties of numbers represented with rods) brings into play two columns to eliminate the upper position in one of them, is prescribed as "an upright division *zhi chu* 直除," while the latter is a plain division *chu*. In this context again, the process of computation shapes a relation of similarity between this execution and that of a division. What is striking is that the data arranged in the lower row are referred to as "dividends," whereas the data arranged in the upper square are referred to using a synonym of "divisor"—namely, "measure *cheng* 程."[15] This identification of the shaping of a similarity using positions and terms enables us, then, to interpret the name that *The Nine Chapters* gives to the operation that this algorithm executes: "divisors/measures in square *fangcheng* 方程." In other words, the operation appears to be a generalization of the division *chu*. Instead of having a single divisor and dividend, "measures in square" opposes a square of divisors to a row of dividends, and the operation is executed using the key process of division first vertically, and then horizontally.

To summarize, the same practice on the calculating surface, which relies in an essential way on how data are arranged in positions, and the same (and related) use of the terminology shape and state the operation "measures in square" as similar to that of division. In this context, we find again the same group of features that we have met in all the contexts in which these practices were in play in our corpus: positions forming place-value notations on the calculating surface; the use of the same terms or of related terms to designate the elements from two different operations that were brought into relation; the establishment of a relationship between the processes of computation.

In all the examples from *The Nine Chapters* that we have evoked, we have seen that one of the two fundamental operations that were opposed to each other—that is, the division *chu*—played a cardinal role, since it was

---

15. Both terms refer to the idea of "norm" with respect to which one will shape a given quantity, and thus measure it.

used as a basis to which the processes of execution of other operations were reduced. More generally, we see that the pair of opposed operations and the practice of computation on the calculating surface that were learned at the beginning of the elementary curriculum played a key part for the knowledge that would be taught later. This knowledge included not only actual algorithms but also the understanding of a structure in a set of operations. To grasp this structure, students had to know the two operations of multiplication and division, and also to understand the way of reading their relation of opposition directly on the processes of execution. Both aspects formed the cornerstone of the knowledge they would acquire later.

So far, we have uncovered a practice of searching for relations between algorithms executing operations, whose conduct and expression used two types of tools: on the one hand, the processes of computation on the calculating surface and the relationships that could be established between them using positions in a specific way, and on the other hand, the terminology referring to positions and prescribing operations. What this search appears to have established is that a certain number of algorithms could be shown to be reducible to the division *chu*—that is, one of the two poles of a pair of opposed processes.

Ontological Statements, Material Practices, and the Differences in Ontological Ideas Between Different Clusters of Texts

In this section, I propose a hypothesis concerning the possible connection between the practices in *The Nine Chapters* and certain philosophical—indeed, ontological—statements in Liu Hui's commentary, and then point to a contrast in a second corpus of mathematical texts that have recently come to light. In both cases I must emphasize the tentative character of my proposals.

The conclusions of the previous section have an echo in a statement that the third-century commentator Liu Hui formulates in the preface to his commentary on *The Nine Chapters*. He writes that in that work, "I observed the dividing of *Yin* and *Yang* and I synthesized the source of mathematical procedures." Taken out of context, this terse statement is hard to interpret. But one possibility may be suggested using the background described above.

The mention of *Yin* and *Yang* evokes philosophical developments in China that took their reference point in the *Book of Changes* (*Yijing* 易 經) and the ancient commentaries that were handed down with this writing, notably the "Great commentary" (*Xici zhuan*), which seems to have assumed the form under which we know it in the first half of the second century BCE. Reflections putting *Yin* and *Yang* into play, such as those we can read in the "Great commentary," approached realities from the viewpoint of processes of transformation at play in them. In this context, *Yin* and *Yang* featured polarities enabling observers to account for how processes unfolded as the interplay of fundamental and general patterns of transformation opposed to one another. The scope of this type of analysis in the "Great commentary" encompasses the natural world, social interactions, and cultural artifacts. Liu Hui's mention of *Yin* and *Yang* in the context of mathematics suggests that some practitioners of this discipline also thought about mathematics from the same ontological viewpoint. This assumption is supported by the multiple quotations of the *Book of Changes* and the "Great commentary" that we read in the commentaries on *The Nine Chapters*.[16]

In this context, one possible interpretation of Liu Hui's statement in his preface would derive from establishing a connection between the pair *Yin/Yang* and the two operations of multiplication and division, with their execution on the calculating surface. Given the analysis developed above, it seems natural to suggest that multiplication and division have embodied fundamental and general patterns of transformation, opposed to one another, by reference to which other processes of transformation could be analyzed. Another piece of information supports this interpretation: in his commentary, Liu Hui refers to the flow of transformations that algorithms carry out on numbers using one of the general terms referring to change in the "Great commentary"—that is, *bianhua* 變化.[17]

---

16. Chemla (1997) analyzes one such quotation in its context. The analysis that I develop (and will not repeat here) implies that the choice of a title in *The Nine Chapters*, which this quotation echoes, might entail that even in *The Nine Chapters*, we might perceive a reference to the "Great commentary." If this assumption holds true, the commentator would only make explicit what he reads in the canon. Moreover, the analysis developed in this other study shows that mathematical entities were also approached from the viewpoint of their transformations, and not only computations. However, here I will only focus on the aspect that will enable me to establish a contrast between the corpus under consideration and other mathematical writings.

17. In Chemla (1999), I have analyzed this reference in context. Let me insist on the fact that I do not claim to offer the only interpretation possible, nor do I mean to have exhausted the meaning of these terms and sentences in this discussion.

According to this interpretation, Liu Hui's statement would refer (in particular, but probably not only) to how one might observe the interplay of multiplication and division in processes of computation.[18] The statement might also refer to the pair of elementary and fundamental operations that are in play in the processes executing multiplication and division as in many other natural processes. Indeed, "moving forward" 進 *jin* and "moving backward" 退 *tui* are terms that regularly occur in the "Great commentary," as are "yield" 得 *de* and "lose" 失 *shi*). Finally, when Liu Hui claims to have "synthesized the source of mathematical procedures" it may be that he has in mind his uncovering of elementary and fundamentally opposed operations to which all the other processes of computation can be reduced.

These interpretations have two main consequences of importance for my purpose here. First, whatever the precise reference of the statement might have been, the interpretations that I have sketched all suggest that mathematical realities like computations would thus systematically have been viewed as processes. This ontological assumption went hand in hand with a program of research: as was the case for other processes of change, this program aimed at identifying fundamental processes to which all other processes could be reduced, through an inquiry comparing processes with one another and searching how they related to one another. In this case, like in other contexts, this search seems to have uncovered that fundamental processes and key patterns of transformation could be arranged into pairs of opposed operations (multiplication and division, moving forward and backward, yielding and losing, etc.).

It is important to note that this search was carried out using specific practices, like the material practice of computation with rods that we have restored on the calculating surface. This brings me to the second consequence that is essential for us and that concerns the type of relationship that practices and ontological assumptions have to one another. Indeed, the ontological assumption that mathematical entities can be viewed as processes and the type of search that corresponded to this assumption are *reflected* in practices that actors shaped to work on mathematics. One such practice is the use of "positions" on the calculating surface, thanks to which flows of transformation could

---

18. I have given an interpretation of the part played by multiplication and division in another range of phenomena in mathematics, and also on a longer time span in Chemla (2010).

be shaped, analyzed, and compared. This latter practice interestingly echoes the use of trigrams and hexagrams in the context of the *Book of Changes*. Another practice is the use of terminology, which shaped networks of similarities and oppositions. Perhaps, in fact, actors did *shape* these practices in *relation* to their ontological assumption and the related program that it led them to pursue. This would account for why to some extent practices bespeak the ontological assumptions actors held. After all, it is about the processes of multiplication and division, shaped using positions and terms in a specific way (our two practices), that *Mathematical Canon by Master Sun* asserts that they are "exactly opposed" to one another—that is, that the canon inserts a statement that relates to an interest in polarities in mathematics. These practices can also be identified in *The Nine Chapters*, and I have emphasized that they were taught (probably with the corresponding approach to processes of computation) at the beginning of the elementary curriculum. We have seen that the commentator Liu Hui referred explicitly to the related ontological assumption. The occurrence of the same practices in *The Nine Chapters* invites us to assume that the same ontological assumption and the same program already existed at the time when *The Nine Chapters* was completed.

The hypothesis that mathematical practices reflect (at least to some extent) ontological assumptions provides to us a method to approach such assumptions in the context of writings that contain no explicit statement about them. I will now use this method to show that none of the mathematical manuscripts from early imperial China so far published (my second cluster of texts) seem to reflect ontological assumptions similar to those I have associated with the elementary curriculum.

At the present day (2017), these manuscripts include *Writings on Mathematical Procedures* (*Suan shu shu* 算數書), which was found in a tomb sealed circa 186 BCE, at Zhangjiashan,[19] and *Mathematics* (*Shu* 數), which was bought on the antiquities market and which its editors date from no later than circa 212 BCE.[20] Both appear to be related to the same milieus for they present tight connections with the practice of administrative regulation. They also include other manuscripts,

---

19. Peng Hao 彭浩 (2001) published the first annotated edition of the text. English translations can be found in Cullen (2004) and Dauben (2008).

20. The first annotated edition was provided in Xiao Can 蕭燦 (2010). The slips are reproduced, transcribed, and an annotated edition is given in Zhu Hanmin 朱漢民 and Chen Songchang 陳松長 zhubian 主編 (2011).

which were not yet published. However, I will also mention the published part of the manuscripts from early imperial China (the Qin dynasty) kept at Beijing University. All these manuscripts attest to mathematical practices and knowledge presenting some similarities with those in our first corpus. They refer to the use of rods, and to the positioning of numbers on a surface to compute. The mathematical terminology they use has a lot in common with what we find in *The Ten Canons*.

The key point about these manuscripts concerns the operation of division. Although all other arithmetical operations (including multiplication) are usually prescribed by verbs, the division to which the manuscripts attest (by contrast with what we have described above) is only prescribed using whole sentences (this holds true of every bit of manuscript so far published).[21] In particular, even if the verb *chu* occurs in them, at the time it only had the meaning of subtraction (including repeated subtraction). This suggests that the executions of multiplication and division are not related to one another. I have offered a reconstruction of the execution of a division at the time, which confirms this assumption. But there is more.

Several manuscripts contain an algorithm to extract a square root.[22] This algorithm does not rely on a decimal expansion of the number whose root is sought, and it does not have any relationship with an algorithm of division of the type we have mentioned above for writings in our first corpus. More generally, nowhere do we have any hint that a place-value notation would be used. In particular, in contrast to the writings in the first corpus, nowhere do we find a division or a multiplication by ten carried out using a shift rightward or leftward of the rods representing a number. However, this is an aspect of a much more general phenomenon: the manuscripts do not attest to the use of positions in the execution of computations similar to what we have described for our first corpus. Finally, nowhere does an interest in the relations between algorithms come to the surface.

---

21. I have been exploring this issue in Chemla (2013b, 2014, and forthcoming). More publications will follow.
22. See in particular Han Wei 韓巍 (2013: 38–39), which shows that the manuscripts kept at Beijing University have the same procedure as *Writings on mathematical procedures*. This suggests that this procedure enjoyed a certain stability at the time.

These elements strongly suggest that these manuscripts do not reflect any program of searching for elementary and fundamental operations within processes of computation similar to the one to which *The Ten Canons* attests. By contrast, these mathematical texts seem to reflect the use of operations as means to reach a result rather than as processes to be pondered. If so, this suggests that the ontological assumptions about processes of computation were not the same.[23]

Conclusion

Whether a similar analysis applies to other mathematical traditions must wait on further study, which I hope this study might inspire. For the time being, let me simply emphasize the general issues that the inquiry presented here invites us to ponder.

The two sets of documents that I have considered (one more extensively than the other) testify to two (partly) different ways of practicing mathematics, which related to different material and terminological practices. Accordingly, I have suggested that in the two contexts, mathematical processes of computations were shaped and explored in different ways, with significant consequences for the knowledge produced. This has led me to conclude that the related ontologies of mathematical processes were different in the social backgrounds in which the two clusters of texts were produced and used. The evidence is not enough to allow us to dig further into ontological assumptions held by the actors who used the manuscripts. However, it suffices to point out a contrast in this respect between the two clusters of texts.

The hypothesis we are led to propose on this basis is the following. Ontological assumptions are not solely determined by written or spoken language. In our case, although all the actors wrote (and most probably spoke) in Chinese, they seem to have embraced at least partly different ontological ideas about mathematical entities.

---

23. I could develop the same argument relying on the corpus of mathematical writings that Zhu Yiwen uncovered in seventh-century commentaries on Confucian canons—that is, in writings composed more or less at the same time as Li Chunfeng's annotated edition of *The Ten Canons* (Zhu Yiwen 朱一文 2016). In this case, actors never seem to place rods on a calculating surface for mathematical work.

I have insisted that ontological ideas can be approached both through the technical terminologies the actors shaped and through the material practices that can be reconstructed from their writings. The reason for this is that these three facets of mathematical activity are interrelated. In this latter respect, perhaps we can go one step further.

Indeed, since the two clusters of texts that I have considered had several features in common, we know they are somehow related to each other. In case, in the future, we can prove that they are historically more closely related—that is, that the mathematical practices and knowledge to which the manuscripts attest in fact developed into mathematical knowledge and practices to which *The Ten Canons* testifies—this would have an interesting consequence for our topic. It would indeed point out that ontological assumptions of the type we have analyzed in *The Ten Canons* took shape in correlation with the shaping of mathematical practices that reflect them and enable actors to work with and explore them. In this case, we would be in a position to observe how ontological assumptions change and how this process relates to actual practices that actors design for their mathematical activity.

Acknowledgments

A first version of this article was presented at the Science in the Forest, Science in the Past meeting, organized in Cambridge by Sir Geoffrey Lloyd, Aparecida Vilaça, Mauro William Barbosa de Almeida, and Manuela Carneiro da Cunha, May 31–June 2, 2017. I benefited from the hospitality of the Institute for the History of Natural Sciences (CAS, China) to write this essay in May 2017; at the moment of completion, I am at the Max-Planck Institute, Department II (Dir.: Lorraine Daston). It is a great pleasure to thank my hosts for their hospitality, and the organizers of the meeting and the participants for their feedback, which proved very helpful as I revised this contribution. The referees have also provided very helpful comments. However, the essay would not have been what it is without the selfless support and generous help of Sir Geoffrey Lloyd, to whom I express my deepest gratitude. Aparecida Vilaça's magical stroke left its imprint on the article as well, and I have pleasure in acknowledging it. Last but not least, many thanks are due to Michelle Beckett, who edited this essay very competently.

References

Chemla, Karine. 1994. "Similarities between Chinese and Arabic mathematical writings: I: Root extraction." *Arabic Sciences and Philosophy. A Historical Journal* 4 (2): 207–66.

―――. 1997. "What is at stake in mathematical proofs from third-century China?" *Science in context* 10 (2): 227–51.

―――. 1999. "Philosophical reflections in Chinese ancient mathematical texts: Liu Hui's reference to the *Yijing*." In *Current perspectives in the history of science in East Asia*, edited by Yung Sik Kim and Francesca Bray, 89–100. Seoul: Seoul National University Press.

―――. 2000. "Les problèmes comme champ d'interprétation des algorithmes dans les *Neuf chapitres sur les procédures mathématiques* et leurs commentaires. De la résolution des systèmes d'équations linéaires." *Oriens Occidens: Sciences Mathématiques et Philosophie de l'Antiquité à l'Age Classique* 3: 189–234.

―――. 2010. "Mathematics, nature and cosmological inquiry in traditional China." In *Concepts of nature in traditional China: Comparative approaches*, edited by Guenther Dux and Hans-Ulrich Vogel, 255–84. Leiden: Brill.

―――. 2013a. "Ancient writings, modern conceptions of authorship: Reflections on some historical processes that shaped the oldest extant mathematical sources from ancient China." In *Writing science: Medical and mathematical authorship in ancient Greece*, edited by Markus Asper, 63–82. Berlin: de Gruyter.

―――. 2013b. "Shedding some light on a possible origin of the concept of fraction in China: Division as a link between the newly discovered manuscripts and *The Gnomon of the Zhou [dynasty]*." *Sudhoffs Archiv* 97 (2): 174–98.

―――. 2014. "Observing mathematical practices as a key to mining our sources and conducting conceptual history: Division in ancient China as a case study." In *Science after the practice turn in the philosophy, history, and social studies of science*, edited by Léna Soler, Sjoerd Zwart, Michael Lynch, and Vincent Israël-Jost, 238–68. New York: Routledge.

―――. 2017. "Changing mathematical cultures, conceptual history and the circulation of knowledge: A case study based on mathematical sources from ancient China." In *Cultures without culturalism in the making of scientific knowledge*, edited by Karine Chemla and Evelyn Fox Keller, 352–98. Durham, NC: Duke University Press.

————. Forthcoming. "Working on and with division in early China." In *Cultures of computation and quantification*, edited by Karine Chemla, Agathe Keller, and Christine Proust. Dordrecht: Springer. Preprint available at https://halshs.archives-ouvertes.fr/halshs-01954353.

Chemla, Karine, and Guo Shuchun. 2004. *Les neuf chapitres: Le Classique mathématique de la Chine ancienne et ses commentaires.* Paris: Dunod.

Cullen, Christopher. 1996. *Astronomy and mathematics in ancient China: The Zhou bi suan jing.* Needham Research Institute Studies, vol. 1. Edited by Christopher Cullen. Cambridge: Cambridge University Press.

————. 2004. *The Suan shu shu* 筭數書 *"Writings on reckoning": A translation of a Chinese mathematical collection of the second century BC, with explanatory commentary.* Needham Research Institute Working Papers, vol. 1. Edited by Christopher Cullen. Cambridge: Needham Research Institute.

Dauben, Joseph W. 2008. "算數書. *Suan Shu Shu* (A Book on Numbers and Computations). English Translation with Commentary." *Archive for History of Exact Sciences* 62: 91–178.

Euclid. 1956. *The thirteen books of Euclid's elements.* Translated from the text of Heiberg with introduction and commentary by Thomas L. Heath. Vol. 2, 2nd edition. New York: Dover.

Guo Shuchun 郭書春, and Liu Dun 劉鈍. 1998. *Suanjing shishu* 算經十書 (*Ten mathematical classics*). *Guo Shuchun, Liu Dun dianjiao* 郭書春，劉鈍 點校 (*Punctuated critical edition by Guo Shuchun and Liu Dun*). 2 vols. Shenyang 瀋陽: Liaoning jiaoyu chubanshe 遼寧教育出版社. Reprint, Taibei, Jiuzhang chubanzhe, 2001.

Han Wei 韓巍. 2013. "*Beida Qin jian* 'Suanshu' *tudi mianji lei suanti chushi* 北大秦簡'算書'土地面積類算題初識 (Preliminary views on the mathematical problems of the type of the areas of croplands in the slips from the Qin dynasty *Writings on mathematics*, kept at Beijing University)." *Jianbo* 簡帛 8: 29–42.

Lam, Lay Yong, and Ang Tian Se. 2004. *Fleeting footsteps: Tracing the conception of arithmetic and algebra in ancient China.* Revised ed. River Edge, NJ: World Scientific.

Martzloff, Jean Claude. (1997) 2006. *A history of Chinese mathematics.* Corrected second printing of the first English edition of 1997. With forewords by Jacques Gernet and Jean Dhombres. Translated by Stephen S. Wilson. Heidelberg: Springer-Verlag.

Peng Hao 彭浩. 2001. *Zhangjiashan hanjian "Suanshu shu" zhushi* 張家山漢簡 "算數書"注釋 (*Commentary on* Writings on mathematical procedures, *a document on bamboo strips dating from the Han and discovered at Zhangjiashan*). Beijing 北京: Kexue chubanshe 科學出版社 (Science Press).

Proust, Christine. 2007. *Tablettes mathématiques de Nippur: Reconstitution du cursus scolaire. Edition des tablettes conservées à Istanbul. Translittération des textes lexicaux et littéraires par Antoine Cavigneaux. Préface de Christian Houzel, Varia Anatolica.* Istanbul: IFEA, De Boccard.

Qian Baocong 錢寶琮. 1963. *Suanjing shishu* 算經十書 *(Qian Baocong jiaodian* 錢寶琮校點*)* (*Critical punctuated edition of* The ten classics of mathematics). 2 vols. Beijing 北京: Zhonghua shuju 中華書局.

Volkov, Alexei. 2001. "Capitolo XII: La matematica. 1. Le bacchette." In *La scienza in Cina*, edited by Karine Chemla, with the collaboration of Francesca Bray, Fu Daiwie, Huang Yilong, and Georges Métailié, 125–33. Rome: Enciclopedia Italiana.

———. 2012. "Argumentation for state examinations: Demonstration in traditional Chinese and Vietnamese Mathematics." In *The history of mathematical proof in ancient traditions*, edited by Karine Chemla, 509–51. Cambridge: Cambridge University Press.

———. 2014. "Mathematics education in East- and Southeast Asia." In *Handbook on the history of mathematics education*, edited by Alexander Karp and Gert Schubring, 55–72, 79–82. New York: Springer.

Xiao Can 蕭燦. 2010. *Yuelu shuyuan cang Qin jian* "Shu" *yanjiu* 嶽麓書院藏秦簡 "數" 研究 (*Research on the Qin strips* Mathematics *kept at the Academy Yuelu*). PhD. thesis, Academy Yuelu 嶽麓書院, Hunan University 湖南大學, Changsha 長沙.

Zhu Hanmin 朱漢民, and Chen Songchang 陳松長 zhubian 主編 , eds. 2011. *Yuelu shuyuan cang Qin jian (er)* 嶽麓書院藏秦簡（貳）(*Qin Bamboo slips kept at the Academy Yuelu* [2]). Shanghai 上海: Shanghai cishu chubanshe 上海辭書出版社.

Zhu Yiwen 朱一文. 2016. "Different cultures of computation in seventh century China from the viewpoint of square root extraction." *Historia Mathematica* 43: 3–25.

CHAPTER SEVEN

Shedding Light on Diverse Cultures of Mathematical Practices in South Asia: Early Sanskrit Mathematical Texts in Conversation with Modern Elementary Tamil Mathematical Curricula

Agathe Keller

The Politics of Alternate Modernities

Since India's Hindu-nationalist Prime Minister Narendra Modi has been in office, he and other government officials have made headlines with surprising statements concerning the scientific feats of past Hindus: for instance, he proclaimed that ancient Hindus knew how to perform cosmetic surgery, as proved by the existence of Gaṇeśa, the god who has the shape of a human with an elephant head.[1] The Chief Minister of the state of Tripura has recently claimed that at the time of the *Mahābhārata*, Hindus had internet and satellites, since Saṃjaya Galvani could give vivid accounts and updates of the formidable Kurukṣetra battle to King

---

1. https://www.theguardian.com/world/2014/oct/28/indian-prime-minister-genetic-science-existed-ancient-times.

Dhṛtarāṣṭra; and one could come up with other such examples.[2] These laughable claims of Indian officials can be understood as a sign of contemporary India's enchantment and disenchantment with science (Raina 1997). It reveals the complex social, political, but also emotional relation that South Asia has to its past and present knowledge and know-hows. Indeed, part of South Asia's postcolonial identity-building has to do with an engagement with its "science of the past," but also its "science of the forest" (here, forest being understood more largely as "rural India"). The most famous example is the gandhian reclamation of economic autonomy by promoting traditional know-hows, such as *khadi* (hand-spun, hand-woven cloth). Such an engagement carries many diverse political nuances and takes many forms. Many paths, models leading to what could be a new modernity (Prakash 1999) are thus explored. Imagined alternatives of what could be a non-Westernized, non-Christian, non-capitalist, or non-imperialist, et cetera appropriation of science and its power are investigated. Villages and forests, then, can be seen as potentially sowing the seeds of the future society as activists turn to them to learn how to harvest water, find medicinal plants, or teach science classes.[3] As action for the future, the recovering of contemporary local know-how and knowledge also nourishes approaches to history—notably, in the case we will explore here, the history of mathematics.[4]

In 2005 I embarked, with Senthil Babu of the French Institute of Pondicherry, on an ethno-mathematics (lit. anthropology of mathematics) project; we visited some villages of the Nagapattinam area in southeastern India. We were struck at the time by the ways in which numeracy

2. https://economictimes.indiatimes.com/news/politics-and-nation/internet-existed-in-the-days-of-mahabharata-tripura-cm-biplab-deb/articleshow/63803490.cms;
    https://www.bbc.com/news/world-asia-india-43806078.

3. For Babu (2015) this would rather be about different imagined publics for which specific mathematics are shaped.

4. The reappropriation and reactualization of one's scientific history, questioning how to situate it in today's world, are something that has been at work, of course, for a very long time. Studies now document how before India's independence itself, at the end of the nineteenth and beginning of the twentieth century, all sorts of hermeneutical schemes and hybridization were at work, from the adaptive translation of De Morgan's mathematical manuals into Marathi (Raina 2016) to the reading of the Vedas as providing the fundamental elements of chemistry (Dodson 2005), all of which, of course, are to be understood in their specific contexts.

and the ability to make conversions were at the heart of the negotiations between landless, low-caste laborers, and the higher-caste owners. Converting hours of labor, in relation to areas of sowed fields, yielding given capacities of more or less refined grain, would be what would determine the amount that such laborers should be paid. In such transactions, tensions relating to evaluations of fractional parts, of measures falling between standards of measurement, were obvious. Much of the payment was in-kind. Part of the village economy rested on value rates enabling exchanges in-kind with the help of capacity vessels: this amount of rice can pay for that amount of oil or clarified butter. In this system, the capacity measures were local, as were the laborers' measures of areas. The landowner and, crucially, the surveyor knew how to navigate between the local measuring unit system and the metrical system that is officially in use all over India today. Here, then, what numbers you know how to compute with, with what units you know how to make conversions, how much you can convert kind into money, were markers of the power you had or did not have, but also of a knowledge that, if acquired, could empower you. Further, the economy and system of value for the laborer seemed a parallel system to the more mainstream one of the national economy. There could be many economies of values, and as long as they were easily convertible into one another, they could yield power. The questions we had and could not answer were these: Is the laborer's value system entirely convertible into our terms? Should it be?

Both Babu and I were historians of mathematics, improvising as ethnographers. And this experience became a lesson in history writing: it first revealed precisely how mathematical knowledge and practices could be a point of conflict. It also raised the question of how, and with what sources, we were uncovering such a history: Were we writing the history of the winners, of the power holders? We also couldn't help but raise the question—which Marilyn Strathern justly criticizes in her essay—in terms of traditions. What from the past explained the present in this case?

In what follows we will examine what can be said, in the past, of what appears as two separate cultures of computations and measuring: medieval (seventh–twelfth century) Sanskrit mathematical treatises and commentaries and modern (seventeenth–twentieth century) Tamil school primers, before coming back, in the conclusion, to the question of the existence of different mathematical ontologies.

Most of the history of mathematics of South Asia has been written using scholarly documents in Sanskrit. Sanskrit, an Indo-European language, was at first a high-caste Hindu, brahmanical language. By the fifth century CE, the language was used by a certain cosmopolitan elite, which might live outside of South Asia, might not be a Hindu, and not necessarily be a Brahmin. Not much is known of the institutions of learning in which such texts were produced, studied, or copied. Astral science is believed to have been both a scholarly field of study and a family-related occupation. Training would have been attended to either within one's family or through prestigious schools (Plofker 2009: 178–81). For the most part, however, the contextual information—including what we can glean about teaching—is embedded in the texts themselves.[5] In all cases, Sanskrit mathematical texts represent highbrow mathematics. Two different types of texts have been transmitted to us. The first, the most prestigious, is in the form of chapters of theoretical astronomical texts. These were mostly transmitted by continuous copying. Another kind of text, much less copied, often referred to as "mathematics for worldly practices" (*loka-vyavahāra*), is known to us by the chance find of one or two manuscripts. These sources document different mathematical practices, but they also share many common technical tools and topics. One of the characteristics, and important values of what Sheldon Pollock (2006) labels the "Sanskrit Knowledge System," is its aim at being universal. Sanskrit treatises and their commentaries do not want their scholarly production to rest on circumstances of time and place, which are regularly erased. Until roughly the seventeenth and eighteenth century, the mathematical texts we have articulate and think of themselves as an immemorial discipline (*gaṇita*): a new text is always the reframing of a preceding treatise or of an orally transmitted doctrine (*śāstra*). This can partly explain why histories of mathematics in Sanskrit have provided a very homogeneous and ahistorical point of view on this literature.[6] We know that astral and mathematical texts written in Sanskrit in the fifth, seventh, or twelfth century were still in circulation in different parts of South Asia during the eighteenth and nineteenth century. However, this Sanskrit literature lived side by side with texts in other Indian languages, generically called "vernaculars." Sources documenting past mathematical practices in Telugu,

---

5. The problem, then, is to find ways of retrieving such information from them. Ganeri (2008) and Keller (2015) use Speech Act Theory to do so.

6. Of course, other reasons can be added to this one, such as the importance of constructing a national scientific heritage, or the belief that when dealing with exact sciences historicity is not what is at stake but rather the technical contents of a text.

Bengali, Tamil, Marathi, Malayalam, Persian, and in various forms of Prakṛt exist, ranging mostly from the seventeenth century onward, except for the Jain Prakṛt texts that were canonized in the sixth–seventh century of our era. The texts have been edited and sometimes studied in the last fifty years, but the mathematics they testify to has remained in the margins of the writings on the history of mathematics in South Asia. Circulation of mathematical and astral knowledge between the vernacular and the Sanskrit is documented essentially as transmissions from the Sanskrit to the vernacular (Sarma 2011). It is possible, however, to imagine that the reverse could at times be true as well—notably, through the circulation of mathematical problems and riddles. We will discuss these transmissions below. Babu (2015) documents the elementary schooling in Tamil in the early nineteenth century in mathematics and shows that brahmanical and rich children were not schooled in the same way as other children. This is discussed in further detail in the next section. India has long been perceived as the champion of arithmetics, the continent from which zero and our way of computing with decimal place value notations have come. Do vernacular documents show alternative systems of noting numbers and dealing with values and measuring units? Do they contrast with what can be found in Sanskrit texts? Do these practices reflect distinct social contexts? And are these systems mutually exclusive: Does adopting one mean you can't convert back to the other?

Computing or Not with the Decimal Place Value Notation

In what follows, I present what may have been two very different cultures of quantification and culture that can be documented in South Asia—more specifically, in the Tamil world of the seventeenth century and until the late nineteenth century. The decimal place value notation was a technical and scholarly device found in Sanskrit lore from at least the fifth century CE all over the Indian subcontinent. In addition, another mode of noting numbers existed: the "Tamil numerals," a decimal notational nonpositional system, including special signs for small fractions, which, Babu suggests, was widespread among "practitioners" (accountants, surveyors, etc.).[7] To execute operations on values noted with Tamil

---

7. The existence of this numerical system is well attested. Other numerical forms as well, including very ancient systems of numerical noting, which might predate the decimal place value notation.

numerals, the tables that were part of the elementary Tamil curriculum could be used: operations such as multiplications and division were not "executed" at least; their resolution was made through the more or less elaborate use of the entries of tables. Second, in the Sanskrit corpus, the decimal place value notation figures as a tool for computing on numbers, without paying attention to the unit in which its value makes sense. Yet, by contrast, in the widespread Tamil primer the *Kaṇakkatikāram* (circa fifteenth–eighteenth century), computations were always carried out in such a way that they were meaningful in terms of measuring units each step of the way.

These are very preliminary results, which rest on what is still a very fragmentary access to proper documentation. For instance, the Sanskrit mathematical texts in circulation in Tamil Nadu in the seventeenth–nineteenth centuries need to be adequately documented, to specify more precisely the kind of practices that would have been familiar at that time and place and in real conversation with the Tamil texts. Their practices of value, number, and quantification will be presented while dealing with two common problems: the computing of areas and the purity of melted gold.[8]

Computing approximate areas of quadrilaterals: With or without specific measuring units?
In the mathematical chapter of the *Brahmasphuṭasiddhānta*, a theoretical astronomical text authored by Brahmagupta in 628 CE, the first part of a versified rule in Sanskrit provides the rough area of trilaterals and quad-rilaterals): "BSS 12 21ab. The gross area is the product of half the sum of the sides and counter-sides of a tri (or) quadrilateral" (Dvivedin 1902).

In his commentary on this chapter, Pṛthūdhaka provides some exam-ples of computations of such rough areas. The computations all deal with numbers with no associated measuring unit. The problems, although dealing with *kṣetra*s (lit. "field"), should be understood in this technical

8. A new interest in manuals in vernacular languages should lead to a se-ries of new publications. Here I use the very fragmentary elements that I have gleaned from Babu (2015). Hopefully, this thesis will be followed by more substantial and extensive re-editions and translations. Roy Wagner as the new chair of History and Philosophy of Mathematical Sciences at the ETZH (Swiss Federal Institute of Technology) in Zurich is also translating similar material in Mayalayam. Both have launched on a new program to create a census, edit, and study the vernacular sources of South India.

152

context as concerned with "geometrical figures." Since the chapter contains also a rule defining the decimal place value notation, and rules to compute multiplications, cubes, and cube roots with this notation, we can assume that the simple and more complex computations with fractions all used the decimal place value in this case. This is indeed how it can be found in the late manuscripts we have of this text. This rule was subsequently found throughout Sanskrit texts devoted to mathematics, outside of the realm of astronomy.[9] The measuring units used in Sanskrit mathematical and astronomical texts were standard, and could also be found in other texts of Sanskrit literature—notably, in treatises of state administration.[10] According to Sreeramula Rajeswara Sarma, they were called the "Magadha Units" (*māgadhamāna*) and were maybe part of the reverence shown by the discipline to its past.[11] Were these measuring units just theoretical ones, or were they those standardly used in South Asia, as part of the means for the educated to convert and compute, whatever their local circumstances? In the texts to be examined subsequently, the lengths are given in the famous linear measure, *hasta* (forearm, sometimes translated cubit), which measures twenty-four linear *aṅgulas* (breadth of a finger). The square *hastas* in the following problems are made of twenty-four square *aṅgulas*: the ratio is the same as in the linear case. Thus, square *hastas* are not made of linear *hastas*, as explained in the appendix on measures at the end of this essay.

In the anonymous and undated commentary on the *Pāṭīgaṇita* of Śrīdhāra, problems are formulated in words with measured values. They are solved by translating these problems into numerals with no associated measure, on which computations are carried out. The result of the computation can then be restated, with an associated measuring unit and

9. As noted in Shukla (1959: 87 n. 2), in the *Pāṭīgaṇita* of Śrīdhāra (eighth–tenth century) (in verse 111cd); in the *Gaṇitasārasaṃgrāha* of Māhavīra, (vii, 7ab), in the *Mahāsiddhānta* of Āryabhaṭa (xv, 66) or the *Gaṇitakaumudī* of Nārāyaṇa (II, verse 8), etc.

10. Those used in what follows are presented in an Appendix at the end of this essay.

11. Sarma: "The Sanskrit texts on arithmetic employ in their sums the so-called *Māgadhamāna*, i.e., units of measurement, weight, and coinage, which are said to have been prevalent in Magadha in ancient times (probably when Āryabhaṭa was writing at Kusumapura) and not the contemporary units" (2011: 204). This remark can be nuanced, as close study shows that units were far from being as homogeneous as they seem.

a certain shape (fractions are not generally found alone). In what follows, the computation of the area of a rectangle is carried out: "PG.115. Ex.123. Tell me the computation when a rectangle's base and mouth amount to five and a half *hastas*, while the flanks and middle height are three *hastas*" (Shukla 1959; Sanskrit p. 161–62).

The rectangle's sides in this example are named as conventionally as those of any quadrilateral, with an implicit orientation: the base (*bhū*) is usually horizontal, the face (*vadana*) is its opposite side, there are both flanks-sides (*pārśva-bhuja*), and a height (*lamba*), which extends from the middle of the base and the face, since it is a rectangle.[12]

The edition of the text provides a diagram, which notes the measures of each length, as shown in Figure 7.

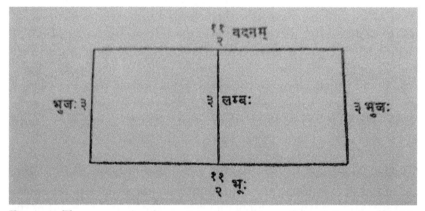

Figure 7. The rectangular diagram in the problem of the *Pāṭīgaṇita* (Shukla 1959).

The treatise's rule states that "the product of half the sum of the sides and counter-sides" should be taken. The "base" and its opposite side, "the face," is according to the statement of the problem, five and a half *hastas*, which is noted   5
               1
               2.

The two other opposite sides measure 3 *hastas*.

---

12. The resolution of the problem also extends to the case were only the value of the height is considered.

The computation, then, following the rule stated by Brahmagupta and restated by Śrīdhāra, first computes the sum of each couple of sides, (5 + ½) + (5 + ½) = 11, 3 + 3 = 6, and then their halves, 1½, 3, and then the product of both: 33/2. This is then converted, and since 33/2 = 16 + ½, and since 1 square *hasta* is 24 square *aṅgula*, the result obtained is "sixteen [square] *hastas* twelve [square] *aṅgulas*."

The resolution literally reads as follows:[13]

Procedure: the base is	5	the mouth	5
	1		1
	2		2

(. . .)

(The sum of both sides and opposite sides 11|6), their half 11| 3, their product 33

                                 2   2

from which the result is just that: sixteen *hastas*, twelve *aṅgulas*. (Shukla 1959; Sanskrit p. 132)

The numbers in the diagram, like those of the computation that follows, are noted, for their integral part, with the decimal place value notation. No mention is made of their units. The result of the computation is stated twice, once in a numerical form, then restated and converted specifying its measuring units in words. It is also striking that in the diagram the number associated with the "base" and the "face" is not 5 + ½ but 11/2. Indeed, the value stated in the text of the problem is first converted into numbers noted on a working surface. Here, the resolution does not seem to require the transformation of the fractional form of an integer increased by a fraction smaller than one (5 + ½), into a simple fraction with numerator and denominator (11/2), but the edited diagram does.[14]

It is not clear why such elementary computations are detailed here, amid much more complex problems, but they do highlight an articulation between values that are stated in problems and answers, on the one hand, and numbers noted in specific manners to compute with, on the other hand. Further, the two texts taken as examples can easily be seen

---

13. () indicates the editorial additions made by K. S. Shukla. (. . .) indicates that part of the text has been skipped.

14. This might be the choice of the editor, Shukla, or that of a scribe. The location of this unique manuscript of this commentary is not known today, so it is difficult to check.

as exhibiting some of the spectrum within the Sanskrit corpus itself: on the one hand, a prestigious theoretical astronomical text of the seventh century, and on the other hand, an undated (but seemingly quite late) commentary on a tenth century text concentrating on mathematics as a topic of worldly affairs. However, they both share a way of emphasizing the computations on numbers over measured values.

As mentioned above, a corpus of mathematical texts in Tamil, a Dravidian language of southeastern India, has been edited and studied in the last fifty years. This corpus encompasses texts of different kinds and times.[15] In what follows, a mathematical text written in classical versified Tamil, which might have been a canonical primer if not an actual textual genre, the *Kaṇakkatikāram* (hereafter abbreviated as *KK*) will be used as a source.[16] A first author of such a text, Kāri Nāyaṉār, would have lived in the fifteenth century in what is today the Nagapattinam district of Tamil Nadu (Babu 2015: 32), while manuscripts from the eighteenth century onward can be found throughout Tamil Nadu, suggesting a widespread textbook. The edited text, which attempts to collect in one text all the variations of thirty-three different manuscripts, presents itself as an "exposition of mathematics to the world," and is composed of rules in classical Tamil verses and problems, some versified, others in prose, and some cursory resolutions. Among the standard topics it treats, problems of land measuring and alloys will be singled out here. The mathematical practices documented in this text will be associated with the two texts that formed in the early nineteenth century (and probably before that) the basis of education/learning, in rural areas, for non–high caste children: the lexical lists, called *Poṉṉilakam* and the multiplication tables, called *Eṇcuvaṭi*. Babu (2015: 127) has shown how they were important parts of the village schools (also known as veranda or *Tiṇṇai* schools) that English observers sometimes called the "multiplication schools." Babu (2015: 83–103) further argues that the *KK* should be understood as a textbook to train practitioners such as the surveyors (*veṭṭiyāṉ*), the tax collectors, or accountants (*kaṇakkaṉ*).

Tamil numerical notations extended to higher numbers and to fractions smaller than one, in many forms. And, as demonstrated by Babu

---

15. For a preliminary study of computations in Tamil inscriptions, see Subbarayalu (2012) and Selvakumar (2016).

16. Three editions of the texts are noted by Babu: Satyabama (1998), Subramaniam (2007), Satyabama (2007) For the status of the text, see Babu (2015: 32–33).

(2015: 119ff.), the teaching associated learning by heart, learning how to write the notations, and learning their values. The *Eṇcuvaṭi* tables, as edited by Babu, are hybrid in terms of numbers and measured values. Some state the measuring unit of the numbers considered. Further, the tables incorporate examples of how to find the value of a product when such a multiplication is not directly tabulated. For example, as shown in Figure 8, to multiply 17 x 17 *kuḻi* (an area measuring unit described below as well as in the appendix at the end of this essay), the value is found by considering the entries for 10 x 10, 10 x 7 (twice), and 7 x 7, and by adding them progressively.

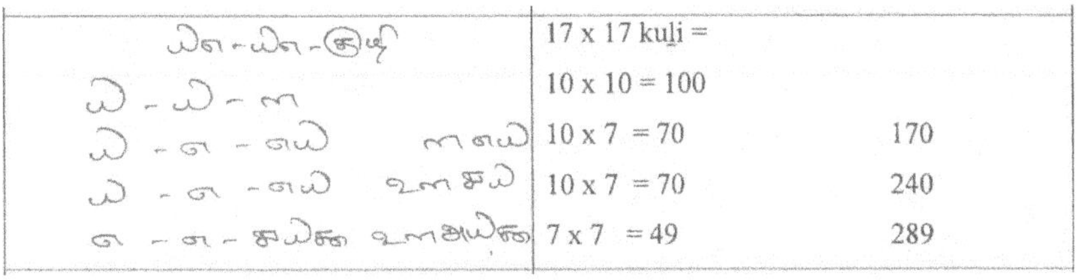

	17 x 17 kuḻi =	
	10 x 10 = 100	
	10 x 7 = 70	170
	10 x 7 = 70	240
	7 x 7 = 49	289

Figure 8. The entry for 17 x 17 *kuḻi* in the *Eṇcuvaṭi*, edited in Babu (2015).

In the *Kaṇakkatikāram* we can see how an approximation of quadrilateral areas was computed:

KK. 81 Add one side to another and halve and multiply the resulting side by the larger one. If you do so, you will obtain all the areas (*nilaṅkaḷ*) of the world like the rays of the sun spreading on earth. (Babu 2015: 46, quoting Subramaniam 2007: 125)

The general rule thus approximates the surface of any quadrilateral by approximating it to the area of a rectangle whose sides would be half the sum of the quadrilateral's opposite sides. As in Sanskrit texts, orientations of figures are provided by cardinal directions.

In South India, before and during the Chōḻa rule (850–1250) the *kuḻi* was an important area measuring unit. The *kuḻi* corresponds to a square having for side the length of a measuring rod (in linear measures of *kōl*). The *kuḻi* served as a surface unit by which other surface units could be determined (Subbarayalu 2012: 83; Babu 2015: 135). The rule stated above is followed by a problem and its resolution:

right/South *kōl* 13 left/North *kōl* 11 therefore *kōl* 24, half of that is
12; West/lower *kōl* 9 East/upper *kōl* 19, therefore *kōl* 28, its half is 14;
multiply this 10 x10 = 100, 4 x 10 = 40, 2 x 10 = 20, 2 x 4 = 8. Therefore <the result is> 168 *kuḻi*; this is how you say it. (Babu 2015: 46,
quoting Subramaniam 2007: 125)

In this problem a quadrilateral has four sides measured in *kōl*, whose
values are given as couples of opposite sides. The "flanks" of the quadrilateral in the Sanskrit text are here its South and North sides, respectively 13 and 11 *kōl*. The opposite "base" and "faces" are here the West
and East sides, 9 and 19 *kōl*.

The rule provided above involves first: "Add one side to another and
halve." Thus, for the first pair of sides, the computation is carried out,
13 + 11 = 24 *kōl*, its half is 12. For the second pair, 9 + 19 = 28 *kōl*, its
half is 14. The next step of the process is then: "multiply the resulting
side by the larger one." Although it is unclear what this means in terms
of assessments of the respective "mean sizes" just computed, we understand that the product of 12 by 14 has to be carried out. Here, as in the
multiplication table examined above, the product of $(10 + 2) \times (10 + 4)$
is carried out, the individual products are made explicit and their sum
100 + 40 + 20 + 8 = 168 computed. This last computation provides the
result.

In this resolution, the execution is such that at each step the measuring unit of what is being computed is always known. And this is often
(although not always) stated. When the area is computed, however, and
the product of 12 by 14 is carried out, the detailing of how values are
taken from a table seems to be noted, as in multiplication tables. Here,
then, when using multiplication tables, the computation is carried out on
numbers, with which measuring units are not associated. But as soon as
the result is input into the resolution of the problem it exists as a measured value again, and the result is too.

Another problem deals with proportions of areas and their different
uses:

If the total *vēli* is 1000, and if ⅒th has been sown; ⅛th has been
transplanted; ¼th has nurseries and ½ has matured paddy, how much
was the wasteland and how much was the cultivated area? (Babu
2015: 49, quoting and translating Subramaniam 2007: 160)

The solution of this problem involves computing 1000 x ⅒, 1000 x ⅛,
1000 x ¼, 1000 x ½, and adding all the results. At each step of such a

computation the results would always be in *vēli* (another area measuring unit). It is possible to arrive at a resolution using the tables, the lexical lists (*Poṉṉilakam*), and the multiplication tables (*Eṉcuvaṭi*) to retrieve the value of each product.[17]

These examples illustrate how tables of multiplication could have been used to execute more complex products, without the decimal place value notation. We can thus contrast the following: Sanskrit sources (the *Brāhmasphuṭasiddhānta* and the *Pāṭigaṇita*, for example), which compute using the decimal place value notation and whose emphasis is on the different operations executed on numbers not associated with measuring units when computing areas, with the *Kaṇakkatikāram* in which the area is computed with an attention given to the measuring units linear and square at every step. Numbers—for example, values without a measuring unit—would come into play in the intermediate steps of retrieving values in multiplication tables when computing products.

"Gold computations"

Similar contrasts of practices with numbers, measured values, and computations can be documented in problems about the fineness of gold, its price, or the mixing of silver and gold. It is striking that in the Sanskrit texts dealing with this quite standard topic (*suvarṇa-gaṇita*) (Sarma 1983), computations are carried out mechanically with numbers. For instance, in the canonical arithmetical *Līlāvatī* by Bhāskara (b. 1104), a problem of the cost of gold is solved by an inverse Rule of Three (*vyasta-trairāśika*). After the quantities are displayed on a grid on a working surface, represented by a "setting" (*nyāsa*) clause in the text, a multiplication is carried out on the left and a division is made on the right. The answer here is given in noted numbers, with no measuring unit associated with

---

17. 1/10th of a 1,000 can be obtained by reading the multiplication table from right to left of *Encuvatti Mēlavai ilakkam*, and retrieve 100 (Babu 2015: appendix III, 52). 1/8th is a standard fraction, having its own sign in the "Tamil numeral system"; 1000 x 1/8 = 125 is the last line of the part devoted to 1/8th in *Mēlavai ciṟṟakkam* (Babu 2015: appendix III, 62). 1/4th is also a standard fraction; it also has its own multiplication table. 1000 x ¼ = 250 is the last line of the part devoted to 1/4th in *Mēlavai ciṟṟakkam* (Babu 2015: appendix III, 67). 1000 x ½ = 50 is the last line of the part devoted to 1/2 in *Mēlavai ciṟṟakkam* (Babu 2015: appendix III, 68). How additions (100 + 125 + 250 + 500 = 975) and subtractions (1000 − 975 = 25) were computed is not made explicit here.

them. The *varṇa* (lit. color) of gold stands for its purity, a measure not unlike the carat, the *gadyāṇaka* is a measure of weight, and the *niṣka* a gold coin (Āpaṭe 1937: 75; Colebrooke 1817: 35, 46–47).

> An example concerning the price of gold according [to its] *varṇa*:
> If a ten *varṇa* gold [weighing] a *gadyāṇaka* is bought for a *niṣka* say then how much [can be bought, with the same amount of money of a] fifteen *varṇa* gold?

> Setting
> 10 | 1| 15|
> the result is   2
>   3

Here then, 1 x 10 (multiplication on the left) was divided (on the right) by 15, and a fraction obtained, ⅔. No measuring unit is stated for the result, which is implicitly in *gadyāṇaka*s.

In the portion of the same treatise devoted to "gold computations" (*suvarṇa-gaṇita*), a similar phenomenon can be found: a tabular display enables the mechanical carrying out of a problem. First a rule is stated, to solve a problem where several parcels of gold of different weights w_i and purity v_i are melted together. The weight of the melted result is assumed to be the sum of the previous weights (Σw_i). The purity of the new lump of gold, V, is computed with a procedure that amounts to $V = \Sigma\ w_i v_i \backslash \Sigma w_i$.[18] The procedure then amounts to computing the sum of the products $w_i v_i$, then the sum of w_i, and divide the first by the second.

The rule is followed by a solved example (Āpaṭe 1937: 99, verse 104–5; Colebrooke 1817: 35, 46–47):

> An example:
> Parcels of gold weighing severally ten, four, two, and four *māṣās*, and of *varṇa* thirteen, twelve, eleven, and ten respectively, being melted

---

18. The sum of the products of the *varṇa* and [weight of several parcels] of gold being divided by the [weight of the melted] gold, the value of the *varṇa* of the [melted] gold [is obtained]. The *varṇa* is [obtained] when [the previous result is] divided by the [weight of] the purified gold, the amount of purified gold when divided by the *varṇa* (Āpaṭe 1937: 99, verse 103; Colebrooke 1817: 35; 46–47, verse 102–3). Colebrooke's verse numbering has been adopted here and in what follows. Note that gold and weight of gold are one and same word here.

together, tell me quickly, merchant, who art conversant with the computation of gold, what is the *varṇa*s of the mass? (. . .)

Setting: 13   12   11   10
             10   4   2   4

The measure of the *varṇa* of gold obtained when melted, 12.

Here, the setting shows how the computation can be done mechanically. The *varṇa*s (v_i) are on the top row, the weights (w_i) of each parcel on the lowest row. To compute the weight of the whole melted gold, the sum of the cells of the lower row is made (20). The product of the numbers in each column can be made (13 x 10 = 130, 12 x 4 = 48, 11 x 2 = 22, 10 x 4 = 40) and the sum of the products computed (130 + 48 + 22 + 40 = 240), to be able then to divide the latter by the first (240/20) and obtain the result (12). The products and their sum are typically numbers to which no specific measuring unit can be associated.

Similar but different "gold computations" can also be found in the Tamil *Kaṇakkatikāram*. In this context, the *māttu* is a gold weight as well as a way of measuring the purity of gold, the *kalañcu* and *paṇavetai* measures of weight, and the *paṇam* a coin.[19] In the problem given in this treatise here, and the rule that follows, the computation that involves first a division and then a multiplication ensures that at each step the measuring unit of what has been computed is known:

If the cost of one *kalañcu* of gold with ten *māttu* is fourteen *paṇam*, what would be the cost of an eight *māttu* gold? Then you divide the *paṇam* by the *māttu* of the given gold and multiply it by the other given *māttu*. (Babu 2015: 51, quoting Subramaniam 2007)

The problem is seen here as a kind of Rule of Three since the weight of gold is stable. The first division gives you the price of gold per *māttu*, and the second the price sought.[20]

It is well established that Sanskrit sources of diverse times and contexts dealing with areas or gold computations (but the topics could be

19. For weight standards as documented in Tamil texts and epigraphy see Babu (2015: 7–8); for gold computations, see Babu (2015: 50); Sarma (1983). For the *paṇa* (tamil *paṇam*), see the appendix at the end of this essay.
20. 14/10 = 1 + 2/5 *paṇam*s, which multiplied by 8 would have been, 9 + 3/5 *paṇa*s. We do not know if such a result accounts for *paṇam* denominations. Divisions may have beeen carried out by inversing tables of multiplications.

largely extended) all use the decimal place value notation to compute. These computations are carried out with numbers whose value and relation to measuring units can be made explicit when stating a problem or providing the final result, but not while the different steps of the computation are executed. In the *Kaṇakkatikāram*, which we have associated with the lexical and multiplication tables that were taught to children in Tamil Nadu from the eighteenth century, some problems seem to be solved in such a way that each step of the computation accounts for the units of the values considered. Only when products are carried out, and multiple entries of a multiplication table need to be retrieved and added, would numbers be considered with no associated measuring unit.

We have thus seen here a testimony of what might have been two different mathematical cultures belonging to different social contexts: the scholarly world of Sanskrit mathematical lore opposed to elementary school texts in Tamil.[21]

Is It Tamil Versus Sanskrit?

Should we see these two cultures as exclusive of one another and characterized by the language they use? Things are not so simple, of course. Thus, in this example from the *Kaṇakkatikāram* (Subramaniam and Satyabama 1999; see also 2005), the fineness *māttu* of an alloy is measured against its weight in standard *paṇaveṭai*:

> When 4 *paṇaveṭai* of gold with 7½ *māttu* are mixed with one *paṇaveṭai* of silver, what will be a *māttu* of the resulting gold? The original *māttu* has to be multiplied by its weight to be divided by the total weight, to yield the final refinement *māttu*. 7½ x 4 *paṇaveṭai* = 30; weight of gold 4 and silver 1- (their sum is) 5; 5 is the total weight in *paṇaveṭai*; the new *māttu* is 30/5 = 6. (Babu 2015: 51, quoting Subramaniam 1999: 224–26)

Here, then, in contrast to the result seen in the previous section, but using a procedure that resembles the one we have seen in the *Lilāvatī*,

---

21. For Babu (2015: 83), this would perhaps be better phrased as a "world of texts" as opposed to a "world of practice."

the procedure to find the fineness of a gold and silver alloy requires computing:

- the product of fineness and weight of the gold $w_i v_i$;
- the sum of the weights w_i of the gold and silver;
- the division of the product by the weight: $w_i v_i / w_i$;
- which would provide the fineness of the alloy.

Here, then, the purity $7 + \frac{1}{2}$ *māttu* and a measure of weight (4 *paṇaveṭai* of gold) are multiplied by one another. The product obtained is a number with no associated measuring unit, $4 \times 15/2 = 30$. The sum of measures of weight of the gold and silver (4 *paṇaveṭai* of gold + 1 *paṇaveṭai* of silver = 5 *paṇaveṭai*) is computed and then the division of the product by the sum (30/5) provides the "new *māttu*," 6. Here, then, one step of the process is not associated with a measuring unit, not unlike what is common in Sanskrit mathematical texts.

Further, among Tamil sources, the *Kaṇitanūḷ*, a text known in one manuscript at the Government Oriental Manuscript Library (in Chennai) seems to be closer to Sanskrit sources for its emphasis on computations with numbers than to the kind of practices found in the *Kaṇakkatikāram*. Here is a problem for the payment of wages:

Finding the gold in 6 *māttu* for one who worked for five days, when one worked for fifteen days and gets 4 *paṇaveṭai* gold of 9 *māttu*. The last quantity of 9 *māttu* gold and its weight 4 are multiplied which is 36. This has to be multiplied by the number of days of the first, which is 5 = 180. Now divide this by the last given number of days which is 15, 180/15 = 12. Now divide this by the first *māttu* which is 2 *paṇaveṭai*. (Babu 2015: 52, quoting Subramaniam 1999: 226–29, verse 70–73)

We can recognize here a Rule of Five, a familiar tool of Sanskrit mathematical texts: To find the weight of gold w_n paid to somebody who worked for n days, for a payment in gold of refinement m_n, knowing that a work of x days, with a gold refinement of m_x is paid w_x, the procedure amounts to computing: $w_n = (n m_x w_x)/x m_n$. The computation carried out, first computing $n m_x w_x = 9 \times 4 \times 5 = 180$, and then dividing this sum first by x = 15 and then by m_n = 4, thus finding the result 2 *paṇaveṭai*, articulates well how the initial values each have a separate associated measuring unit, but the intermediate steps are numbers to which no distinct measure can be associated.

Here is an alloy problem, whose numerical values seem to echo one we have seen above:

When a 8 *māttu* gold weighing 2 *paṇaveṭai* and another 7 *māttu* gold weighing 2 *paṇaveṭai* are melted, what would be the resulting *māttu*? The method is to multiply the *māttu* and *paṇaveṭai* of each gold and add them. That is (8 x 2) + (7 x 2) = 16 + 14 = 30. Add the weights, 2 *paṇaveṭai* + 2 *paṇaveṭai* = 4 *paṇaveṭai*. Now, divide the previous 30 by this 4 to get 7½. Therefore, the resultant *māttu* gold will have a *māttu* of 7½. (Babu 2015: 50–51, quoting Subramaniam 1999: 212, verse 58)

We recognize here the same process as the one found in the *Kaṇakkatikāram* and the *Līlāvatī*, in which to find the fineness of an alloy, the sum of the products of weights and purity is divided by the sum of weights ($V=\Sigma w_i v_i/\Sigma w_i$). The emphasis here is first on the application of a general abstract rule ("to multiply the *māttu* and *paṇaveṭai* of each gold and add them"), which is applied. It is striking that the elements of the process to which no measuring unit can be associated are not articulated, while those to which an interpretation in terms of measures can be made, are. The resulting value of *māttu* 7½, is the same as in the *Kaṇakkatikāram*. Would these two texts be in dialogue with one another?

The recognition of this circulation of problems and practices, within the Tamil sources and with some of the Sanskrit canons, hints at the fact that probably these ways of computing and practicing mathematics were not separate geographically one from another. In his study of the local village schools in South-East Tamil Nadu, Babu notes that Brahmin children would go to funded Sanskrit schools, while other children would rather be schooled in the Tamil ones. Implicitly, there seems to have been a separate space for Sanskrit lore within Brahmin *maṭhas*. Babu (2015: 116) also shows how these worlds interacted: some teachers of the village schools knew Sanskrit mathematical texts. Translations are also known from the Sanskrit to the Tamil. There is a trope of exchange—when we come to the relations of Sanskrit with the vernaculars—in mathematics. Thus, in his pioneering essay on the topic, Sarma states:

It is certain that these exchanges were never one-sided, i.e., from the "Great Tradition" of Sanskrit to the "Little Traditions" of regional languages. The two traditions were mutually complementary. While mathematical ideas and processes were systematized in Sanskrit manuals, the broader dissemination of these ideas took place in the regional languages. Conversely, Sanskrit has also absorbed much from the local traditions. (Sarma 2011: 221–22)

Implicitly, a social role is devoted to both tradition. Sanskrit is understood as the realm of the highbrow elite, while Tamil is used for the "dissemination" of the knowledge created in Sanskrit. In the cases we have found here, the Sanskrit texts seem to want to build a mathematical understanding and a more general mathematical context for the rules applied in the *Kaṇakkatikāram*.

Similarly, the fact that even in the seventeenth century computations could be carried out without using the decimal place value notation may explain why computations in Sanskrit texts also hint at methods not involving this notation.[22] Time and space prevent me from developing the point here, but it seems that a whole range of rules that were interpreted as expressing the commutativity, associativity, and distributivity of multiplication may, in fact, be read as providing general procedures when computing with numerals that do not use place value notations.

A problem quoted by Sarma (which seems to have traveled widely from Europe to Japan) alludes both to how multiple exchanges could take place across language and social barriers and also to how the knowledge was kept mostly to the Brahmins, in an atmosphere not at all civil:[23]

Fifteen Brahmins and fifteen thieves had to spend a dark night in an isolated temple of Durga. The goddess appeared in person at midnight and wanted to devour exactly fifteen persons, since she was hungry. The thieves naturally suggested that she should consume the fifteen plump Brahmins. But the clever Brahmins proposed that all the thirty would stand in a circle and Durga should eat each ninth person. The proposal was accepted by Durga and the thieves. So the Brahmins arranged themselves and the thieves in a circle, telling each one where to stand. Durga then counted out each ninth person and

22. Keller and Morice-Singh (forthcoming) considers the use or not of decimal place value notations while observing techniques of multiplication in Sanskrit texts.
23. For a more in-depth study of the problem and its circulations, see Sarma (1987).

devoured him. When the fifteen were eaten, she was satiated and dis-appeared, and only Brahmins remained in the circle. The problem is, how did the Brahmins arrange themselves and the thieves in a circle? (Sarma 2011: 210, also quoted in Babu 2015: 1)

Conclusion: What Speaks to Ontological Differences?

I borrow the concept of mathematical practices and culture from Ka-rine Chemla, Renaud Chorlay, and David Rabouin (2016), and more largely to a group in Paris that reflects on these questions. Mathematical cultures in this understanding, which associates shared practices with shared values, are fundamentally plural. Of course language and local contexts come into play in ways that need to be described as well, but it is striking that sometimes across language and space people with the same occupations develop similar practices which can be very different from the practices and values of people sharing the same language but not the same occupation. From what we have seen in this essay, it is reasonable to believe that it was not two cultures of mathematics but many that have existed in the Indian subcontinent during its very rich, vast, and long history. If we do not know of many of these cultures as of today, it is because they have been overlooked. Indeed, for a very long time, what counted as valuable was what was similar to present day mathematics on the one hand, and the practices of a cultivated elite on the other hand. If we come back to the situation of the Nagapattinam region of Tamil Nadu evoked in the beginning of this essay, the question will be first to understand the social contexts that these mathematics are an emanation of: the story that brought this situation into being. Second, if we consid-er this situation as testifying to contemporary and geographically close but differing mathematical cultures, we may want to raise questions that might help us think of how different these mathematical practices are: Does the adoption of one exclude the other? Can these mathematical practices cross-fertilize each other, can they produce a hybrid? Have they done so in the past? Could this serve as a criterion of ontological difference?

But in the context of South Asia today what would it mean to hold that different mathematical cultures have different mathematical on-tologies? Those who brandish ontological differences today are those who want to see Hindu, Christian, and Muslim cultures as ontologically different. The current fundamentalist and nationalist government would like to promote the idea of Indian traditional sciences as alternatives to Western secular-Christian-Muslim science, very much insisting on the fundamental difference and power that come from exploring science with mystical and religious tools. In this very political atmosphere, let us leave the question of the existence of different mathematical ontologies open, but remember that there have been and still are different cultures of how we deal with values and numbers, cultures of measure, and dealings with shapes. Some are still alive today. They are studied by ethnomathematics and should be thought of as a cultural heritage in danger that needs to be preserved.

Appendix: Measuring Units

Here, I explain the different measuring units found in the extracts discussed in this essay.

A. Measuring Units in Sanskrit Sources

Measures of lengths and areas
lengths
24 *aṅgulas* (breadth of a finger) make a *hasta* (forearm, cubit).
areas
24 square *aṅgulas* make a square *hasta*.
The ratio is the same as in the linear case. Consequently, the square *aṅgula* cannot be thought of as being constructed from linear *aṅgulas*. Indeed, a square linear *hasta* should contain 24 x 24= 576 square linear *aṅgulas*. 24 is not a perfect square; consequently, this square *hasta* seems to be a theoretical unit.

Measures relating to gold
purity is measured not in *carats* but in *varṇa* (colors)
weight of gold involves small specialized measuring units such as the *gadyāṇaka*. The *māṣa* is a more standard weight. The text does not specify how they are related.
prices are given in *niṣkas*, a gold coin, in the *Līlāvatī*. The treatise provides a rule from which we know that there would have been 256 (16 x 16) *paṇas* in a gold *niṣka*.

B. Measuring Units in Tamil Sources

Measures of lengths and areas

<u>lengths</u>

kōl is the name of a measuring rod, and also of a unit of length.

<u>areas</u>

1 *kuḻi* is a square whose side is 1 *kōl*

Many relations of the *vēli* to the *kuḻi* are documented, probably the cholas imposed the following:

2000 *kuḻi* make a *vēli*

Measures relating to gold

<u>fineness</u> measured in *māttu*

<u>weight</u> measured in *kalañcu* and *paṇaveṭai*

<u>coins</u> are evoked through the *paṇam* here. Silver and coper punch-marked *paṇa*s are known to have been used as early as the Mauryan empire in South Asia (321 BCE–187 CE). In the *Līlāvatī*, a rule explains that there would have been 256 (16 x 16) *paṇas* in a gold *niṣka*.

References

Āpaṭe, Dattātreya Viśṇu. 1937. *Līlāvatī with the commentaries Buddhivilāsanī by Gaṇeśa Daivajña and Vivaraṇa by Mahīdhara*. 2vols. Ānandāśrama Sanksirt Series 107. Pune: Vināyaka Gaṇeśa Āpaṭe, Ānnadāśrama Sanskrit Series.

Babu, Senthi. 2015. "The culture of science and politics in colonial Tamil Nadu c. 1860–c. 1940." PhD diss., Jawahral Nehru University, Centre for Historical Studies, School of Social Sciences, New Dehli.

Chemla, Karine, Renaud Chorlay, and David Rabouin. 2016. *The Oxford handbook of generality in mathematics and the sciences*. Oxford: Oxford University Press.

Colebrooke, Henry Thomas. 1817. *Algebra, with arithmetic and mensuration, from the Sanscrit of Brahmegupta and Bhàscara*. London: J. Murray.

Dodson, Michael S. 2005. "Translating science, translating empire: The power of language in colonial North India." *Comparative Studies in Society and History* 47 (4): 809–35.

Dvivedin, Mahāmahopaḍhyāya Sudhākara. 1902. *Brahmasphuṭasiddhānta and Dhyānagrahopadeṣādhyāya by Brahmagupta; Edited with his own com-*

mentary. Reprint from the Pandit. Vol. 24, no. 12. Benares: Medical Hall Press.

Ganeri, Jonardon. 2008. "Contextualism in the study of Indian intellectual cultures." *Journal of Indian Philosophy* 36 (5–6): 551–62.

Keller, Agathe. 2015. "Ordering operations in square root extractions, analyzing some early medieval Sanskrit mathematical texts with the help of speech act theory." In *Texts, textual acts and the history of science,* edited by Karine Chemla and Jacques Virbel, 183–218. Cham: Springer.

Keller, Agathe, and Catherine Morice-Singh. Forthcoming. "Multiplying integers: On the diverse practices of medieval Sanskrit authors." In *Cultures of computation and quantification in the ancient world,* edited by Karine Chemla, Christine Proust, Cécile Michel, and Agathe Keller. Cham: Springer. https://halshs.archives-ouvertes.fr/halshs-01006135

Plofker, Kim. 2009. *History of mathematics in India.* Princeton, NJ: Princeton University Press.

Pollock, Sheldon. 2006. *The language of the gods in the world of men: Sanskrit, culture and power in premodern India.* Berkeley: University of California Press.

Prakash, Gyan. 1999. *Another reason: Science and the imagination of modern India.* Princeton, NJ: Princeton University Press.

Raina, Dhruv. 1997. "Evolving perspectives on science and history: A chronicle of modern India's scientific enchantment and disenchantment (1850–1980)." *Social Epistemology* 11 (1): 3–24.

———. 2016. "The phased institutionalization of mathematics education and research in late colonial India (1850–1950)." *Archives Internationales d'Histoire des Sciences* 66 (176): 225–41.

Sarma, Sreeramula Rajeswara. 1983. "Varṇamālikā system of determining the fineness of gold in ancient and medieval India." In *Aruna-Bharati: Professor A. N. Jani felicitation Volume,* 369–89. Baroda: Essays in Contemporary Indological Studies.

———. 1987. "The Pāvulūrigaṇitamu: The first Telugu work on mathematics." *Studien zur Indologie und Iranistik* 13–14: 163–76.

———. 2011. "Mathematical literature in the regional languages of India." In *Ancient Indian leaps into mathematics,* edited by B. S. Yadav and Man Mohan, 201–12. New York: Bikhäuser.

Satyabama, Kamesvara. 1998. *Kaṇakkatikāram-Tokuppu Nūl.* Thanjavur: Sarasvati Mahal.

————. 2007. *Suriyapūpaṉ Kaṇakkatikāram (Pakuti II)*. Thanjavur: Sarasvati Mahal.

Selvakumar, V. 2016. "History of numbers and fractions and arithmetic calculations in the Tamil region: Some observations." *International Journal of Research in Humanities and Social Sciences* 3 (1): 27–35.

Shukla, Kripa Shankar. 1959. *Pāṭīgaṇita of Śrīdharācarya*. Lucknow: Lucknow University.

Smadja, Ivahn. 2015. "Sanskrit versus Greek 'proofs': History of mathematics at the crossroads of philology and mathematics in nineteenth-century Germany." *Revue d'Histoire des Mathématiques* 21 (2): 217–349.

Subbarayalu, Yellava. 2012. *South India under the Cholas*. New Delhi: Oxford University Press.

Subramaniam, P., and Kamesvara Satyabama, eds. 1999. *Kāṇita Nūl: A treatise on mathematics*. Part I. Chennai: Institute of Asian Studies.

————. 2005. *Kāṇita Nūl: A treatise on mathematics*. Part II. Chennai: Institute of Asian Studies.

————. 2007. *Kaṇakkatikāram*. Chennai: Institute of Asian Studies

CHAPTER EIGHT

Antidomestication in the Amazon: Swidden and its Foes

Manuela Carneiro da Cunha

It might come as a surprise that I would enlist agriculture as a science in and of the forest. Is it a science? Here's a quotation from the *Oxford English Dictionary* (*OED*): "If we estimate dignity by immediate usefulness, agriculture is undoubtedly the first and noblest science."[1] In the second edition of the *OED*, agriculture is still being defined as a science: "The science and art of cultivating the soil; including the allied pursuits of gathering in the crops and rearing live stock; tillage, husbandry, farming (in the widest sense)."[2] However, the third edition, twenty-three years later, considers that earlier usage to have become rare: "(a) Originally: the theory or practice of cultivating the soil to produce crops; an instance of this (now rare); (b) Later also (now chiefly): the practice of growing crops, rearing livestock, and producing animal products (as milk and eggs), regarded as a single sphere of activity; farming, husbandry; (also) the theory of this."[3] If the *OED* change of heart is any indication, it looks

---

1. Johnson Rambler (1751) No. 145. ¶3.
2. *Oxford English Dictionary*. 1989. 2nd ed. Vols. 1–20. Oxford: Oxford University Press.
3. *Oxford English Dictionary*. 2012–. 3rd ed. Vols. 1– Oxford: Oxford University Press. Continually updated at http://www.oed.com/.

as if agriculture is being demoted from science to mere practice. And yet, somewhat puzzlingly, *OED* adds the theory of the practice of agriculture to its (b)-level definition.

There is no doubt that the scientific establishment tends to keep the label *science* to itself. A depreciation of local communities and Indigenous peoples' agriculture is transparent in a distinction that is sometimes made between knowledge and empirical know-how, something the French separate into *savoir* and *savoir-faire* (Caplat 2016).

I take it that we can agree that the term *science* is applicable to traditional peoples' agriculture. But then, how can I call it a science *in* or *of the forest*? How can one reconcile agriculture with the forest, since the former is blamed for having caused the very destruction of the latter? True, some definitions of agriculture include forestry, but this is not what I am talking about. What I mean is high forest, a forest that looks pristine to nonexpert eyes, even though it might well be anthropogenic to some degree (Balée 1994, 2013; Heckenberger and Neves 2009).

It is somewhat ironic that among many South American Lowland Indigenous peoples, the forest is often conceived of as itself cultivated. True, not necessarily cultivated by present-day humans but rather by other "people," animals, spirits, masters, even planted and cared for by other plants. In a sense, it is as if agriculture were the norm, wilderness being residual. Thus, the Wajãpi notion of human space is restricted to their gardens and fallows while the forest is made by other beings cultivating their own food (Gallois 1986; Cabral de Oliveira 2012). In Jamamadi Indigenous universe, there are no such things as wild plants, since everything is cultivated but by some "other" cultivator (Shiratori 2018: 136). Jarawara follow a similar view, yet admit a degree of remaining wilderness (Maizza 2014: 504). Several Amazonian Indigenous peoples credit agoutis for cultivating Brazil nuts. Sometimes the forest is reconfigured as the garden planted by the Creator himself.

This might correlate with a puzzling and often noted absence among Indigenous peoples as well as Amazonian rubber-tappers of a general term for designating the *Plantae* kingdom. A *plant* for humans is literally what humans have planted.[4] But animals and other beings can

---

4. In a similar fashion, for older Wajãpi, wild fruit was designated by an exclusive term that could not be extended to cultivated fruit. Under outside influence, the scope of the term now covers both wild and cultivated fruit (Cabral de Oliveira 2012: 77). What this might indicate is that in the

and do also plant, hence they have their own plants—that is, those they cultivate. Knowledge of animal food preferences is truly encyclopedic (Cabral de Oliveira 2012: 73ff.).[5] An animal's plant roughly corresponds to its food, though such food might be edible for several different animals and humans alike. Just as many animals partake in what is produced in human gardens, so humans may also eat what was produced by animals: wild food. One could speculate whether this would favor human trekking seasons and abandoning cultivation once and for all. In a sense, therefore, every sentient being could be a gardener or an agriculturalist.

In contrast with such notion of a wide prevalence of cultivators, be they humans or otherwise, John Locke never acknowledged any agriculture at all among "Americans": "In the beginning all the world was America." This somewhat odd quote comes from John Locke's *Second treatise of government* (1690: chap. 5, sec. 49) and needs some explanation. America and aboriginal Americans stand, in Locke's scheme, for an age of universal undivided commons. Individual property (and hence its "conveniences") does not exist just as was the case when humankind lived in the Garden of Eden.

> *Sec. 41.* There cannot be a clearer demonstration of any thing, than several nations of the Americans are of this, who are rich in land, and poor in all the comforts of life; whom nature having furnished as liberally as any other people, with the materials of plenty, i.e. a fruitful soil, apt to produce in abundance, what might serve for food, rayment, and delight; yet for want of *improving it by labour*, have not one hundredth part of the conveniencies we enjoy. (Locke 1960: chap. 5, sec. 41; emphasis added)

The reasoning is: labor being absent, property has not yet emerged. Primeval labor was cultivation, and cultivation implied "subduing."

> And hence *subduing or cultivating the earth, and having dominion, we see are joined together. The one gave title to the other* (Locke 1960: chap. 5, sec. 35; emphasis added)

---

nomenclature criteria of old, actions and relations to plants trumped form and function.

5. It exceeds its hunting utility that allows one to anticipate when and where one can expect to find specific game by following the ripening of fruit or seeds.

Half a century after Locke's *Second treatise of government*, the joint issue of agriculture as the paradigmatic form of labor and hence the basis of rights of dominion over land had firmly taken root.[6] Cultivation for Locke is subduing the earth.

Not just any kind of agriculture, however. Agriculture in its full sense was deemed to be practiced in permanent fields and preferably with a plow. A plow no doubt "subdues the earth" more effectively than a stick. That those "Americans" merely "scratched the land" and ignored tillage could be grounds for asserting that their title to property was dubious at best.[7]

It looks as if in the eighteenth century, issues of style of agriculture, domestication, sedentarization, property, and progress had become entangled in a single syndrome. A similar syndrome seems to appear in archaeology, when Neolithic revolution conflates pottery with domestication of animals and plants. As archaeologist Eduardo Neves has pointed out, the distinct dimensions of the syndrome are disjointed in the Amazon. Pottery is older than agriculture and not necessarily found together with cultivated plants. Hence, there was never a Neolithic revolution in Lowland South America, as the author puts it (Neves 2016).

As for livestock or any other animal domestication, Amazonian Indigenous peoples are famous for their love for wild animals as pets as well as for their avoidance of animal domestication (Erikson 1987, 1997; Fausto 1999). Taming is one thing, domestication is quite another. Furthermore, pets or any creature one has fed are generally not to be eaten.[8]

Amazonian agriculture is a vibrant topic of research (Carneiro da Cunha 2017). This is not the place to review such things as the changing historical importance of maize relative to manioc in different societies and linguistic stocks, nor what presently appears as a primary domestication of sweet (i.e., nonpoisonous) manioc in southwest Amazonia to be followed by selection favoring toxic manioc spreading in other

---

6. The word itself, *labor*, comes from old French *Labour*, which meant tillage using a plow.

7. Such an argument could be brought up in later colonial conquests such as Australia, but was (fortunately) never used in earlier European colonial empires.

8. An example of the same attitude is brought out by an attempt in the 1990s by an NGO at breeding fish on the upper Rio Negro. Women starkly refused to eat fish they had been feeding (Estorniolo 2012).

areas of the region (Arroyo-Kalin 2010; Santos-Mühlen et al. 2013).[9] While some debate persists on regional issues, there is presently a general recognition of the Amazon being a major center of plant domestication (Clement et al. 2015; Levis et al. 2017). Recently, even rice on the Guaporé was added to an already large list of plants domesticated in Amazonia (Hilbert et al. 2017). Archaeological research in Amazonia has produced evidence of several large sites with long-term intensive agriculture in the forest (Heckenberger and Neves 2009). A formidable Indigenous contribution to agrobiodiversity has been stressed, covering an astounding number of varieties of sweet potatoes, gourds, beans, peanuts, et cetera, not to forget, of course, manioc (Carneiro da Cunha and Morim de Lima 2017).

In short, this is a time for academic celebration of Indigenous agricultural techniques and exploits. And yet, a number of Amazonians' attitudes toward agriculture look somewhat puzzling.

As Claude Lévi-Strauss very early pointed out in the *Handbook of South American Indians* (Lévi-Strauss 1950), people knew and relied at least as much on cultivated as on wild plants. In the myth usually called "The origin of cultivated plants" among the Ramkokamekra-Canela of Eastern Timbira, Star-Woman not only donates seeds and teaches Amerindians to cultivate plants but she also introduces them to edible wild food: before Star-Woman, people ate "rotten wood" (Miller 2015: 385–90). It is as if the two modes of procurement, which are so starkly distinguished by us, were never really separated.

Present-day foragers like the Maku-Nukak (Politis 2009) will cultivate some manioc for special occasions, while not letting cultivation hinder their mobility. A significant number of former agriculturalists, such as the Western Parakanã, the Awá (or Guajá), the Sirionó, the Ache, have reverted to foraging (Carneiro da Cunha and Morim de Lima 2017). Conversely, some Gê-speaking societies, who were deemed "marginal" in the 1950 *Handbook of South American Indians* for their little agriculture, have presently turned into obsessive gardeners. Ramkokamekra-Canela

---

9. Sweet manioc is pervasive on the Juruá River (Acre and Amazon states). On the Purus River basin, Indigenous people who cultivated sweet manioc claim to have only recently learned of toxic manioc and manioc flour from itinerant river traders. In Northwestern Amazonia, in contrast, the word *mandioca* refers only to the toxic varieties and sweet manioc is considered a wholly different species, sometimes assimilated to a "fruit" and is called *macaxeira*.

and Krahó are examples of that move (Miller 2015; Morim de Lima 2016). Trekking periods are enjoyed even among strong agriculturalists.

There is abundant worldwide evidence of cultivated plants as "people" requiring special attention and coaxing. Anne-Christine Taylor (2007) and Philippe Descola have described Achuar women's extreme maternal dedication to their plants (Descola 1986). Rio Negro women endeavor to make their manioc children happy in the gardens by providing to them companion species who should play music and comb their hair (Emperaire, van Velthem, and Oliveira 2012).[10]

Kraho people seem to take this cultivars' independence and demands to the next level. Their plants have their own volition and demand special attention. If discontent, sweet potato tubers will migrate on their own and establish themselves in gardens of more attentive farmers (Morim de Lima 2016). Again, this kind of relationship to cultivated plants is hardly seen as the dependency on plants implied in domestication. It might look like domestication to us, but it doesn't seem to look like it to them. There is no (ideological at least) subduing implied. Marilyn Strathern (2017, this volume) gives several New Guinea examples of similar personal relations.[11]

Even as the Amazon is presently recognized as a major center of plant "domestication," it is as if Amazonians would maintain a virtual if not actual possibility of escaping being fully domesticated themselves. For agriculture and livestock, as I have argued recently, go both ways: they fix and tie down the domesticated as much as the domesticator (Carneiro da Cunha and Morim de Lima 2017).

Granted, foragers are commonly despised by more sedentary Lowland societies. The Kaapor and Guajajara agriculturalists in the state of

---

10. Stephen Hugh-Jones (this volume) rightly points out that, according to context and situation, very similar attitudes are present in people whose ontologies are deemed naturalist as against animist. I recall this old Portuguese lady who pitied her cabbages: "my cabbages are sad, poor things." The more general point of whether one can compare everyday attitudes to explicit ontologies provides a bitter ongoing debate.

11. "In the eyes of many Papua New Guineans, however, planting does not axiomatically ensure that the plant stays there; once in the care of particular gardeners, who may or may not pay them sufficient attention, the souls of both taro and yam may have reason to wander away. If they have come from somewhere else they can go off too, in a kind of reverse movement" (Strathern 2017: 33n11).

Maranhão looked down on the Guajá before they settled down in villages.[12] Similarly, the Hupda (Maku) are looked down upon by the more sedentary Tukanoans.[13] And yet Tukanoans themselves enjoy seasonal mobility for fishing or foraging. Central Brazil Gê-speaking societies, for all their present-day agricultural activity, have not relinquished their seasonal trekking expeditions.

Would there be something like a (so to speak) menu available to neotropical Lowlanders offering a gradient ranging from full sedentarization to an option for mobility? In support of such view, let us stress that many mobile societies seem to share regional space with more sedentary ones. It is as if their spatial contiguity could be thought of as jointly forming a meaningful unit, much in the way as the articulate coexistence of Jivaros and their neighbors, as Taylor (2007) once pointed out.

The term *domestication* and the expression *domestication process* are loosely used based on more or less stringent definitions. Yet many natural scientists will argue that proper domestication is that state of affairs that demands that the very life and reproduction of a species be strictly dependent on human care. Hence, the notion is one of absolute subjection of the domesticated to the domesticator. Volition, demands, and even initiatives by plants in Lowland agriculture ideology hardly conforms to that definition. What I mean is that Indigenous peoples, for all their exploits in what we call domestication of plants, might not think of themselves as domesticators.

Swidden, Manioc, and Colonial Concerns

Manioc, also known as cassava among many other names, has several virtues: it grows on poor soils, such as Amazonian ferrosols; it can be quite precocious (as little as six months to maturity) as well as very long-lived (up to two years, according to varieties); and it does not require storage arrangements, as it remains stored in the field itself. By now, manioc or cassava, which is native to the Amazon, has become staple food for some eight hundred million people, mainly in Africa.

Manioc is cultivated in tropical countries around the world in a system known as swidden. Swidden is "an agricultural system in which fields

---

12. Uirá Garcia, personal communication.
13. They are often accused of pilfering in agriculturalist fields. Yet Hupda are used as occasional laborers by Tukanoans.

are cleared by burning and are cropped discontinuously, with periods of fallowing which are always longer than periods of cropping" (Fox et al. 2000). Fallow—that is, regeneration—is an integral part of the system. Yet swidden is often defined (for example, in *OED*) solely by its use of fire, obliterating the importance it places on fallow.

Here is a very general and rough model for Indigenous agricultural system in the Amazon: every year, at least one new field is cleared for planting manioc, corn, squash, pineapples, sweet potatoes, bananas, and a wealth of other plants. Primary or secondary vegetation is cut and burned and logs are left in place. The plot will still be productive the following year, with varieties that can mature more slowly. However, weeds and secondary vegetation are already present, and weeding is a very demanding task. By the third year, as soil fertility has declined, weeding and cultivation will cease, but not the visits to the plot and the rights over it.

In many neotropical societies, there is an elaborate management of gardens and fallows initiated even before anything is planted. It starts with the opening of a new plot and persists long after the garden's last crop is reaped. Fruit and other useful trees, tolerated or protected when clearing will be growing in there, competing for light with fast-growing secondary vegetation. Useful trees comprise not only those that bear fruits that humans eat but also fruit trees appreciated by game (and hence that attract game when fruit is ripe), trees for attracting birds that disperse forest seeds (Bahuchet and Betsch 2012), besides a number of other plant species used for construction, health, and all kinds of other purposes.

William Denevan (1992) suggests that manioc cultivation exploded as steel axes became available in colonial times. Stone axes made felling trees much more exerting, but we should remember that there were other precolonial Indigenous techniques for felling trees, such as cutting out a bark ring on a big tree, causing it to die. That tree would be able to take down some others when it fell, and thus open up a clearing in the forest.

In any case, the system required opening up at least one new field per year, and led (and still leads) to moving from one place to another every so many years when gardens become too distant from villages. Other factors, which include game depletion, political disputes, and permanent schools and health and administration facilities that function as attractors are taken into consideration when considering moving. But whatever other reasons there were, gardens on their own acted as inducers of territorial movement.

Colonial settlers in the hinterland were quick to adopt manioc culti-vation, while urban settlers tried to stick a little longer to a rarefied diet of wheat, wine, and olive oil. Jesuits sent queries to Rome asking if com-munion with manioc host was acceptable.

Settlers who had slaves took swidden cultivation to a much greater scale. To this day, *mutatis mutanda*, the change in scale is a major cause of huge deforestation in the region. Yet, at the time, in contrast with what happens now, people were not concerned with deforestation. Officials were rather concerned with settlers who moved about too much, settlers who did not actually settle down, and who did not produce what was expected to stand as cultivation—namely, permanent fields leading to permanent homes and villages.

A somewhat extreme measure was advocated by a Jesuit priest. Padre João Daniel S.J., born in 1722, had first arrived in the Amazon at the age of nineteen and had spent some sixteen years in the region. As Jesuits were being thrown out of the Portuguese Empire under Prime Minister Pombal, Padre João Daniel was incarcerated. While rotting in prison where he died nineteen years later, he wrote a remarkable treatise on the Amazon, posthumously published under the title *Tesouro Descoberto no Máximo rio Amazonas*, which can be roughly rendered as "A treasure unveiled in the greatest River Amazon" (Daniel [1757?–1776] 2004).

The manuscript described all kinds of Amazonian riches and pro-ceeded to suggest governmental colonial measures. His odd recom-mendation was that Amazonian colonial settlers should be barred from planting manioc and should turn instead to cereals. There were several reasons the prisoner expounded for prohibiting manioc. Most impor-tantly, manioc meant swidden agriculture, itinerant agriculture meant itinerant population. Cereals were much more desirable from a colonial government point of view since they were supposed to fix people on their land.

His recommendation was actually shared by eighteenth-century co-lonial authorities. The issue of settling the settlers, fixing them to a spe-cific portion of land, and even better, urbanizing landowners to some extent, appears to have been a permanent concern of the eighteenth-century colonial state.

By then, manioc was popular almost everywhere in what is today's Brazil. A contemporary of imprisoned Padre João Daniel, the fourth Morgado de Mateus (Earl of Mateus) was, by contrast, well regarded by the all-powerful Prime Minister Pombal of Portugal. For ten years (1765 to 1775) he governed a large part of Southeast Brazil (the then captaincy of São Paulo) and became known for the many urban settlements he was able to create. He issued ordinances requiring landed citizens to build a proper house in town and . . . to abstain from cultivating manioc. Again, manioc was considered a hindrance for fixing the population and establishing title to land (Monteiro 2012).

Swidden in High Modern Times

Swidden agriculture still has a bad name, in more than one sense. True, its most common earlier designation, "slash and burn," which is reminiscent of the infamous "search and destroy," is slowly being abandoned. Itinerant or shifting agriculture is a more politically correct expression.[14]

Yet, to this day, discussions still go on about swidden's good or bad effects. In Southeast Asia, there is a lively, ongoing dispute about the overall prohibition of the practice, as many traditional peoples are being pushed into abandoning it in favor of palm oil plantations (Padoch and Pinedo-Vasquez 2010; Ribeiro Filho et al. 2013). All kinds of state policies, including the separation of forest and agricultural land have contributed to the demise of swidden in Southeast Asia (Fox et al. 2009).

The Food and Agriculture Organization of the United Nations (FAO) bears a strong responsibility on that front. The very same year it published the remarkable work by Harold Conklin (1957) on Hanunoo swidden agriculture, it delivered a scathing indictment of the very same practice. They referred to the practice as "the greatest obstacle not only to the immediate increase of agricultural production, but also to the conservation of the production potential for the future, in the form of soils and forests. . . . Not only a backward type of agricultural practice . . .[but] also a backward stage of culture in general" (FAO Staff 1957). However, Conklin's study had ended with no suggestions for improvement of the system, for, as the reviewer E. Biasutti Owen stated, no

---

14. The NGO Survival International gives a more updated definition and explanation: "Swidden agriculture, also known as shifting cultivation, refers to a technique of rotational farming in which land is cleared for cultivation (normally by fire) and then left to regenerate after a few years. Governments worldwide have long sought to eradicate swidden agriculture, which is often pejoratively called "slash-and-burn," due to a mistaken belief that it is a driver of deforestation." https://www.survivalinternational.org/about/swidden.

suggestions were in order, since this was a case of a good, stable equilibrium. So, which is it?

Almost sixty years later, in 2015, in what looked like a reversal of opinion, the FAO, the International Work Group for Indigenous Affairs (IWGIA), and the Asia Indigenous Peoples Pact (AIPP) jointly published a book defending swidden agriculture in Southeast Asia (Erni 2015). However, FAO still discreetly refrained from endorsing the views of the authors.

Prejudice against swidden endures. Starting in 1994, a long-term program that went on at least until 2004 and was led by an international agroforestry research organization was suggestively named "Alternatives to slash and burn" (Pollini 2009). It was richly endowed on the promise to inject a massive dose of hard science and agroforestry technology: one of its recommendations was enriching fallows, something that a large number of Indigenous peoples already do.

Swidden agriculture is largely practiced in tropical countries around the world, with several variations. Tropical poor soils will use as nutrients the ashes of the vegetation that was cleared and burned down. While the cropping techniques have been extensively described, much less attention was paid to techniques related to fallow. These were often thought to be merely abandoned on account of the excess of invasive weeds. A remarkable paper, published online in 2012 and already cited, provides a minute description of an Amazonian fallow creation technology by the Wayana people on the Maroni River in French Guiana and their sophisticated method for establishing fallows (Bahuchet and Betsch 2012). Fallows will eventually result in a biodiverse and high biomass forest. *Swidden is not only a cultivation system in the forest, it is as well and very importantly a procedure for high forest regeneration.* "Swidden cultivation is an old paradigm built around the temporary removal of trees but not of the forest" (Fox et al. 2000).[15]

William Balée (1993, 1994, 2013) has published very interesting results on the importance of biodiversity that can be found on mature fallows. Further, by now archaeologists and botanists are claiming that a significant part of the Amazon is anthropogenic, based on the presence of plant species that indicate secondary forest and on the large distribution of ADEs, Anthropogenic Dark Earths (for example, Levis et al.

---

15. As neotropical agriculture cannot be thought in isolation from forest production, many researchers prefer to call such systems agroforestry rather than simply agriculture.

2017). ADEs are highly fertile soils, produced by anthropic remains, including food remains and pyrogenic carbon four thousand to ten thousand years old. They are often considered a model for the development of modern soil fertility in the tropics. Some ADEs may be quite extensive and their presence supports the claim for high density archaeological agricultural populations in the Amazon.[16]

Do Ontologies Account for People Seeing the Trees while Not Seeing the Forest?

Shifting cultivation under every other name is still outcast as promoting destruction of forests and land degradation. People see (felling of) trees yet they do not seem to see (the regeneration of) forests.

Among Amazonian Indigenous peoples, humans' rights in the forest certainly do not follow Locke's theory of dominion. Everything has its own "master" or "mother" (Fausto 2008). Wayãpi people, to take an example, consider that the human domain is restricted to the clearings and plots they cultivate, which by definition are transient (Gallois 1986). Everything else has its own masters. Wild pigs or tapirs are obtained as prey only through shamanic transactions with their specific masters. Moreover, everywhere in Amazonia (and newcomers such as rubber-tappers learned to behave in the same manner), game carcass and remains are to be treated with "respect" and should not be disposed of carelessly (Almeida 2013). In the Amazon, forest-dwellers are supposed to follow all kinds of rules and prohibitions that curtail use of resources. As noted earlier, even cultivated plants have their own volition and require to be pampered (Emperaire, van Velthem, and Oliveira 2012; Morim de Lima 2016). There is no Lockean talk about "subduing and cultivating the earth."

Locke went on:

> *Sec. 32.* But the chief matter of property being now not the fruits of the earth, and the beasts that subsist on it, but the earth itself; as that which takes in and carries with it all the rest; I think it is plain, that property in that too is acquired as the former. As much land as a man

---

16. Very similar systems using fire and resulting in enhanced soil fertility and centered around maize cultivation are reported for the Maya forest milpa tradition (Nigh 2008).

tills, plants, improves, cultivates, and can use the product of, so much is his property. He by his labour does, as it were, inclose it from the common. (Locke 1960: chap. 5, sec. 32)

Again, this does not apply in Indigenous Amazonia. Surely, people have a number of rights over their crops, their fields, and their fallows, but these do not extend to rights of property over the land itself.[17]

What seems to have occurred? What kind of science in the forest were and are some Lowland Indigenous people still practicing?

Descola has argued that Amazonians never domesticated wild pigs because wild pigs, as every other animal and realm of nature, had their own masters (Descola 1994). I think the argument can be extended: it looks like Amazonian humans did not give preeminence to their own interests, making it the "primary organizing principle" of the forest. In that sense, their aim was not to colonize the forest.

Domestication is first and foremost a mode of inhabiting the world by occupying it. Occupation here is meant in the settler-colonial sense. Indeed, from an inter-species perspective, every human occupation is an act of settler colonialism since one occupies a space that is always already occupied by other domesticators, whether insects, animals, plants or trees. Each of these inhabits the world with some degree of instrumentalization too: a tree spreads itself above and below the ground in its struggle to extract nutrition, sun, and so on. Ants also organize and transform their surroundings in a specific way. What defines human generalized domestication is the act of occupying a space by *declaring one's own interest as its primary organizing principle.* As such it relates to prior occupiers of the same space according to how their being can be harnessed to the advancement of our own being. What comes in the way is excluded or exterminated. (Hage 2017: 94-95; emphasis added)

Charles Clement describes landscape domestication by Amerindians as making it "more productive and congenial to humans" (Clement 1999: 190). What about every other sentient being? Lowland Indigenous peoples, with their theory of generalized cultivation, assume that

---

17. Groves and immature crops are usually not left behind by a departing dweller without bestowing them to someone else, either to keep or to look after. Most of the times, all that is required to access an area on which some other family enjoys rights is to ask its permission.

such sentient beings too are organizing the land in order to make it more productive and congenial to *themselves*. What makes Amerindian ways different from human domestication in Ghassan Hage's sense is that Amerindians refrain from making their organization of the land into the "primary organizing principle" of the forest. In short, one could say that they do not submit the forest to human generalized domestication.[18] They no doubt made the forest more favorable to human life but did not colonize the forest.

Swidden and Antidomestication as a Science of the Forest

As Balée has first pointed out, Lowland Indigenous societies who strictly resort to foraging are dependent on the preexistence of anthropogenic forests (Balée 1989). For the wandering Huaorani, those enriched forests are assumed to be the footprints of their own forebears (Rival 2002). It looks as if to be able to lead a totally foraging mode of life, one is best served by previously enriched forests and/or agriculturalist neighbors for resources.

Could it be that the management and enrichment of fallows in swidden agriculture are among the main mechanisms that allow for the very possibility of foraging societies?[19] For most hunting and foraging societies in the Lowlands (if not every hunting an foraging society), there seems to be a move out of a previous agriculturalist way of life, as Lévi-Strauss early suggested (Lévi-Strauss 1952). Such is the case for the Western Parakanã (Fausto 2001), the Hi-Merimã (Shiratori 2018), among many other known examples. Rather than being an involution or necessarily the outcome of disaster, foraging would be maintained as a possibility by the very management practices of Indigenous agriculturalists. It would be as if their kind of agriculture—opening forest plots for

---

18. Saying this is starkly different from the still-lingering tropes about Indigenous peoples "living in harmony with Nature." For one thing, the very concept of Nature as we know it is foreign to Amazonians.

19. Among other important techniques: archaeology as well as forest-dwellers are familiar with "indian bread" (*pão de índio*) an elaborate product of wild plants preserved in the forest for food in wandering moments or trekking expeditions (Shiratori 2018: 140n49).

gardens and enriching fallows—would account for being able to abandon agriculture itself.[20]

What comes out of the peculiarities of neotropical swidden agriculture is that it resists so-called progress—namely, that irreversible "evolution," assumed by theorists to be universal, from foraging to domesticated life. Indigenous societies seem to have conceived of a forest that they inhabit with nonexclusive rights. As do those other species that dwell in the same forest, they try to favor their own interests. It looks like their aim is to be able, given different historical circumstances or mere choice, to turn to a foraging existence.[21] At times, they enjoy trekking through the forest in small family groups, at others, living in their villages and tending their gardens. They retain the possibility of reverting ad libitum to different forms of life, to the pleasure of fishing, hunting, and eating wild fruit as well as to the enthusiasm of participating in beautiful crowd village rituals. As much as former wanderers can become enthusiastic gardeners, agriculturalists seem to be able to morph into foragers. Their science, as much as their messy gardens that mimic the forest, contradicts what we thought we knew about agriculture: that once one has it, there is no turning back; that progress is domestication of plants, animals, landscapes, and as a result, humans themselves.

There is another lesson here. Sharing rights over the land with other sentient beings; avoiding hegemony of human interests for exploiting the territory; abiding to a wealth of rules and restrictions; refusing to be wholly domesticated could well be the recipe for a good life in a lively forest.

Acknowledgments

I wish to thank Stephen Hugh-Jones for his pertinent remarks and thorough discussion of a previous version of this essay. Any mistakes are, of course, my own responsibility. I also thank Marcus Schmidt for suggesting Serge Bahuchet and Jean-Marie Betsch's paper (as well as

---

20. Such interdependence between foragers and agriculturalists reinforces my earlier suggestion of interdependent clusters of foraging and agricultural Lowland societies.
21. See Carlos Fausto's excellent discussion of foraging apropos the Western Parakanã case (Fausto 2001: 150-74) and Luiz Costa's summary of the literature (Costa 2009).

other related papers) on swidden, and Ludivine Eloy for recommending Jacques Pollini's paper. Eduardo Viveiros de Castro provided me with the important text by Hage.

References

Almeida, Mauro. 2013. "Caipora e outros conflitos ontológicos." *Revista de Antropologia da UFSCar* 5 (1): 7–28.

Arroyo-Kalin, Manuel. 2010. "The Amazonian formative: Crop domestication and anthropogenic soils." *Diversity* 2 (4): 473–504.

Bahuchet, Serge, and Jean-Marie Betsch. 2012. "L'agriculture itinérante sur brûlis, une menace sur la forêt tropicale humide?" *Revue d'ethnoécologie* 1. https://journals.openedition.org/ethnoecologie/768.

Balée, William. 1989. "The culture of Amazonian forests." In *Resource management in Amazonia: Indigenous and folk strategies*, edited by Darrell Posey and William Balée, 1–21. New York: New York Botanical Garden Press.

———. 1993. "Indigenous transformation of Amazonian forests: An example from Maranhão, Brazil." *L'Homme* 33 (2–4): 231–54.

———. 1994. *Footprints of the forest: Ka'apor ethnobotany—The historical ecology of plant utilization by an Amazonian people*. New York: Columbia University Press.

———. 2013. *Cultural forests of the Amazon: A historical ecology of people and their landscapes*. Tuscaloosa: University of Alabama Press.

Cabral de Oliveira, Joana. 2012. "Entre plantas e palavras: Modos de constituição de saberes entre os Wajãpi." PhD diss., Universidade de São Paulo.

Caplat, Jacques. 2016. "Savoir-faire ou savoirs?" *Histoire & Sociétés Rurales* 46 (2): 125–53.

Carneiro da Cunha, Manuela. 2017. "Traditional peoples, collectors of diversity." In *The anthropology of sustainability: Beyond development and progress*, edited by Jerome Lewis and Mark Brightman, 257–72. New York: Palgrave Macmillan.

Carneiro da Cunha, Manuela, and Ana Gabriela Morim de Lima. 2017. "How Amazonian Indigenous peoples enhance biodiversity." In *Knowing our lands and resources: Indigenous and local knowledge of biodiversity and ecosystem services in the Americas*, edited by Brigitte Baptiste, Diego Pacheco, Manuela Carneiro da Cunha, and Sandra Diaz, 63–81. Knowledges of Nature 11. Paris: Unesco.

Clement, Charles. 1999. "1492 and the loss of crop genetic resources: I. Crop biogeography at contact." *Economic Botany* 53 (2): 203–16.

Clement, Charles, William M. Denevan, Michael Heckenberger, André B. Junqueira, Eduardo G. Neves, Wenceslau G. Teixeira, and William Woods. 2015. "The domestication of Amazonia before European conquest." *Proceedings of the Royal Society Biological Sciences* 282 (1812). doi: https://doi.org/10.1098/rspb.2015.0813.

Conklin, Harold C. 1957. *Hanunoo agriculture: A report on an integral system of shifting cultivation in the Philippines.* Rome: Food and Agriculture Organization of the United Nations.

Costa, Luiz. 2009. "Worthless movement: Agricultural regression and mobility." *Tipití: Journal of the Society for the Anthropology of Lowland South America* 7 (2): 151–80.

Daniel, João, S.J. (1757?–1776) 2004. *Tesouro descoberto no máximo Rio Amazonas.* Vols. 1 and 2. Rio de Janeiro: Contraponto.

Denevan, William. 1992. "Stone vs. metal axes: The ambiguity of shifting cultivation in prehistoric Amazonia." *Journal of the Steward Anthropological Society* 20 (1–2): 153–65.

Descola, Philippe. 1986. *La nature domestique: Symbolisme et praxis dans l'écologie des Achuar.* Paris: Éditions de la Maison des Sciences de L'Homme.

———. 1994. "Pourquoi les Indiens d'Amazonie n'ont-ils pas domestiqué le pécari." In *De la préhistoire aux missiles balistiques: L'intelligence sociale des techniques*, edited by Bruno Latour and Pierre Lemonnier, 329–44. Paris: La Découverte.

Emperaire, Laure, Lúcia Hussak van Velthem, and Ana Gita Oliveira. 2012. "Patrimônio cultural imaterial e sistema agrícola: o manejo da diversidade agrícola no médio Rio Negro (AM)." *Ciência e Ambiente* 44: 154–64.

Erikson, Philippe. 1987. "De l'apprivoisement à l'approvisionnement: Chasse, alliance et familiarisation en Amazonie amérindienne." *Techniques et cultures* 9: 105–40.

———. 1997. "On Native American conservation and the status of Amazonian pets." *Current Anthropology* 38 (3): 445–46.

Erni, Christian, ed. 2015. *Shifting cultivation, livelihood and food security: New and old challenges for indigenous peoples in Asia.* Bangkok: Food and Agriculture Organization of the United Nations, International Work Group For Indigenous Affairs, and Asia Indigenous Peoples Pact.

Estorniolo, Milena. 2012. "Laboratórios na Floresta: Os Baniwa, os peixes e a piscicultura no alto rio Negro." Master's diss., University of São Paulo.

Fausto, Carlos. 1999. "Of enemies and pets: Warfare and shamanism in Amazonia." *American Ethnologist* 26 (4): 933–56.

———. 2001. *Inimigos fiéis: História, guerra e xamanismo na Amazônia.* São Paulo: EDUSP.

———. 2008. "Donos demais: maestria e domínio na Amazônia." *Mana* 14 (2): 329–66. doi: https://dx.doi.org/10.1590/S0104-93132008000 200003.

FAO Staff. 1957. "Shifting cultivation." *Unasylva* 11: 9–11. http://www.fao. org/3/x5386e/x5386e07.htm.

Fox, Jefferson, Dao Minh Truong, A. Terry Rambo, Nghien Phuong Tuyean, Le Trong Cuc, and Stephen Leisz. 2000. "Shifting cultivation: A new old paradigm for managing tropical forests." *BioScience* 50 (6): 521–28.

Fox, Jefferson, Yayoi Fujita, Dimbab Ngidang, Nancy Peluso, Lesley Potter, Niken Sakuntaladewi, Janet Sturgeon, and David Thomas. 2009. "Policies, political-economy, and swidden in Southeast Asia." *Human Ecology* 37 (3): 305–22.

Gallois, Dominique. 1986. *Migração guerra e comércio: Os Waiapi na Guiana.* Antropologia 15. São Paulo: FFLCH-USP.

Hage, Ghassan. 2017. *Is racism an environmental threat?* London: Polity Press.

Heckenberger, Michael, and Eduardo Góes Neves. 2009. "Amazonian archaeology." *Annual Review of Anthropology* 38: 251–66. https://www.annualreviews.org/doi/abs/10.1146/annurev-anthro-091908-164310.

Hilbert, Lautario, Eduardo Góes Neves, Francisco Pugliese, Bronwen S. Whitney, Myrtle Shock, Elizabeth Veasey, Carlos Augusto Zimpel, and José Iriarte. 2017. "Evidence for mid-Holocene rice domestication in the Americas." *Nature Ecology & Evolution* 1 (11): 1693–98.

Lévi-Strauss, Claude. 1950. "The use of wild plants in tropical South America." *Physical Anthropology, Linguistics and Cultural Geography of South American Indians.* Vol. 6 of *Handbook of South American Indians,* edited by Julian H. Steward, 465–86. Washington, DC: Smithsonian Institution.

———. 1952. "La notion d'archaïsme en ethnologie." *Cahiers Internationaux de Sociologie* 12: 3–25.

Levis, Carolina, Flávia R. C. Costa, Frans Bongers, Marielos Peña-Claros, et al. 2017. "Persistent effects of pre-Columbian plant domestication on Amazonian forest composition.: *Science* 355 (6328): 925–31.

Locke, John. 1690. *Second Treatise of Civil Government.* Chapter 5. https://www.marxists.org/reference/subject/politics/locke/ch05.htm.

Maizza, Fabiana. 2014. "Sobre as crianças-planta: o cuidar e o seduzir no parentesco Jarawara." *Mana: Estudos de Antropologias Social* 20 (3): 491–518.

Miller, Theresa. 2015. "Bio-sociocultural aesthetics: Indigenous Ramkokamekra-Canela gardening practices and varietal diversity maintenance in Maranhão, Brazil." PhD diss., Oxford University, Institute of Social and Cultural Anthropology.

Monteiro, Allan R.A. 2012. "Povoamento e formação da paisagem em São Luiz do Paraitinga." PhD diss., UNICAMP, Universidade Estadual de Campinas.

Morim de Lima, Ana Gabriela. 2016. "'Brotou batata para mim': Cultivo, gênero e ritual entre os Krahô (TO, Brasil)." PhD diss., Universidade Federal do Rio de Janeiro.

Neves, Eduardo Góes. 2016. "Não existe neolítico ao sul do Equador: as primeiras cerâmicas amazônicas e sua falta de relação com a agricultura." In *Cerâmicas arqueológicas da Amazônia: rumo a uma nova síntese*, edited by Cristiana Barreto, Helena Pinto Lima, and Carla Jaimes Betancourt, 32–39. Belém: IPHAN, Ministério da Cultura.

Nigh, Ronald. 2008. "Fire and farmers: Making woods and soil in the Maya forest." *Journal of Ethnobiology* 28 (2): 231–43.

Padoch, Christine, and Miguel Pinedo-Vasquez. 2010. "Saving slash-and-burn to save biodiversity." *Biotropica* 42 (5): 550–52.

Politis, Gustavo G. 2009. *NUKAK ethnoarchaeology of an Amazonian people.* London: Left Coast Press; University College London Institute of Archaeology Publications.

Pollini, Jacques. 2009. "Agroforestry and the search for alternatives to slash and burn." *Agriculture, Ecosystems and Environment* 133 (1–2): 48–60.

Ribeiro Filho, Alexandre Antunes, Cristina Adams, and Rui Sergio Murrieta. 2013. "The impacts of shifting cultivation on tropical forest soil: A review." *Boletim do Museu Paraense Emílio Goeldi. Ciências Humanas* 8 (3): 693–727.

Rival, Laura. 2002. *Trekking through history: The Huaroani of Amazonian Ecuador.* New York: Columbia University Press.

Santos-Mühlen, Gilda, Alessandro Alves-Pereira, Charles R. Clement, and Teresa Losada Valle. 2013. "Genetic diversity and differentiation of Brazilian bitter and sweet manioc varieties (*Manihot esculenta* Crantz,

Euphorbiaceae) based on SSR molecular markers." *Tipití: Journal of the Society for the Anthropology of Lowland South America* 11 (2): 66–73. http://digitalcommons.trinity.edu/tipiti/vol11/iss2/8.

Shiratori, Karen. 2018. "O Olhar Envenenado: da metafísica vegetal Jamamadi (Médio Purus, Amazônia)." PhD diss., Museu Nacional, Universidade Federal do Rio de Janeiro.

Strathern, Marilyn. 2017. "Gathered fields: A tale about rhizomes." *Anuac* 6 (2): 23–44.

Taylor, Anne-Christine. 2007. "Sick of history: Contrasting regimes of historicity in the Upper Amazon." In *Time and memory in indigenous Amazonia: Anthropological perspectives*, edited by Carlos Fausto and Michael Heckenberger, 133–68. Gainesville: University Press of Florida.

CHAPTER NINE

Objective Functions: (In)Humanity and Inequity in Artificial Intelligence

Alan F. Blackwell

This essay offers observations and reflections from within a rather distinctive scientific culture—that of the artificial intelligence (AI) engineer. The AI engineer is a figure who appears mundane in person (a geek at a computer keyboard) while apparently also harboring the kind of dark creative imagination through which scientist-inventors such as Rotwang in Fritz Lang's *Metropolis*, Nathan in Alex Garland's *Ex Machina*, or Dr. Gall in Karel Čapek's *R.U.R.* habitually endow machines with souls, and tempt men to fall in love with their sexy robots. AI engineering is a field that is both dull and fascinating.

I come to this project as the mundane kind of AI engineer, having little contact with robots, whose perspective is distinctive primarily as that of a technologist. The perspective of a professional engineer stands in contrast to many philosophers and critics, for whom technology generally appears as a found object, a given, an object of critique. For many commentators on AI, technology is something that *happens* to them, not something that they *do*. For engineers, of course, the world seems different. Technologies are things that we made and that we are still in the process of making. As technologists, we engineers possess a *technè*, a practice. To the extent that AI engineers also engage in reflection on their own work, a fervent rallying call is for them to exercise a *critical technical practice* (Agre 1997), in which their technology research is not purely making but questioning, informed by the epistemological and ethical questions that often pervade such work.

Despite such advocacy, engineers are not generally commentators. They are ontologically interventionist, bringing into existence real things, whether new computers, information systems, or the knowledge economy. Yet this work means that engineers must also live as prospective inhabitants of the future that they intend to bring about. Like any of us, engineers will inhabit this future when it arrives. But engineers also live in the future right now, as their work necessarily proceeds through the exercise of imagination to bring into existence novel artifacts.

One might ask whether exercise of the imagination should be considered a kind of science. British academics are accustomed to speaking of STEM—science, technology, engineering and mathematics—as representing one of the "Two Cultures" that C. P. Snow observed in public life (Snow [1959] 2012). Within this putative shared culture of science-and-technology, scientists easily think of themselves as technologists, and engineers think of themselves as scientists. If they pursue a common enterprise, it is the use of measurement and mathematical calculation to construct objective bodies of knowledge—positivist proofs and discoveries whose future legacy is not simply the transient and contingent practical products of the engineer, but universal and immutable laws of science.

Despite this shared aspiration, engineering is not a natural science. AI engineers do not study natural phenomena, but only what we make ourselves—as named by Herbert Simon, this is a "science of the artificial" (Simon 1996). In reflecting on the scientific practices of AI engineers such as myself, I am concerned with the nature of knowledge, with the ways that engineering researchers represent reality, and with the differing ways that words are used to reflect states of affairs as perceived by different academic communities. Even more centrally, I am concerned with what engineers achieve through making descriptions—with knowledge as a sociotechnical process rather than a private cognitive achievement.

Like all computer science, AI offers an especially intriguing prospect, because of the ways that knowledge itself (as information and data) becomes a mathematical object subject to mechanical manipulation. Despite the fact that computer scientists prefer to align themselves with the positivist traditions of STEM, through representational strategies in which binary 1s and 0s correspond to truth and falsity, much computer science research might be better characterized as a kind of mechanical sophistry, in which only the processing of information matters, and not any sense in which that information corresponds to the world outside the computer. As a subfield within the artificial science of computing, the epistemological and ontological status of AI deserves close attention.

The Relationality and Subjectivity of AI

To summarize the case I will be making in this essay, I will be focusing on the ways in which operational definitions of AI must always be constructed in relation to humans. The most famous operationalization of AI, the "Turing Test," draws attention to the potential and/or desire for intersubjectivity in relations between a person and a machine (Collins 2018). An AI that passes the Turing Test will have demonstrated a degree of intersubjectivity. But in order to be a scientific accomplishment, this subjectivity must be objectively measurable. My argument explores the resulting relationship between objectivity and subjectivity, and the distribution of agency or obligation that might be implicit in that relationship.

It is also useful to keep in mind the fact that, as I have explained, AI as an engineering discipline is largely an exercise of the imagination. Particular qualities of desire may be acquired in the imaginary domain. As noted in the introduction, the artificial construction of simulated humans in fiction seems often to become powerfully gendered, perhaps alluding to the gendered nature of all human procreation. The figure of the AI engineer building sexy robots and falling in love with them has many fictional precursors, including that of Pygmalion. Indeed the Turing Test itself was first posed as an Imitation Game in which the challenge assigned was not for a computer to imitate a man but for a man to imitate a woman.

These transgressive imaginary relationships through which engineers fall in love with their own gendered creations are often accompanied by guilt and moral retribution. In science fictions the sexy robot, having gained the status of a subjective agent, often becomes an agent of punishment. The transgression of the engineer is one of hubris, whether exhibited as a travesty of naturally gendered procreation or usurpation of a divine creator that bestows soul on matter. When engineers aspire to the divine, the imagined potential retribution becomes increasingly apocalyptic and eschatological, including the emergence of the superintelligent AI Singularity originally posited by science fiction author Vernor Vinge (1993).

If the Turing Test is interpreted as a competition, then in *total* victory the winner will not only have achieved the goal of imitating a human but will surpass it, building a machine that becomes *more* than human. The imagined goal, as for Pygmalion, Frankenstein, Geppetto, and all their fictional successors, is to create an artificial being that achieves some kind of intersubjective agency, whether exhibited as a conscience, soul, or erotic love. But what could it mean for a machine to be more human than the Turing Test—not only demonstrating intersubjectivity but being *more* subjective? We understand that machines are often stronger, faster, and more durable than human bodies, and this does not cause us to fear retribution for our hubris. Similarly, we are comfortable with digital computers that calculate, measure, remember, and react more efficiently and effectively than we do.

If the attributes of subjectivity are to be the measure of success for AI research, how could the competitive scientific achievement be *objectively* recorded, verified, and replicated? It is necessary to find a domain in which human subjectivity is quantified—and board games such as chess and Go are repeatedly identified as an ideal research domain that is both competitive and quantified. If board games are taken to represent a measurable outcome of human subjectivity, then scores beyond those attained by any human represent a kind of supersubjectivity, a source of anxiety constantly reported in newspaper headlines following demonstrations such as the victory of computer player AlphaGo over the (human) world champion: "Stunning AI breakthrough takes us one step closer to the singularity" (Dvorsky 2017) or "How the demon plays Go: AI advances that will render us obsolete" (Ahuja 2017).

Here, the transgressive imagination of the AI engineer is seen to result in dangerous new kinds of subjectivity, objectively measured as beyond human capacities, to an extent of superhuman performance resulting in domination and subjection, through which the Singularity becomes the ultimate sexy robot that betrays us all. Others have suggested that sex and subjectivity may be even further entangled, and that the enterprise of AI itself is fundamentally gendered (Adam 1998). Leaving that question for now, I return to the question of subjectivity.

Quantifying Intelligence with an Objective Function

This essay has until now presumed that the AI system is indeed, as claimed by its developers and press commentators, behaving in ways that emulate human performance. According to this perspective, the numerical outcome of the Go game (the player who has surrounded the largest number of board positions within their territory) is an incidental quantification used to measure the degree of human-like performance that has been achieved. Yet for many AI systems, and arguably for AlphaGo also, this measure is not incidental. In fact, the performance of game-playing systems depends fundamentally on the definition of some measure that the system will be programmed to (or will "learn" to) optimize.

Modern "machine learning" methods are techniques for generating simple choices in the presence of complex data. A common requirement is simply to predict a single numerical output value, using a much larger amount of stored input data. A typical challenge might be to predict tomorrow's stock price, based on a great deal of potentially relevant information (today's price, past prices, the weather, articles in the financial press, company accounts, political announcements, Twitter messages from the company's customers, and so on). The input information might be enormously complex, but the output appears very simple—just one number (the price) or even a one-bit binary decision (buy/sell). We must note, as a point of caution, that many demonstrations of such systems are simply tested against historical data, which we might describe as retrodiction—as Woody Allen observed, prediction is difficult, especially when it applies to the future.

If the software can further predict how a number might change in response to its own alternative actions, then it will be able to choose the action most likely to result in the number that will make it appear intelligent (in the case of a board game, this would be a final score in which the automated player has won the game). Predictive models of this kind can be tested and refined within the software by playing huge numbers of games against itself—automatically running through many alternatives—to learn as much as possible about the relationship between different actions and their possible numerical outcomes.

The numerical function that measures and thus defines the desired outcome for an AI system is effectively a master specification, determining the goals and objectives that the system will have, and according to which it will choose its actions. Technically, this is described as an *objective function*, and as indicated in the title of this essay, understanding the nature of the objective function is critical to understanding many AI systems. As apparent from the title, the phrase *objective function* can be read in two ways: either specifying a goal (the correct technical meaning), or making an objective judgment in an otherwise subjective situation (which would be a claim deserving careful epistemological scrutiny). As noted by Philip Agre (1997), this is not the only word (or phrase) associated with AI research that has a double meaning. There are a number of other technical terms, directly related to the objective function, worth exploring further.

Statistical Machine Learning: Two Kinds of Regression

The process of predicting a single number, based on patterns that have been learned from previous data, is described generically as a "regression" task.[1] The statistical regression techniques used in machine learning, as with much of modern statistics, originate in the mathematical study of heredity associated with eugenics. Francis Galton (1886) first formulated the principle of "regression towards mediocrity" as the observation that the children of exceptional parents are less likely to be exceptional themselves.

"Regression" continues to be a core principle of machine learning. The machine observes a series of data points, whether stock market prices, gene sequences, or board-game moves. Individual points might fit no obvious pattern, but over time, some kind of trend can be found, as the regression function tends back to an underlying average. This is only slightly oversimplified. If many kinds of data must be observed, the trend relating them becomes much harder to visualize because the lines must be drawn in a multidimensional space (one dimension for every variable). Nevertheless, the principle remains the same—that the "machine learning" system predicts some quantity on the basis that it is the most mediocre explanation after all exceptions to the pattern have been discounted.

The second kind of regression is "logistic regression," in which the machine learns to predict a categorical observation (yes/no, buy/sell, or animal/vegetable/mineral) rather than a numerical one. Once again, the term first appeared in the eugenics literature, being used to predict the likelihood over time that a parent will have a genetically defective child (Haldane and Smith 1947). The word *logistic* is slightly problematic. As used by statisticians, the "logistic function" is a logarithmic population curve, originally described by Belgian Pierre François Verhulst (1845) as a *fonction logistique*. While it seems that modern French uses this word *logistique* mainly in the sense of freight transportation logistics, Verhulst was referring to Napier's logarithms.

---

1. Or perhaps retrodicting.

Logarithm itself is an odd word, coined by Napier to describe his method of manipulating ratios. It seems that Napier himself did not explain his coinage, and the Oxford English Dictionary suggests alternative derivations related to arithmetic (*ars metrica*, the art of metrication), and also to logos. *Logistic* might previously have described the ratio between two numbers, a rational process, or a rhetorical argument, in addition to its potential use as a mathematical term. So in modern usage, we might consider a logistic function that offers a logical approach to the logistics of formal logic. It may be derived from Napier's exploration of ratio, associated with rationalizing, rationality, and rational (ratio-nal) numbers. In the mathematical foundations of computer science, terminology seems constantly to drift between associations of quantification and of linguistic argumentation.

Whether or not the behavior to be achieved falls within the general categories of linear or logistic regression, the epistemology underlying exciting new AI developments, such as "deep learning," often addresses issues that would be familiar from school mathematics. Every school student is taught to reduce "big data" to a single quantity by calculating the average ("mediocre"), to estimate the trend line through a sequence of varying observations ("linear regression"), or assess whether a repeatedly tossed coin is fair or not ("logistic regression"). These simple intuitions start to falter only where there are many dimensions of data. In many dimensions, there are many possible ways to draw a line between points, or to construct a boundary dividing the set of fair coins from that of loaded ones. Many possible lines or boundaries must be assessed, in order to see which is the best of the many objective outcomes, even though each is simple in itself. The process of assessment involves searching through the many alternatives, turning this way and that as each possible explanation seems marginally more likely than the last.

This search process represents a theory of knowledge, in which a variety of possible explanations ("models") are tested against huge amounts of data to see which of them fits it best. The quality of the fit is the central epistemological feature in this theory of knowledge. Fit quality must be expressed numerically, in order that one possibility can be tested against another in an optimization equation. This equation too can be described as an objective function—apparently more complex than the simple win/lose outcome of a game of chess or Go, but equally valuable in allowing brute force repeated evaluation of the function, through many reviewed and simulated games, to find the best fit.

Ultimately, the procedure of "logistic" regression, as guided by an "objective" function, is not at all the objective and logical foundation of knowledge that these words might seem to imply. As I have shown, the terminology of machine learning has developed via engineering applications from the mathematics of eugenics, and has only minimal relevance to the philosophical questions that theorists of artificial intelligence hope to address. It is not that mathematicians misunderstand the words they use. If pressed, any expert in the field would explain that the technical term *objective* should not be taken to mean "objectivity" in any sense, and that *logistic* certainly does not imply "logical." Unfortunately, such careful clarifications are seldom necessary among mathematicians themselves. Many computer scientists are poorly trained in basic principles of epistemology, while many philosophers are poorly trained in basic principles of engineering, meaning that they happily talk at cross-purposes with the aid of ambiguous terminology that neither properly understands.

Oracles and Ground Truth

At this point, we can look more closely at how the objective function is applied. Recall that the purpose of a statistical machine learning system is to find a model that best predicts or categorizes possibly simple regularities within a large amount of varying data. In order to compare possible alternative models, the objective function may act as an "oracle" (another technical term) judging which is the better. As with all prediction, this is far more easily done if we already know the answer.

This is precisely how AI systems are trained—by showing them past cases in which we do know the answer, so that the objective function may compare each possible model to this "ground truth" (the technical term for this comparison process is *supervised learning*). Where might ground truth come from, in these supervised machine learning systems? The surprisingly mundane answer is often that thousands of people have been paid pennies to help the AI understand how to measure truth by providing labels for large data sets of training examples. These workers are likely to be recruited via "crowdsourcing" systems such as Amazon's Mechanical Turk—a surprisingly direct reference to an earlier mechanical intelligence hoax. In this case, the "objective function" is no more or less than a comparison of the trained model to previous answers given by the Turkers (as the workers are called). If the artificially intelligent computer appears to have duplicated human performance, in the terms anticipated by the Turing Test, the reason for this achievement is quite plain: the performance appears human because it *is* human!

The identity of the Turkers is kept secret, and this is the whole point (Irani and Silberman 2013). The researchers and entrepreneurs who collect the big data, store and process it in server farms, and replay the "ground truth" of human interpretation have no desire to attribute their artificially intelligent creations to low-paid digital pieceworkers. The irony of this situation is that the behavior of the "objective function" appears impressively intelligent only to the extent that it replays human *subjective* judgments. The artificial intelligence industry is a subjectivity factory, appropriating human judgments, replaying them through machines, and then claiming epistemological authority by calling it logically "objective" through a double reading of historically ambiguous mathematical terms.

Logistic Regression and Objective Categorization

Logistic regression seems appealing in situations where machine judgment is necessary for the purposes of "objective" classification. A typical ambition for an AI system commissioned by a government agency might be to ask the question "Is this person a criminal?" where this question should be answered objectively either yes or no. If we have information about all persons known to be convicted criminals—such as their bank balance, educational history, shoe size, head circumference, length of nose, color of skin, and so on—and corresponding information about people who are *not* criminals, then we might train a logistic regression system to tell us whether a given person on the street is, or is not, likely to be a criminal.

Some of these pieces of information (noses, skin, etc.) may be more or less useful in predicting which people are criminals or not, but this is not a problem if we have plenty of cheap computer memory. We can store all of this "big data" information—ideally, as much as possible—and leave the optimization search algorithm to find which of it is useful and how it should be weighted. More of a problem is the ground truth on which the objective function is based. Are we confident that the ground truth, whether based on convictions or prison sentences, is wholly reliable? It is disappointingly easy to introduce circular reasoning when large data sets have been collected just in case they might be useful. Imagine if an arrest record were taken as part of the ground truth. It might easily be the case that being arrested is associated with having dark skin, in which case the objective function leads to the conclusion that a person with dark skin should be arrested. The old adage that correlation does not imply causation applies just as surely to the correlations underlying AI systems. Embedding the correlation in an "objective function" makes its causal interpretation no more objective!

Unfortunately, the AI methods used in police and security work, although apparently being deployed rapidly, are seldom described or debated in the research literature (Bennett Moses and Chan 2016), so it is hard to assess the degree of caution currently being exercised in their application around the world. Rather than such potentially controversial applications, published research into AI classification tends to involve relatively innocuous logistic regression tasks. Is this a photograph of a horse? Is it a cat? Is it a fish? A deep learning system considers huge numbers of features within an image that might represent fur or water, or anything else, and then correlates these features with previous images that it "knows" (from the ground truth label assigned by a crowd sourcing worker, hard-working graduate student, or Facebook user adding labels to their vacation photographs) to belong to the relevant category.

Distinguishing photographs of fish from photographs of horses may be innocuous, but neither is it particularly impressive. Research subfields of artificial intelligence rely on classifications that are not too offensive, while still being sufficiently interpretive that the results do not seem trivial. One such is "affective computing," in which images of human faces are classified according to whether they seem happy or sad. This can be challenging when the crowdsource workers are not certain whether a given person appears happy or sad. This brings the problem that ground truth may be unreliable, unless collected from an actor who has been instructed to portray an unambiguous emotion. Indeed, many people being photographed (if not actors) find it difficult to tell us whether they themselves are feeling happy or sad, in which case it is necessary to find an objective alternative—researchers therefore consider alternative measures, such as the amount of serotonin in a blood sample, or functional imaging scans that can tell us if our *body* or *brain* is happy, whether we know it or not. These cases draw attention to the problems that are inherent, when we must find an objective measure, with corresponding ground truth, for subjective phenomena.

The need to find an appropriate objective function and ground truth labels is a challenge for AI research, not only in relation to the nature of subjectivity but also in relation to socially normative consensus. For example, it is not unusual for AI researchers to train classifiers, using logistic regression, to determine whether a person being photographed is male or female. The training set consists of photographs that have been labeled as either male or female by crowdsourcing workers. I met a researcher who was pleased with results that achieved a high degree of "accuracy" (which is to say, consistency with those prior labels), and who suggested that such systems would be valuable as an independent assessment of gender. That conversation took place at a time when academic claims regarding gender identity were highly controversial (e.g., Morris 2015). Yet to the AI researcher, having little interest or knowledge of contemporary gender identity issues, the engineering problem seemed to involve straightforward binary classification. Indeed, he was not concerned about such subjective problems, because he believed that the objective "ground truth" of gender could, if necessary, be determined from the body.

Objective Functions and Text

The discussion of statistical machine learning so far has attempted to demystify the prediction of stock markets, and "recognition" of photographic images, emotions, boys and girls, criminals, and so on. Many other headline examples celebrating the achievements of AI are similarly straightforward, in which the objective function must simply replicate a simplified "consensus," replaying the subjective judgments of the researchers or crowdsource workers. Board games such as chess or Go are even more specifically designed to be free from interpretive ambiguity, with formally defined rules ensuring that there will be a clearly defined objective function. So although humans may find some of these tasks difficult because of the large volumes of decisions to be made or consensus labels to be collected, they are all quite clearly mechanical, and thus easily amenable to mathematical description.

However, some of the greatest challenges and apparent achievements for artificial intelligence are related to the processing of text, rather than numbers. How can an objective function be achieved when constructing a text?

Consider the following snippets of conversation between a human on one side, and an advanced artificial intelligence on the other:

HUMAN QUESTION: Why does Juliet die?
COMPUTER ANSWER: Juliet sees Romeo dead beside her, and surmises from the empty vial that he has drunk poison.

HUMAN QUESTION: Tell me what Donald Trump will do next?
COMPUTER ANSWER: Donald Trump looks set to be a controversial
and unpredictable president after an inflammatory election campaign.

These exchanges would be quite unremarkable between two humans.
But between a human and a computer, they do seem surprising and impressive. This conversation certainly seems to pass the Turing Test. However, the exchanges above did not surprise me at the time . . . because this
is the transcription of an actual "conversation" in which I was the human
and the computer application was simply my web browser, which for-
warded the questions I had typed to Google. The "answers" that I report
above are quoted from the text that was returned in my browser window
by the Google search engine.

When viewed in this light, the conversation above is hardly impressive at all. Perhaps fifty years ago these exchanges might have seemed
magical, evidence that AI had been achieved in the terms proposed by
the Turing Test. Today, they are so far from magical as to induce a yawn.
This is not intelligence, it is simply another Google search—an everyday
transaction. Yet the mechanisms by which this once-intelligent, now-
mundane interaction have been achieved are the same kinds of statistical
process already described. Google algorithms work by calculating statistical correspondences between the words that I type and web pages
that might provide pertinent information. The sentence that is returned
appears to have been written by a human, because indeed it has been
written by a human: the author of another web page.

I should note, in passing, that the things I actually saw on my computer screen during this exchange contained many clues that would alert
an observer from fifty years ago to the relative absence of intelligence.
The answers as reported in my transcript above *appear* intelligent as I
quoted them, because of the fact that I transcribed with a degree of
interpretation—for example, I had to ignore the Google logo that appeared at the top of the screen; I had to know where to type; I needed
judiciously to ignore the text of an advertisement that was "clearly" (to
me) not relevant to my question; and so on. I am able to make all of
these interpretive judgments routinely and unconsciously, precisely because Google searches are so familiar to me. For the 1970 observer, my
own interpretation and transcription of the text appearing on my screen
might seem as foreign (or even more foreign) than the responses provided by the search engine. This fundamental property of interaction with
machines is described by Harry Collins and Martin Kusch (1999) as

Repair, Attribution, and all That (RAT)—human users constantly "repair" the inadequacy of computer behavior, then attribute the results to intelligence on the part of the machine, while discounting the actual intelligence that was supplied in the process of repair.

So to return to the transcribed "conversation" above, now that we know the "answers" are simply text copied from a Google search result, it is quite obvious that the original texts were written by human authors. For the first question in my transcription, we may surmise that the words appearing in the search result were written by the author of a school study guide. For the second question, the words seem to have been written by a professional journalist or political commentator. If an *employee* of Google were to pretend that he or she was the actual author of these words, then this pretense would be (morally) plagiarism and (commercially) an infringement of copyright. On the other hand, if we pretend that the Google *algorithm* was the author, as I did initially when presenting the example, then would this algorithmic "artificial intelligence" be equally guilty of plagiarism or copyright infringement? Can an algorithm be guilty of anything? It is not morally culpable, and cannot be tried in a court of law, despite the fact that using the term *artificial intelligence* as a noun phrase seems to imply some kind of legal personhood.

In the case of the relatively simple and honest behavior of the Google search engine, the question does not arise. Google is quite clear in stating (and ample legal precedent has confirmed) that it is simply providing an indexing service, not claiming to be the author of the content it delivers. (This despite the fact that the text I quote above was copied directly from the Google search results page, never visiting the sites created by the actual authors, with the consequence that the index has to some extent *become* the text through my reading of it).[2]

---

2. Jonathan Swift famously explained the profit that may be obtained from indexes like Google as follows:

    We of this age have discovered a shorter, and more prudent method, to become scholars and wits, without the fatigue of reading or of thinking. The most accomplished way of using books at present is two-fold: either first, to serve them as some men do lords, learn their titles exactly, and then brag of their acquaintance. Or secondly, which is indeed the choicer, the profounder, and politer method, to get a thorough insight into the index, by which the whole book is governed and turned, like fishes by the tail. . . . Thus physicians discover the state of the whole body, by consulting only what comes from behind." Swift (1704, §VII: *A digression in praise of digressions*)

The situation is more complex when an algorithm "mashes up" text that was written by multiple authors rather than a single identifiable person. It is quite routine to create algorithms that generate text, on the basis that after a short sequence of words, it is statistically straightforward to predict the next word. This behavior is seen every day, in our search bars and web browsers. If I type "How may I . . . ," Google helpfully offers to complete my sentence: "How may I assist you," on the basis of statistical likelihood. Presumably some actual person (more likely many) has previously typed these words so that Google may respond with this "intelligent" assistance. It would be silly to suggest that Google has infringed their individual copyrights, or plagiarized the work of a multitude, who themselves have only repeated a cliché.

On the other hand, if I type "It is a tr. . . ," Google immediately offers "It is a truth universally acknowledged." We know that Jane Austen is the author of this phrase, but this is not attributed or acknowledged. Undoubtedly, many people have typed these words since Austen did, but it is Google that offers them to me, with no mention of the original author. It might be suggested that Google is providing me with an "intelligent" plagiarist, to be defended on the convenient mathematical principle that we have only engaged in a statistical transaction, with no intention that the result should be passed off as the work of a creative novelist.

Summary

We are often told that in an imminent era of automated "general intelligence," computers will acquire creative capabilities, acting on their own initiative, and perhaps even presenting a threat to the future of the human race, as they decide autonomously to act in their own interests rather than ours. Yet this essay has argued that the "intelligent" behavior of machines is no more than human behavior reflected back to us. The ground of mutual intelligibility, between the artificially intelligent ontologies of the machine world and our embodied experience of the human one, may not be as hard to discover as one would suppose.

On the contrary, one might argue that a computer using "deep learning" techniques to produce text or music is no more displaying intelligence than a television is interpreting Beethoven during a broadcast from the Albert Hall. The human orchestra still exists—it is simply playing elsewhere. The machine is simply a transmission and filtering medium, not an interpreter. It might take us time to recover from the surprising form of new technologies, and to recognize the ways in which they yet again reconfigure social relations. Nevertheless, this is all that is happening in AI. The objective ground truth can usually be traced to subjective judgments, made by a person or persons who are more or less hidden from view, and more or less rewarded for their contribution to the commercial or scientific achievements of AI.

I introduced this essay with the suggestion that interlocking questions of (a) translatability/mutual intelligibility and (b) ontology/reality might be explored, in relation to the phenomena of "big data," "machine learning," and "artificial intelligence." If we are going to consider artificial intelligence as a matter of philosophical interest, then we must pay more attention to the actual algorithmic basis through which reality is represented, ontologies are constructed, and human observers interpret the interactions that they experience with complex systems (Blackwell 2015).

I have also discussed the way that words pass among disciplines, acquiring new connotations that may represent wishful thinking on the part of researchers, and overexcitement among critics, rather than rigorous analysis. The "objective function" is perhaps the most problematic case, sliding from a purely mathematical optimization principle to an anachronistically positivist interpretation of statistical machine learning. Common narratives of general artificial intelligence, derived more from science fiction than from cognitive science, all too often serve to obscure the real people whose work is hidden from view, in favor of celebrating the companies whose profits are derived from that work.

It is interesting to note how many such companies choose to describe their software creations as though the software is itself a person (Watson, Alexa, Siri). Are companies doing this purely as a marketing device, or is there some other advantage in arguing that artificial persons are being created? Press coverage of self-driving cars pays constant attention to the supposed importance of ethical decisions that would have to be taken by such person-cars—for example, resolving the moral dilemma of whether to drive into various numbers of babies or of pensioners after the brakes have failed. But if software services, or vehicles, truly did become autonomous, then this capacity of the machine to act as a moral agent could be used to indemnify those responsible for their design and operation. In the same way that claims to objectivity might represent a "view from nowhere," so the philosophically objective-subjectivity of the autonomous AI allows moral accountability for an action to be avoided through the defense that no-body did it.

Reducing intelligence to the consequences of an objective function, whether undertaken for the purpose of scientific investigation or commercial advantage, results in a problematic understanding of what intelligence might be. If the Turing Test is a competition, then the easiest way to "win" it is not by making computers more intelligent but by making humans more stupid. The danger of such a surrender, as recently analyzed with far more detail and sophistication by Harry Collins (2018), must not become a serious basis for AI research and investment. A contextualized, qualitative, and interpretive social science is needed to defend the true complexity and diversity of embodied and situated human experience.

References

Adam, Alison. 1998. *Artificial knowing: Gender and the thinking machine.* London: Routledge.

Agre, Philip E. 1997. "Towards a critical technical practice: Lessons learned in trying to reform AI." In *Social science, technical systems and cooperative work*, edited by Geoffrey Bowker, Susan Leigh Star, and William Turner, 131–57. Mahwah, NJ: Lawrence Erlbaum.

Ahuja, Anjana. 2017. "How the demon plays Go: AI advances that will render us obsolete." *Financial Times*, October 25, 2017. https://www.ft.com/content/5fb68a9e-b80b-11e7-bff8-f9946607a6ba

Bennett Moses, Lyria, and Janet Chan. 2016. "Algorithmic prediction in policing: Assumptions, evaluation, and accountability." *Policing and Society* 28 (7): 806–22.

Blackwell, Alan F. 2015. "Interacting with an inferred world: The challenge of machine learning for *humane* computer interaction." In *Proceedings of critical alternatives: The 5th decennial Aarhus conference*, edited by Shaowen Bardzell, Susanne Bødker, Ole Sejer Iversen, Clemens N. Klokmose, and Henrik Korsgaard, 169–80. Aarhus: Aarhus University Press.

Collins, Harry. 2018. *Artifictional intelligence: Against humanity's surrender to computers.* Cambridge: Polity Press.

Collins, Harry, and Martin Kusch. 1999. *The shape of actions: What humans and machines can do.* Cambridge, MA: MIT Press.

Dvorsky, George. 2017. "Stunning AI breakthrough takes us one step closer to the singularity." *Gizmodo*, October 18, 2017. https://gizmodo.com/stunning-ai-breakthrough-takes-us-one-step-closer-to-th-1819650084.

Galton, Francis. 1886. "Regression towards mediocrity in hereditary stature." *Journal of the Anthropological Institute of Great Britain and Ireland* 15: 246–63.

Haldane, John B. S., and Cedric A. B. Smith. 1947. "A simple exact test for birth-order effect." *Annals of Eugenics* 14 (1): 117–24.

Irani, Lilly C., and M. Six Silberman. 2013. "Turkopticon: Interrupting worker invisibility in Amazon Mechanical Turk." In *Proceedings of the SIGCHI conference on human factors in computing systems*, edited by Wendy E. Mackay, Stephen Brewster, and Susanne Bødker, 611–20. New York: ACM Press.

Morris, Steven. 2015. "Germaine Greer gives university lecture despite campaign to silence her." *Guardian*, November 18, 2015. https://www.theguardian.com/books/2015/nov/18/transgender-activists-protest-germaine-greer-lecture-cardiff-university.

Simon, Herbert A. 1996. *The sciences of the artificial*. Cambridge, MA: MIT Press.

Snow, Charles Percy. (1959) 2012. *The two cultures*. Cambridge: Cambridge University Press.

Swift, Jonathan. 1704. *A tale of a tub*. London: John Nutt.

Verhulst, Pierre François. 1845. "Recherches mathématiques sur la loi d'accroissement de la population." *Nouveaux mémoires de l'académie royale des sciences et belles-lettres de Bruxelles* 18: 14–54.

Vinge, Vernor. 1993. "The coming technological singularity: How to survive in the post-human era." NASA VISION-21 Symposium: Technical report NASA CP-10129. https://edoras.sdsu.edu/~vinge/misc/singularity.html.

CHAPTER TEN

Modeling, Ontology, and Wild Thought: Toward an Anthropology of the Artificially Intelligent

Willard McCarty

I come back to ostranenyi, *how we freshen things that have become banal, rather than banalize things that have become revolutionary.*
—Jerome Bruner (1988)

Raw and Strange

"We shape our tools and thereafter they shape us" is a good place to begin (Culkin 1967: 54). Whether it is true of all tools at all times, John Culkin's principle fits the reciprocity between the remarkable adaptability of the digital machine and our own.[1] It suggests how we come to respond to intelligently designed interfaces as if they were "intuitive" by nature, not seeing the characteristics of the machine behind them.

---

1. In most instances, by "digital machine" I mean the kind we use daily, but sometimes all devices conforming to von Neumann's architecture ([1945] 1993). Thanks to the common design, much of what I have to say applies to all of them. Context should make clear which is intended when clarity is needed.

In Michael Polanyi's terms, with exposure to the machine we become increasingly able to "attend from" it to the work at hand, thinking with rather than about it (1983). More so than with earlier tools, engineering behind the scenes makes less and less common the phenomenological "breakdown" that would otherwise cause us to "attend to" the mechanics, and so be reminded of those characteristics. For this reason, digital appliances are or quickly tend to become part of the furniture, their digitality imperceptible.

Here I want to come back to the primary consequences of design responsible for those unseen characteristics: the radical translation that the machine requires and the combinatorial "blind thought" (Leibniz's *cogitatio caeca*) that follows. These bear centrally on the anthropological question of intelligence that I explore in this essay.

Anthropology and Computing

Anthropologists were among the earliest to take an interest in computing. Their engagement with it began in conversations at Stanford in 1960–61. These led the next year to an international conference whose aim, Dell Hymes wrote, was to place the virtues and prospects of the computer "not in speculative isolation, but in real relation" to the anthropological disciplines (1965). But the stage had already been set by the early 1940s with the multidisciplinary and hugely influential field Norbert Wiener named "cybernetics" (1948a), from which the sciences of cognition and computing have inherited a great deal. Wiener took the name from the Greek *kŭbernḗtēs* ("steersman"), invoking the embodied kinesthetic intelligence of a skilled person interacting with what James Gibson would later call its "affordances" ([1977] 1986). Wiener had worked with this kind of intelligence in the feedback mechanisms of antiaircraft fire-control systems during World War II (Galison 1994).

Theoretically, Wiener wrote, cybernetics aimed "to find the common elements in the functioning of automatic machines and of the human nervous system," or what he called "control and communication" when done by machines and "thinking" when performed by humans (Wiener 1948b: 14). From their nascent theorizing, the early cyberneticists proposed to fashion these elements into a far-reaching, radically interdisciplinary science. Anthropologists Gregory Bateson and Margaret Mead were keen, seeing in cybernetics, as Mead later wrote, the prospect of "a form of cross-disciplinary thought which made it possible for members of many disciplines to communicate with each other easily in a language which all could understand" (Mead 1968: 2).[2] Cybernetics, in other words, appeared to offer fulfillment of the age-old quest for a universal language that would overcome the distortions and inhibitions of our lapsarian tongues (Eco [1993] 1995; cf. Steiner [1975] 1992). Artificial intelligence (AI) research pursues this quest in its search for a perfect programming language (Blackwell 2017).

What is AI from the "relations everywhere" perspective of social anthropology (Strathern 2005: 37)? In simplest terms, it is an engineering project that reifies personality in interactive, relational machinery; in consequence, it estranges and defamiliarizes that which it models. To borrow Philippe Descola's words from his commentary on Eduardo Kohn's *How Forests Think* (2013), AI is "the project of repopulating the . . . sciences with nonhuman beings"—or, in an echo of the related Artificial Life project, of creating the human *in silico*. AI thus joins the larger shift of focus "toward the interactions of humans with (and between) animals, plants, physical processes, artifacts, images, and other forms of beings" (Descola 2014: 268). Thus, Alfred Gell: "The entire historical tendency of anthropology has been towards a radical defamiliarization and relativization of the notion of 'persons.' Since the outset of the discipline, anthropology has been signally preoccupied with a series of problems to do with ostensibly peculiar relations between persons and 'things' which somehow 'appear as,' or do duty as, persons" ([1998] 2013: 9). As an art, working in material forms, AI becomes in Polish artist Bruno Schulz's words, "a probe sunk into the nameless" murk of human potential, *in statu nascendi*, premoral, barely conceptual, rapidly changing, and potentially revelatory (Schulz [1935] 1998: 369–70; McCarty 2009).

---

2. Mead and Bateson were present at the earliest gathering in 1942, then participated as core members of the yearly Macy Conferences on Cybernetics from 1946 to 1953, the first of which included a session on "Anthropology and how computers might learn how to learn" (Heims 1991: 14–17 and *passim*; Mead 1968). Bateson's dialogue with Wiener proved highly fruitful (Heims 1977; Ramage 2009). For Bateson's connection of his early anthropological work with cybernetics, see "Epilogue 1958" (Bateson [1936] 1958: esp. 287ff.) and "Foreword" (Bateson [1972] 1987). Other prominent anthropologists took up cybernetic theory; see, for example, Talcott Parsons and Lévi-Strauss (Geoghegan 2011) and the index to Geertz ([1973] 1993). Pickering (2010: chap. 2) argues that ontology was central to cybernetics.

In computer science from the 1950s into the early 1980s, recognition of the machine as such a "person"—an "acting and interacting other"—was established; work began on identifying and implementing the "human factors" it needed to have (Suchman 1998: 5). Serious theorizing followed mid-decade with three landmark studies that drew *inter alia* on phenomenology, neurobiology, anthropology, and social science to conceptualize human-machine interaction (Koschmann 2003). The most influential of these, Lucy Suchman's *Plans and Situated Actions* (1987), gave its name to research of this kind. Her work from that book onward, with its focus on the relationality of machine and human rather than their convergence, is central to my topic (Duguid 2012).

Mimesis and Alterity

Within the analogical frame of human-machine relations, my emphasis falls in this essay almost exclusively on differences between the two. The mimetic agenda of technological research, its progressive success in fitting digital circuitry to the appliances of modern life, and our own readiness to accept them argue effectively enough for similarities.

Let us suppose, then, an artificial intelligence with which, or with whom, we communicate in a probing and critical conversation. Let us assume this AI is fully realized, not in our terms but in its own. (While it is premature to say what exactly the intelligence at play might be and what it means to reason in the context of AI, we can look to the differences between how we reason biologically and how the machine acts in taking full advantage of its digital circuitry. I will return to this question later.) Let us assume further that in relation to ourselves it is neither servant nor master, neither simply inferior nor superior but different, a new kind of being, though with ancient ancestry (Riskin 2016). Undiscouraged by Wittgenstein's lion (2009: 235, §327), let us assume we converse with it in an effort to learn and understand what this "probe sunk into the nameless" has to tell us. Let us think of it and ourselves as situated on opposite sides of a Galisonian "trading zone" (Gorman 2010) or separated by a beach we would cross with Greg Dening (2004), then attempt to strike up a conversation. How would we proceed? What might we learn and understand?

The structure I propose closely resembles two well-known scenarios: Alan Turing's "imitation game," which he devised to attract attention to artificial intelligence (Whitby 1996; Gandy 1996: 124); and ELIZA,

Joseph Weizenbaum's simulation of a psychoanalyst's responses to the user as patient (1976: 1–16). My proposal differs: I assume realization of that which Turing invited others to explore, and I want to focus specifically on a full-frontal encounter that preserves critical distance. In other words, in parallel with recent work in ethology (Cheney and Seyfarth 2007; de Waal 2016; Godfrey-Smith 2017), I want to pluralize intelligence. I want to raise it not as a criterion to be met but a question to be asked, so that we may meet creatures unlike ourselves with some possibility of understanding them in their terms rather than bending them to ours—without moving the goalposts to preserve human separateness (Darwin 1871: 47). Again, an analogical investigation is called for, using the similarities so easily spotted and differences we must work to identify to strike sparks off each other.

The computer scientist Peter Wegner has said of Alan Turing's original design, from which the machine we have is derived, that it is "autistic in precluding interaction" beyond itself (Wegner 1998: 318; cf. Blackwell 2010; Zuboff 1988: 86). This autism was overcome with the machine's first implementation, but it continues in our conception, application, and deployment of the machine *insofar as we think of or configure it as isolated*, as merely taking input and delivering results. One consequence is the tendency to conceive the artificial kinds of intelligence as utterly alien (that is, *nothing* whatsoever to do with us) rather than other (enigmatically and unresolvably both like and unlike us). A former colleague, an ex-pat who had lived in a European country for decades, once remarked to me that the longer he lived there, the better he knew its people and the stranger they became. He was a misanthrope, but he had a valuable point about what depths lie beneath superficial similarities. His is the sense of relatedness I would apply to the machine.

Ontology and Modeling in Computer Science

Anthropology, we are told, has taken an "ontological turn" (Salmond 2014) that radically pluralizes the conventionally singular if incompletely accessible account of "what there is" (Quine 1948) familiar to us from the natural sciences. The core anthropological idea is that we cannot rightly speak of a single ontology about which there are multiple perspectives but must recognize multiple, problematically related ontologies. This raises the question of whether ontological pluralization has anything to do with the practice in computer science of resolving a domain of interest into a more or less adequate "ontology," hence different "ontologies" for different domains and conceptions of them.[3]

The term *ontology* came to be used in computer science about forty years ago to denote a particular formal description or many of them. An ontology in the computational sense is thus indeterminate, one of an indefinite number, each one shaped by choice, interpretation, and the affordances of the computer-language into which problem and source material are encoded. This "ontology" is basis for an interpretative "model." These two words can and often do overlap in meaning, but in the sense used here an ontology is to a model as a map is to an itinerary.[4] A model may achieve a stable form and be accepted as a standard research tool (as usual for mathematical models, for example, in economics), but since the late twentieth century, technological improvements have made composing and changing software on the fly ever easier. This has foregrounded the dynamic, exploratory process of "modeling," hence the computer itself as a modeling machine with which *serio ludere* ("seriously to play"). Programmers will recognize this playfulness in what they often do.

It seems plausible if not obvious that the computer would simultaneously influence and reflect how we conceive and engineer the world we live in. Furthermore, it seems plausible that although the modeling machine is largely a tool of the established order, a net effect of its use over the last many decades would have been not only to work against the status quo but, as it were, to liquefy it, or come to express and accelerate its liquefaction. Argument for the place of our "machine for doing thinking" (Mahoney 2011: 87) in such a shift of emphasis from the stable, well defined, and uniform to the mutable, transgressive, and diverse is beyond my scope here, but I suggest it has played and is playing a part. One rather crude bit of evidence is the surge in occurrences of "model" and its inflected forms in English from circa 1950 to the present alongside an equally dramatic surge in occurrences of "ontology."[5]

---

3. Efforts at designing a comprehensive ontology in computer science proved impractical from the beginning, were largely ignored, and have more or less been abandoned (Smith 2004: 159).

4. This is a highly simplified version of the relationship between "ontology" and "model." For model in the human sciences, see Flanders and Jannidis (2018); for ontology in computer science, see Gruber (2009; cf. 1995), and in digital humanities, see Eide and Smith Ore (2018).

5. The Google Ngram Viewer (https://books.google.com/ngrams) may be used to show this—with caution: word-frequency is a very blunt instrument

Less dramatic though also less problematic evidence comes from the transformations computing has wrought within the physical and life sciences (Gramelsberger 2011; cf. Keller 2003). Again, however, my concern is with possible relations between the digital machine on the one hand and anthropological interests on the other. My argument will be that the machine and the ontological turn in these disciplines are complementary. What underlies both, draws them together, or associates them is a teasing question I cannot answer and suspect is best left as is. The digital machine has become the great (and quite amoral) engine of civilization since its implementation mid-twentieth century, but the rapidity of its diversification and strength of its appeal suggest a technological response to something else—a *Zeitgeist*? Robin Gandy's "something in the air which different people catch" (1995: 53)?

I have noted the relative youth of the term *ontology* in computer science: it was, in fact, not poached from philosophy until circa 1980 and not formalized until the 1990s. Nevertheless, the ontological question was from the very beginning implicit in the design of the stored-program computer (the kind we have). Hence the ease with which "ontology" slipped noiselessly into the discourse of computer science.[6] But as it did so, it changed from denoting a philosophical account of "what there is" to a practical inventory in a schema. Ontological disagreements have divided philosophers since the Presocratics (or earlier, and elsewhere), but the computational redefinition pluralized ontology in a different sense by substituting an indefinitely large and proliferating number of engineered objects for an ultimate referent: metaphysically, not different conceptions of *the* world but different ("toy") worlds. Ontology in this sense became part of how computing redefines whatever research

---

for probing ideas or concepts; mistakes in OCR affect accuracy; and "metaphysics" is sometimes used as a synonym for "ontology." Since "model" is highly polysemous, searching for "model of" and "model for" will reduce false positives (although the shape of the curve for "model" alone is the same). To compare the shapes of the graphs and so rates of change in usage, scaling is recommended: none for "model," a factor of 4 for the other model-words, 80 for ontologies et al., 20 for "ontology" and "ontological." The rough point is that something quite dramatic happened circa 1945–50.

6. For early examples see Kosslyn (1978) and especially McCarthy (1980). See also Alexander et al. (1986). Formal definition came with Gruber (1995; cf. Sowa 2000: 51–131; Zúñiga 2001).

questions it embraces, at least those in the human sciences: as a locus of indeterminate approximations that sum to a statistical result.

"Ontology" was first pluralized in Anglo-American philosophy of the mid- to late 1940s by Willard van Orman Quine.[7] Quine understood the digital machine theoretically, from its mathematical origins in the work of Turing and others, the design of logic circuitry for actual machines (in which he participated), and the challenges of programming as "mechanical brains come to be adapted to purposes farther and farther beyond mere arithmetical calculation" ([1960] 1966: 40; 1955). He concludes, "the utterly pure theory of mathematical proof and the utterly technological theory of machine computation are thus at bottom one, and the basic insights of each are henceforth insights of the other." While it is true that he regarded physical science as providing best access to knowledge of "what there is," in his work on language he argued that our individual accounts of it are indeterminate and incommensurable ([1960] 2013: chap. 1 and 2). Quine's ontology remains a matter of different takes on a singular world, but by ruling out the possibility of resolving them, his hugely influential position undermined ontological singularity just at the point at which the computing machine began its own subversive work.

Quine famously made his point by analogy to an anthropological linguist attempting to produce a definitive translation of an imagined native's utterance, arguing that although the natural sciences give us the most reliable account, only incompatible versions of the one ontology are possible. Subsequently his influence on anthropology seems to have been slight, but the connection his work made between the digital machine and social anthropology is suggestive.[8]

Forests

The connection between the anthropological experience of the disturbingly different human and of the disturbingly different machine made by

---

7. For the state of ontology at the end of WWII see Feibleman (1949). Serious attention to ontology and its proximity to the digital computer happened earlier in Germany (see Heidegger [1927] 2001: §3; Steiner 1978: 79–80; see also Zuse 1993: chap. 3). Heidegger's work became known in Anglophone computer science with Dreyfus (1972) and important in that discipline thanks to Winograd and Flores (1987).

8. http://openanthcoop.ning.com/m/group/discussion?id=3404290%3ATopic%3A52720. Accessed November 29, 2018.

humans may be suggested by positioning ourselves with Charles Darwin, in the moment when he first set eyes on a "Savage," as he called him, a "naked Fuegian his long hair blowing about, his face besmeared with paint . . . [with] an expression . . . inconceivably wild." Gillian Beer quotes these words from Darwin's correspondence then comments, "Here no relation, in the sense of a message or narrative, can be established. The other is 'inconceivably wild.' But that which is inconceivable is also here a mirror image" (Beer 1996: 23, 25).

Beer's catoptric metaphor, informed by the long tradition of revelatory, perilously existential mirroring from Greco-Roman times onward (McCarty 1989), fits our anthropomorphic machine. My interest here is not so much in the question of the human that this mirroring provokes, rather more in the possibilities opened up by meeting my AI-as-maybe on level ground. Donald MacKay once commented that attributing intelligence to machines "would not primarily be a matter of using evidence and knowledge, but a matter of having the nerve" (Gandy 1996: 136). Indeed, that nerve will out; it has been driving very well-funded efforts to realize the imaginative possibilities of computing (bad and good) for decades. So I think it not exaggerated to insist that we bring to light the reasoning we are doing in concert with this Heraclitean machine, whose containing mathematics shapes a torrent of proliferating changes into the future.

The historian of computing Michael Mahoney tellingly asked how we get back into the driver's seat of this machine in its proliferating manifestations and interpretations of them. He saw us standing "before the daunting complexity of a subject that has grown exponentially in size and variety, looking not so much like an uncharted ocean as like a trackless jungle. We pace on the edge, pondering where to cut in" (2011: 23). I know exactly what he meant and am likewise daunted by the spreading, metamorphosing, interpenetrating forms of "the" computer and the many takes on them and their effects. But I wonder if the *tracklessness* of that jungle is not a matter of *perspective*. What might it look like to an artificial native? What might *we* look like? Imagine the "semantic stretch" necessary in both directions (Lloyd 2007: 65).

Machines Are (Not) Us

To answer those questions of stretch we need history, specifically the history of how we came to accept (and act on) the notion that this digital native will one day be more rather than differently intelligent. David Hanson, founder of Hanson Robotics, has observed, "people get used to the robots very quickly . . . within minutes" (Guizzo 2010). Even if features of a robot make "getting used to" difficult, one may find oneself drawn in, wanting the robot to be alive.[9] Again, what was once spectacular, spooky, or curious, if successfully engineered, becomes part of the furniture. How has this happened in the case of AI?

Consider the neatly unbroken sequence from Turing's foundational paper of 1936 onward. In that paper Turing, in response to one of David Hilbert's mathematical challenges, proved that there can be no purely algorithmic procedure for deciding whether mathematical statements are universally valid, thus helping to rescue mathematics from a sentence of terminal exhaustion.[10] To do this he invented an abstract machine that allowed him to show in principle what such a procedure could not do. He began with a metaphor: "We may compare a man in the process of computing a real number to a machine which is only capable of a finite number of conditions $q_1, q_2, \ldots q_n \ldots$" (Turing 1936: 231; Wittgenstein 1980: 1096). His machine imitated the mathematician but reduced him to a discrete logical form. A few years later neuropsychologist Warren McCulloch and mathematician Walter Pitts used Turing's abstract machine to design a computational schematic for the human brain (McCulloch and Pitts [1943] 1988). Two years after that John von Neumann used the McCulloch-Pitts schematic and its neurological vocabulary to describe the architecture of the digital machine more or less as we have it now ([1945] 1993). Eventually—I pass over a complex history—a "computational theory of mind" settled into the cognitive sciences and became a standard account if not *the* standard account (Rescorla 2016). Development of neuromorphic chips, hence brain-based robots, has been underway since then (Hof 2014). Thus the coevolutionary human-machine

---

9. See, for example, Alice at https://www.youtube.com/watch?v=G0NLHVJoI_E, an experiment in producing facial expressions.

10. G. H. Hardy wrote, "Suppose, for example, that we could find a finite system of rules which enabled us to say whether any given formula was demonstrable or not. This system would embody a theorem of metamathematics. There is of course no such theorem, and this is very fortunate, since if there were we should have a mechanical set of rules for the solution of all mathematical problems, and our activities as mathematicians would come to an end" (1929: 16).

"looping effect" (Hacking 1995: 21; McCarty 2015: 297–98): from inventor to the invention that bears his imprint; from the invention to a
new human self-image or life-style; from the self-reconfigured human
builders to a new machine; and so on.

Work on neuromorphic chips and the ongoing research in both computational biology (simulation of life *in silico*) and biological computing
(computation done with biological materials) bears out von Neumann's
view of artificial intelligence: always simultaneously an engineering and
a mathematical problem (1958). He had argued in 1949 that to conceive
of automata purely in the abstract was to throw "half of the problem"—
the physical half—"out of the window, and it may be the more important
half" (1966: 77). Among other things, von Neumann's suspicion and the
prehistory of the computational model of mind underscore the importance of the biological turn in computing (Keller 2002, 2003) and the
embodied and socially situated mind in the cognitive sciences (Wilson
and Foglia 2017).

The Machinery

The machine we have is a composite of hardware and of software that
progresses stepwise in layers, from the circuitry that creates and maintains the crisp binary signals so often assumed to be simply a given, to
the ever friendlier, "intuitive" interface that trains as much as reflects
the user's intuition. The low-level details can be left to electrical and
software engineers, but this logic survives through all the layers of abstraction and has much to do with how its resources are applied and
how we are affected (Evens 2015). Furthermore, at all steps at which
a scholarly problem and the resources on which it draws are defined
and encoded, binary logic is the gatekeeper and disciplinarian. For this
reason, *a scholarly understanding of the digital machine begins (but does not
end!) with these terms of reductive translation.* Those who use the machine
as an instrument of critical reasoning need to have the sensitivity of the
princess who feels the hard pea under those many mattresses and cannot
sleep because of it.

In the reception history of computing in the human sciences, that
sensitivity was greatest in the early period, when the small minority of
scholars involved were attempting to sort out what in principle the machine was for. In 1976, the great pioneer Fr. Roberto Busa asked, "Why
can the computer do so little?"; he dismissed the damaging notion that

the machine should be "aimed towards less human effort, or for doing things faster and with less labour," insisting on the greater efforts the computer made possible. Fourteen years earlier, the Cambridge linguist and philosopher Margaret Masterman wrote that the potential of the computer "is so great as to make of it the telescope of the mind" (1962: 39), arguing that to treat it as the "purely menial tool" that others had described was a great mistake. Four years later, the American literary critic Louis Milic argued, "The true nature of the machine is unknown to us," that "its intelligence and ours must be made complementary," and so implied the crucial question of what we take intelligence to be (1966: 4). "Thinking in a new way is not an easy accomplishment. It means," he said, *"reorientation of all the coordinates of our existence"* (1966: 5, my emphasis)—that is, a cosmological reconfiguration. He called his brief article, "The next step." I don't think we've taken that step yet. Several factors, including assimilation of the machine as an appliance of daily life, have dulled us to its fundamentally different, algorithmic way of reasoning—once again, to the hard pea under those mattresses.

The historian of science David Gooding put it like this:

> To digitalize is to represent features of the world, including relation-ships between them, in a manner that establishes and fixes unam-biguous meaning. . . . It is a method designed to achieve two things: to preserve the invariance of tokens in a symbol manipulation system and to make the value of the tokens unambiguous. (2003: 279 and 283n33)

Hence my two axioms of digitization: that everything to be encoded in software, both source material and operations to be done on it, must be rendered with the *complete consistency* and with the *absolute explicitness* demanded by all-or-nothing digital logic. The severity of these axioms makes it difficult to see how the machine has anything to offer beyond clerical assistance, however fast, however accurate. The machine's price of admission may seem entirely too high, offering as reward only some light on whatever cannot satisfy those axioms. It is true that the escapees do help us ask how we know what we know if we cannot spell it out digitally, hence a valuable *via negativa*. But this is cold comfort if that is all that is possible. Indeed, this *via negativa* does not, in fact, require use of the machinery at all.

Digitization, however, is only the first of three stages. Overall, these stages comprise the iterative and exploratory process I have called "modeling." They are illustrated by the diagram in Figure 9.

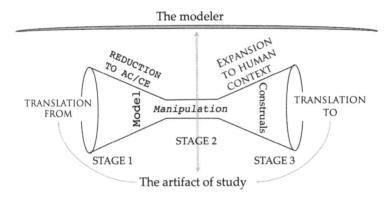

The computational process

Figure 9. Three stages of the computational process (after David Gooding, "Varying the Cognitive Span" [2003], fig. 13.4).

Although in practice these stages can take place rapidly with little demarcation, I will describe them in a clearly distinct sequence. Again, the first and third involve the machine primarily in the abstract, as a set of requirements and as the source of results to be considered. Only the second stage involves the machine directly.

We may think of operations in this middle stage as "mechanical"— that is, not human—but since the machine is a human artifact, it is more productive to ask after the model of thought-processing the machine instantiates—its hardwired "theory of mind," if you will. In the nineteenth century, Charles Babbage's friend Lady Ada Lovelace, commenting on his Analytical Engine, wrote that the machine "can do [only] whatever we *know how to order it* to perform" (Lovelace 1843: 722). In other words, her human correlate was a perfectly obedient servant. In the mid-twentieth century, her long-lived dictum resurfaced in numerous statements to the effect that the digital computer was no more than a "fast moron" (e.g., Soule 1956: 173–74; Andree 1958: 2, 106). IBM supposedly made "fast moron" and similar phrases doctrine, promulgating this doctrine via sales staff in order to salve public fears of artificial intelligence following the successes of the machine at the game of checkers and the ramping up of publicity required to sell the very expensive "giant brain" (McCorduck 1979: 159). The mantra certainly became a stubbornly persistent meme.

But such is *not* the machine they had nor the one we have (the one von Neumann helped to design), nor the one for which he and Herman Goldstine sketched the basics of programming in a very early paper on that subject, "Planning and coding of problems for an electronic computing instrument" (1947). They pointed out that the difference in design (which in effect transcends Lady Lovelace's dictum) is the provision allowing a running program, conditional on the outcome of previous operations, to deviate from the linear sequence of instructions or to rewrite those instructions on the fly. They explained—note these words well—that coding "is not a static process of translation, but rather *the technique of providing a dynamic background to control the automatic evolution of a meaning*" as the machine follows unspecified routes in unspecified ways in order to accomplish specified tasks (Goldstine and von Neumann 1947: 2; my emphasis; Campbell-Kelly 2011). Thus Herbert Simon: "This statement—that computers can only do what they are programmed to do—is intuitively obvious, indubitably true, and supports none of the implications that are commonly drawn from it" (Simon [1960] 1977: 67; Feigenbaum and Feldman 1963: 3–4). The idea of "machine" behind it is, as Marvin Minsky remarked, "precomputational" (McCorduck 1979: 71).

The high level of complications that result from the design of the stored-program computer, Goldstine and von Neumann went on to note, are "not hypothetical or exceptional . . . they are indeed the norm"; the power of the machine "is essentially due to them, i.e. to the extensive combinatorial possibilities which they indicate" (1947: 2). In essence, as von Neumann suggested four years later, machines "of the digital, all-or-nothing type" work by combining and recombining the data under given constraints until coherent patterns emerge (von Neumann 1951: 16). By design they are combinatorial. Hence, in a nutshell, the core benefit they confer is their *recombinatorial potential*, which does not offer the enquirer closure on truth but generation of unforeseen or unforeseeable possibilities for consideration. Thus, the mathematician Martin Gardner: "When ideas are combined in all possible ways, the new combinations start the mind thinking along novel channels and one is led to discover fresh truths and arguments" (Gardner 1958: 17). That is essentially what Ada Lovelace went on presciently to write after laying down her dictum: that the Engine's power of "mechanical combinations" would throw new light on "the relations and nature of many subjects," leading to more profound investigation of them (1843: 721, 723). In his 1950 paper, Turing quoted her, noting in agreement with Douglas Hartree that she had left open the possibility of an intelligent machine; all that was lacking was memory and speed (1950: 450).

While it is true that interpretative significance does not survive digitization, that the machine sorts only configurations of bits from which this significance has been stripped, meaning stays with the enquirer and, after the Leibnizian *cogitatio caeca* in hardware, is reattributed to the resorted output at the end (Picon 2008: 223).

Hence the emphasis falls on Gardner's "new . . . novel . . . fresh," which deserves further, stronger emphasis—and considerably more attention than I have space for here. The best, most highly developed example for AI is the rapidly evolving AlphaGo system, designed to play the ancient board-game known as *go* in Japanese, *weiqi* in Chinese (Papineau and Black 2001; Fairbairn 2007). AlphaGo's victories are impressive,[11] especially given the antiquity and complexity of the game and the discipline required to master it. The significance for AI, however, is that in the 2017 (AlphaGo Zero) version, it acquired its skill by playing against itself repeatedly, starting off as tabula rasa with no historical knowledge of play beyond the basic rules (Silver, Schrittwieser, and Simonyan 2017), and that in doing so it deployed legal moves that no human player had thought to make in the approximately 2500-year history of the game. Ambitions for the latest algorithm, AlphaZero, are stronger yet: to achieve "superhuman performance in many challenging domains" (Silver, Hubert, and Schrittwieser 2017).

For the question of intelligence that I raise here, these developments are unquestionably important. What they import, however, is not so much a superhuman intelligence but a clearly different kind. However dependent on the rigidly defined rules and structure of this and other games, these developments in AI serve as an existence-proof that, in the lineage of Turing's provocation, draws attention to possibilities of intelligence in the built world, in conversation with us.

Permit me a few wild thoughts. For the future, AlphaGo and progeny raise the question of what happens as the precisely defined limits of the game-board fall away and expand, as the application of explicit and consistent rules relaxes into the playing of roles. For the present they direct

---

11. For the history, see https://en.wikipedia.org/wiki/AlphaGo#AlphaGo_Zero_and_AlphaZero.

us to look toward exploratory experimental work with the machines we have for the conversation happening there, right now. Anthropologically, as the history of board games suggests, they point toward manipulatory ethnomathematical and divinatory practices, which likewise use combinatorial techniques to direct the client toward something other (a subject for another time). It is, in other words, a question of what the AI *does* in concert with us.

Incommensurability?

Back to Darwin's naked Fuegian, inconceivably other but simultaneously a mirror image. On the one hand, the Fuegian cannot have been incommensurable, since that would made any kind of comparison impossible. On the other hand, Eduardo Viveiros de Castro has pointed out, to grant commensurability or guarantee it by presuming continuity short-circuits "the challenge . . . to construct a commensurability (i.e., a reciprocal measurability)" between the kinds (2010: 330). The crucial thing is not to ignore the challenge, however we construe it.

For scholarship, the disciplinary marches—Thomas Kuhn's Gestalt switch (1977), Beer's open (but hazardous) fields of cultural encounter (1996; cf. 2006), Dening's beaches of the mind (2004), Strathern's commons and borderlands (2004), Galison's trading zone (Gorman 2010)— provide preparatory examples close to hand. What these scholars have *not* done is the reason I cite them: they have not underestimated the difficulty or breezily assume an ontologically neutral standing point from which each discipline can be viewed objectively, its ways and means poached at will without error or partiality (McCarty 2016). This error is comparable to Viveiros de Castro's "modern cosmological vulgate": the multiculturalist supposition of "a single world or nature . . . around which different partial cultural views orbit" (2010: 329). Look closely, he argues, and the one nature it supposes turns out to be this cosmology naturalized. Michel Foucault's invocation of Jeremy Bentham's panopticon, with its "sentiment of an invisible omniscience," gives us a fitting image for it.[12] G. E. R. Lloyd's corrective statement, "there is no

---

12. Foucault, "Panopticism" (Foucault [1975] 1995: 195–228; plate 3 shows Bentham's design). See also Bentham (1843: 235–48). The quoted phrase is often attributed to an anonymous architect; see Lyon (2006); Nugent (2011).

theory-free way of accessing an answer to the question of what the world comprises" (2010: 210), throws us back to the question of the relation of theory to the digital machine. I will return to it, but for now I want to focus on the temporal dimension.

Ontologizing

Lloyd continues: "We just have to make the best use we can of such bridgeheads of intelligibility as will enable us to begin to make sense of others." Are these bridgeheads *ontologies*—that is, formal specifications or ethnographies? I don't think this is the best way to conceive of them, and not the most productive, at least for my consideration of a machine that is nothing but a paperweight if not "doing thinking" *with* us.

Lloyd avoids the closure and abstraction a formal ontology would require. Amiria and Anne Salmond note in their commentary on his "History and human nature" (2010) that these bridgeheads "are not 'out there' conveniently to hand, waiting to be discovered, but are rather cultivated over years, often generations" (Salmond and Salmond 2010: 304). *They are processes in time.* In "Historical ontology" Ian Hacking avoids closure by bringing ontology to life in time, allowing it to denote the implicitly changeable and changing "whatever we individuate and allow ourselves to talk about." He points, for example, to new ways of "constituting ourselves *as* so and so" by discovering "possible ways to be a person"—other ways of being human that arise, surge in popularity, then decline and lose their appeal (2002: 1–2; cf. 1995). Viveiros de Castro repeatedly refers to his anthropological project as experimental, with a perpetual revolution intended; *Cannibal Metaphysics*, he says, is "a beginner's guide" to another, endlessly imagined book ([2009] 2014: 39). Thus, Dening: "we write culture in the present participle" (2002: 23). Participles "soften the essentializing quality of nouns with the being and acting quality of the verb" better to express the truth of our experience in a world that is "processural, unfinished" (1993: 84).

What, then, *is* the world in processual experience or representation? The latter—representation—is Quinean, implying a reality out there that in practice can only be severally, separately, incommensurably, approximately represented. With Dening's participle in mind, I have been converging on a suggestion of an ongoing, participatory, asymptotic *ontologizing* that, like Emanuel Schegloff's verbal/nonverbal communication (1982), is normally a commensurating activity—a bridgehead cooperatively under construction from both sides. Note that I have left the world alone. Lloyd has offered a *multidimensional* world but has avoided limiting the number of dimensions, and he has allowed for semantic stretch in how we talk about them. I think his multidimensionality and my ontologizing are complementary.

Back to our face-to-face encounter with that AI. What we are talking about when we talk about AI, then, is not a catoptric sign, a reflection of ourselves, but an emergent manifestation of ourselves differently constituted.

Toward an Anthropology of the Artificially Intelligent?

Why, then, anthropology and AI?

To date, computer scientists have taken an interest in anthropology mostly to inform the design of software better to suit people who use and are affected by it. Anthropologists have tended to come to computing to give structure to and process data and to draw on its formally systematic ways of conceptualizing social behavior. My interest in probing artificially intelligent entities anthropologically is motivated not by the practical effectiveness of ethnographic description to improve the products of computer science nor vice versa but by the theoretical effectiveness of anthropology to illumine a way forward with computing. Simply put, anthropology is where the right sort of questions are being asked so that we may move beyond utility and impact. It is the discipline, Kant wrote in the *Jäsche Logik* (1800), that asks the summative question of philosophy in the "cosmopolitan [*weltbürgerlichen*] sense": "What is man?" (1992: 538). Kant's question is the principal one raised by the disturbingly different machine when, in fits and starts, its disturbing difference emerges and draws us in.

In the late 1980s Terry Winograd and Fernando Flores put the argument toward which I am gesturing most succinctly: "In designing tools we are designing ways of being" (1987: xi). In other words, in its participant observation an anthropology of the artificially intelligent would have to be "a way of knowing from the inside" (Ingold 2013: 10), which would in turn be predicated on a human-machine resonance rather than a symbolically mediated representation of the world.

I conclude by returning to Margaret Masterman's "telescope of the mind." She referred in her clear-sighted article to Newton's instrument, but I think a much more telling one is Galileo's *occhialino*. The question is, to echo Hacking, do we *see* through, or see *through*, such a telescope (1983: 186–209)? Today, just as in the microscopy Hacking studied, optoelectronics interposes a hermeneutic black box between the eye and its object, complicating—but not essentially altering—the philosopher's question. For when Galileo looked through his spyglass, much of what he saw had been seen before, but the differences were enough to make what was "momentarily mutable," stuff of the eye reshaped by his mind into "a compelling argument for Copernicanism."[13]

It's an altogether more interesting challenge we face than we have so often supposed.

Acknowledgments

I am indebted to G. E. R. Lloyd for the wonderfully demanding opportunity to develop this essay and encouragement to stick with it; to my fellow participants and commentators in the "Science in the Forest, Science in the Past" symposium; to Amiria Salmond for her helpful commentary in a long-running email exchange during summer and autumn 2017; to Aparecida Vilaça for later relativizing conversations about the Wari'; and to an anonymous reviewer for pointing out metaphorically what I am doing here: releasing hares to be chased.

References

Alexander, James H., Michael J. Freiling, Sheryl J. Shulman, Jeffrey L. Staley, Steven Rehfuss, and Steven L. Messick. 1986. *Knowledge level engineering: Ontological analysis.* Proceedings of the Fifth National Conference on Artificial Intelligence. Menlo Park, CA: AAAI Press.

Andree, Richard V. 1958. *Programming the IBM 650 magnetic drum computer and data-processing machine.* New York: Henry Holt.

Bateson, Gregory. (1936) 1958. *Naven: A survey of the problems suggested by a composite picture of the culture of a New Guinea tribe drawn from three points of view.* Stanford, CA: Stanford University Press.

---

13. Thanks to Crystal Hall (Bowdoin College) for the commentary on Galileo (email message, June 1, 2017). The literature is extensive (see especially Biagioli 2006: chap. 2; Lipking 2014).

———. (1972) 1987. *Steps to an ecology of mind: Collected essays in anthropology, psychiatry, evolution, and epistemology*. Northvale, NJ: Jason Aronson Inc.

Beer, Gillian. 1996. *Open fields: Science in cultural encounter*. Oxford: Oxford University Press.

———. 2006. "On the challenges of interdisciplinarity." Institute of Advanced Study, Durham University. March 15, 2017. http://www.dur.ac.uk/ias/news/annual_research_dinner/.

Bentham, Jeremy. 1843. *The works of Jeremy Bentham*. Vol. 4, *Panopticon, constitution, colonies, codification*, edited by John Bowring. Edinburgh: William Tait.

Biagioli, Mario. 2006. *Galileo's instruments of credit: Telescopes, images, secrecy*. Chicago: University of Chicago Press.

Blackwell, Alan F. 2010. "When systematizers meet emphasizers: Universalism and the prosthetic imagination." In "History and Human Nature," edited by Brad Inwood and Willard McCarty, special issue, *Interdisciplinary Science Reviews* 35 (3–4): 387–403.

———. 2017. "6,000 years of programming language design: A meditation on Eco's perfect language." In *Conversations around semiotic engineering*, edited by Simone Diniz Junqueira Barbosa and Karin Breitman, 31–9. Berlin: Springer.

Bruner, Jerome. 1988. "Life and language in autobiography." Alfred Korzybski Memorial Lecture, 1988. *General Semantics Bulletin* 57: 14–24. http://www.generalsemantics.org/wp-content/uploads/2011/04/gsb-57-bruner.pdf.

Busa, Roberto, S. J. 1976. "Why can a computer do so little?" *Bulletin of the Association for Literary and Linguistic Computing* 4 (1): 1–3.

Campbell-Kelly, Martin. 2011. "From theory to practice: The invention of programming, 1947–51." In *Dependable and historic computing: Essays dedicated to Brian Randell on the occasion of his 75th birthday*, edited by Cliff B. Jones and John L. Lloyd, 23–37. Heidelberg: Springer-Verlag.

Cheney, Dorothy L., and Robert M. Seyfarth. 2007. *Baboon metaphysics: The evolution of a social mind*. Chicago: University of Chicago Press.

Culkin, John M., S. J. 1967. "A schoolman's guide to Marshall McLuhan." *Saturday Review*, March 18, 1967, 51–53, 70–72.

Darwin, Charles. 1871. *The descent of man, and selection in relation to Sex*. Vol. 1. New York: D. Appleton.

de Waal, Frans. 2016. *Are we smart enough to know how smart animals are?* London: Granta.

Dening, Greg. 1993. "The theatricality of history making and the paradoxes of acting." *Cultural Anthropology* 8 (1): 73–95.

———. 2002. "Performing on the beaches of the mind: An essay." *History and Theory* 41: 1–24.

———. 2004. *Beach crossings: Voyaging across times, cultures and self.* Carleton, Australia: Miegunyah Press.

Descola, Philippe. 2014. "All too human (still): A comment on Eduardo Kohn's *How forests think*." *HAU: Journal of Ethnographic Theory* 4 (2): 267–73. http://www.haujournal.org/index.php/hau/article/view/hau4.2.015/1130.

Detienne, Marcel, and Jean-Pierre Vernant. 1974. *Les ruses de l'intelligence: la métis des Grecs.* Paris: Flammarion.

Dreyfus, Hubert L. 1972. *What computers can't do: Of artificial reason.* New York: Harper & Row.

Duguid, Paul. 2012. "On rereading: Suchman and situated action." *La Libellio d'AEGIS* 8 (2): 3–9.

Eco, Umberto. (1993) 1995. *The search for the perfect language.* Oxford: Blackwell.

Eide, Øyvind, and Christian-Emil Smith Ore. 2018. "Ontologies and data modelling." In *The shape of data in digital humanities: Modeling texts and text-based resources*, edited by Julia Flanders and Fotis Jannidis, 178–96. London: Routledge.

Evens, Aden. 2015. *Logic of the digital.* London: Bloomsbury.

Fairbairn, John. 2007. "Go in China." In *Ancient board games in perspective: Papers from the 1990 British Museum colloquium, with additional contributions*, edited by I. L. Finkel, 133–37. London: British Museum Press.

Feibleman, James K. 1949. "A defense of ontology." *Journal of Philosophy* 46 (2): 41–51.

Feigenbaum, Edward A., and Julian Feldman, eds. 1963. *Computers and thought.* New York: McGraw-Hill.

Flanders, Julia, and Fotis Jannidis, eds. 2018. *The shape of data in digital humanities: Modeling texts and text-based resources.* London: Routledge.

Foucault, Michel. (1975) 1995. *Discipline and punish: The birth of the prison.* Translated by Alan Sheridan. New York: Vintage Books.

Galison, Peter. 1994. "The ontology of the enemy: Norbert Wiener and the cybernetic vision." *Critical Inquiry* 21 (1): 228–66.

Gandy, Robin. 1995. "The confluence of ideas in 1936." In *The universal Turing machine: A half-century survey*, edited by Rolf Herkin, 53–102. Wien: Springer-Verlag.

———. 1996. "Human versus mechanical intelligence." In *Machines and thought: The legacy of Alan Turing*, edited by Peter J. R. Millican and Andy Clark, 125–36. Oxford: Clarendon Press.

Gardner, Martin. 1958. *Logic machines and diagrams*. New York: McGraw-Hill.

Geertz, Clifford. (1973) 1993. *The interpretation of cultures: Selected essays*. London: Fontana Press.

Gell, Alfred. (1998) 2013. *Art and agency: An anthropological theory*. Oxford: Clarendon Press.

Geoghegan, Bernard Dionysius. 2011. "From information theory to French critical theory: Jakobson, Lévi-Strauss, and the cybernetic apparatus." *Critical Inquiry* 38 (1): 96–126.

Gibson, James J. (1977) 1986. "The theory of affordances." In *Perceiving, acting, and knowing: Toward an ecological psychology*, edited by Robert Shaw and John Bransford, 127–43. Hillsdale NJ: Lawrence Erlbaum Associates.

Godfrey-Smith, Peter. 2017. *Other minds: The octopus and the evolution of intelligent life*. London: William Collins.

Goldstine, Herman H., and John von Neumann. 1947. *Planning and coding of problems for an electronic computing instrument*. Report on the Mathematical and Logical aspects of an Electronic Computing Instrument. Part II, vols. 1–3. Princeton NJ: Institute for Advanced Study. https://library.ias.edu/files/pdfs/ecp/planningcodingof0103inst.pdf.

Gooding, David. 2003. "Varying the cognitive span: Experimentation, visualization, and computation." In *The philosophy of scientific experimentation*, edited by Hans Radder, 255–83. Pittsburgh: University of Pittsburgh Press.

Gorman, Michael E., ed. 2010. *Trading zones and interactional experience: Creating new kinds of collaboration*. Cambridge, MA: MIT Press.

Gramelsberger, Gabriele, ed., 2011. *From science to computational sciences: Studies in the history of computing and its influence on today's sciences*. Zürich: Diaphanes.

Gruber, Thomas R. 1995. "Toward principles for the design of ontologies used for knowledge sharing." *International Journal of Human-Computer Studies* 43 (5–6): 907–28.

———. 2009. "Ontology." In *Encyclopedia of database systems*, edited by Ling Liu and M Tamer Özsu, 1963–65. New York: Springer Science+Business Media.

Guizzo, Enrico. 2010. "Who's afraid of the uncanny valley?" *IEEE Spectrum*, April 2, 2000. https://spectrum.ieee.org/automaton/robotics/humanoids/040210-who-is-afraid-of-the-uncanny-valley.

Hacking, Ian. 1983. *Representing and intervening: Introductory topics in the philosophy of natural science.* Cambridge: Cambridge University Press.

———. 1995. *Rewriting the soul: Multiple personality and the sciences of memory.* Princeton, NJ: Princeton University Press.

———. 2002. "Historical ontology." In *Historical ontology*, 1–26. Cambridge, MA: Harvard University Press.

Hardy, Godfrey Harold. 1929. "Mathematical proof." *Mind*, n.s., 38 (149): 1–25.

Heidegger, Martin. (1927) 2001. *Sein und Zeit.* Achtzehnte Auflage. Tübingen: Max Niemeyer Verlag.

Heims, Steve P. 1977. "Gregory Bateson and the mathematicians: From interdisciplinary interaction to societal functions." *Journal of the History of the Behavioral Sciences* 13 (2): 141–59.

———. 1991. *Constructing a social science for postwar America: The cybernetics group, 1946–1953.* Cambridge, MA: MIT Press.

Hof, Robert D. 2014. "Neuromorphic chips." *MIT Technological Review* (May/June). https://www.technologyreview.com/s/526506/neuromorphic-chips/.

Hymes, Dell, ed. 1965. *The use of computers in anthropology.* The Hague: Mouton & Co.

Ingold, Tim. 2013. *Making: Anthropology, archaeology, art and architecture.* London: Routledge.

Kant, Immanuel. 1992. *Lectures on logic.* Translated and edited by J. Michael Young. Cambridge: Cambridge University Press.

Keller, Evelyn Fox. 2002. *Making sense of life: Explaining biological development with models, metaphors, and machines.* Cambridge, MA: Harvard University Press.

————. 2003. "Models, simulation, and 'computer experiments.'" In *The philosophy of scientific experimentation*, edited by Hans Radder, 198–215. Pittsburgh: University of Pittsburgh Press.

Kohn, Eduardo. 2013. *How forests think: Toward an anthropology beyond the human*. Berkeley: University of California Press.

Koschmann, Timothy. 2003. "Plans and situated actions: A retro-review." *The Journal of the Learning Sciences* 12 (2): 257–306.

Kosslyn, Stephen Michael. 1978. "On the ontological status of visual mental images." In *Theoretical issues in natural language processing II*, edited by David L. Waltz. Arlington, VA: Association for Computational Linguistics. Draft entry in the ACL Anthology. Accessed November 29, 2018. http://www.aclweb.org/anthology/T78-1023.pdf.

Kuhn, Thomas S. 1977. "The relations between the history and the philosophy of science." In *The essential tension: Selected studies in scientific tradition and change*, 3–20. Chicago: University of Chicago Press.

Lipking, Lawrence. 2014. *What Galileo saw: Imagining the scientific revolution*. Ithaca, NY: Cornell University Press.

Lloyd, G. E. R. 2007. *Cognitive variations: Reflections on the unity and diversity of the human mind*. Oxford: Oxford University Press.

————. 2010. "History and human nature: Cross-cultural universals and cultural relativities." In "History and Human Nature," edited by Brad Inwood and Willard McCarty, special issue, *Interdisciplinary Science Reviews* 35 (3–4): 201–14.

Lovelace, Lady Ada. 1843. Translator's notes to L. F. Menabrea, "Sketch of the Analytical Engine invented by Charles Babbage, Esq." In *Scientific memoirs, selected from the transactions of foreign academies of science and learned societies, and from foreign journals*, vol. 3, edited by Richard Taylor, 666–731. London: Richard and John E. Taylor.

Lyon, David, ed. 2006. *Theorizing surveillance: The panopticon and beyond*. Cullompton, Devon: Willan Publishing.

Mahoney, Michael Sean. 2011. *The histories of computing*, edited by Thomas Haigh. Cambridge, MA: Harvard University Press.

Masterman, Margaret. 1962. "The intellect's new eye." In *Freeing the mind: Articles and letters from* The Times Literary Supplement *during March–June, 1962*, 38–44. London: Times Publishing.

McCarthy, John. 1980. "Circumscription—A form of non-monotonic reasoning." Stanford Artificial Intelligence Laboratory Memo AIM-334.

Computer Science Department Report STAN-CS-80-788. Stanford, CA: Stanford University.

McCarty, Willard. 1989. "The shape of the mirror: Metaphorical catoptrics in classical literature." *Arethusa* 22 (2): 161–95.

———. 2009. "That uneasy stare at an alien nature." *Digital Studies / Le champ numérique* 1 (1). http://doi.org/10.16995/dscn.135.

———. 2015. "Getting there from here: Remembering the future of digital humanities." In *Advancing digital humanities: Research, methods, theories*, edited by Paul Longley Arthur and Katherine Bode, 291–321. Houndmills, Basingstoke: Palgrave Macmillan.

———. 2016. "Becoming interdisciplinary." In *A new companion to digital humanities*, edited by Susan Schreibman, Ray Siemens, and John Unsworth, 69–83. Chichester: John Wiley and Sons.

McCorduck, Pamela. 1979. *Machines who think: A personal inquiry into the history and prospects of artificial intelligence*. San Francisco: W. H. Freeman.

McCulloch, Warren S., and Walter H. Pitts. (1943) 1988. "A logical calculus of the ideas immanent in nervous activity." In *Embodiments of mind*, by Warren S. McCulloch, 19–39. Cambridge, MA: MIT Press.

Mead, Margaret. 1968. "Cybernetics of cybernetics." *Purposive systems: Proceedings of the first annual symposium of the American Society for Cybernetics*, edited by Heins von Foerster, John D. White, Larry J. Peterson, and John K. Russell, 1–11. New York: Spartan Books.

Milic, Louis T. 1966. "The next step." *Computers and the Humanities* 1 (1): 3–6.

Nugent, David. 2011. "On the study of social optics: Foucault, countersurveillance, and the political underground of Northern Peru." *Review* (Ferdinand Braudel Center): 34 (3): 311–31.

Papineau, Elisabeth, and Michael Black. 2001. "The game of *weiqi*, a Chinese way of seeing the world." *China Perspectives* 33: 43–55.

Pickering, Andrew. 2010. *The cybernetic brain*. Chicago: University of Chicago Press.

Picon, Marine. 2008. "What is the foundation of knowledge? Leibniz and the amphibology of interpretation." In *Leibniz: What kind of rationalist?*, edited by Marcelo Dascal, 213–27. Berlin: Springer Science+Business Media.

Polanyi, Michael. 1983. *The tacit dimension*. Gloucester, MA: Peter Smith.

Quine, Willard van Orman. 1948. "On what there is." *Review of Metaphysics* 2 (5): 21–38.

———. 1955. "A way to simplify truth functions." *American Mathematical Monthly* 62 (9): 627–31.

———. (1960) 1966. "On the application of modern logic." In *The ways of paradox and other essays*, 35–41. New York: Random House.

———. (1960) 2013. *Word and object*. Rev. ed. Cambridge, MA: MIT Press.

Ramage, Magnus. 2009. "Norbert and Gregory." *Information, Communication & Society* 12 (5): 735–49.

Rescorla, Michael. 2016. "The computational theory of mind." *Stanford Encyclopedia of Philosophy*. https://plato.stanford.edu/archives/win2016/entries/computational-mind/.

Riskin, Jessica. 2016. *The restless clock: A history of the centuries-long argument over what makes living things tick*. Chicago: University of Chicago Press.

Salmond, Amiria. 2014. "Transforming translations (part 2): Addressing ontological alterity." *HAU: Journal of Ethnographic Theory* 4 (1): 155–87.

Salmond, Amiria, and Anne Salmond. 2010. "Artefacts of encounter." In "History and Human Nature," edited by Brad Inwood and Willard McCarty, special issue, *Interdisciplinary Science Reviews* 35 (3–4): 302–17.

Schegloff, Emanuel A. 1982. "Discourse as an interactional achievement: Some uses of 'uh huh' and other things that come between sentences." In *Analyzing discourse: Text and talk*, edited by D. Tannen, 71–93. Washington, DC: Georgetown University Press.

Schulz, Bruno. (1935) 1998. "An essay for S. I. Wirkiewicz." In *The collected works of Bruno Schulz*, edited by and translated by Jerzy Ficowski, 367–70. London: Picador.

Silver, David, Thomas Hubert, and Julian Schrittwieser. 2017. "Mastering chess and shogi by self-play with a general reinforcement learning algorithm." arXiv:1712.01815v1 [cs.AI], December 5, 2017. https://arxiv.org/pdf/1712.01815.pdf.

Silver, David, Julian Schrittwieser, and Karen Simonyan. 2017. "Mastering the game of Go without human knowledge." *Nature* 550 (October 19): 354–59.

Simon, Herbert A. (1960) 1977. *The new science of management decision*. Rev ed. Englewood Cliffs, NJ: Prentice-Hall.

Smith, Barry. 2004. "Ontology." In *The Blackwell guide to the philosophy of computing and information*, edited by Luciano Floridi, 155–66. Oxford: Blackwell.

Soule, Gardner. 1956. "The machine that indexed The Bible." *Popular Science* (November): 173–75, 242, 246.

Sowa, John F. 2000. *Knowledge representation: Logical, philosophical, and computational foundations.* Pacific Grove, CA: Brooks/Cole.

Steiner, George. (1975) 1992. *After Babel: Aspects of language and translation.* 2nd ed. Oxford: Oxford University Press.

———. 1978. *Heidegger.* Glasgow: Fontana/Collins.

Strathern, Marilyn. 2004. *Commons and borderlands: Working papers on interdisciplinarity: Accountability and the flow of knowledge.* Wantage, Oxfordshire: Sean Kingston Publishing.

———. 2005. *Kinship, law and the unexpected: Relatives are always a surprise.* Cambridge: Cambridge University Press.

Suchman, Lucy A. 1987. *Plans and situated actions: The problem of human-machine communication.* Cambridge: Cambridge University Press.

———. 1998. "Human/machine reconsidered." *Cognitive Studies* 5 (1): 5–13.

Turing, Alan M. 1936. "On computable numbers, with an application to the Entscheidungsproblem." *Proceedings of the London Mathematical Society,* series 2 (42): 230–65.

———. 1950. "Computing machinery and intelligence." *Mind,* n.s., 59, no. 236 (October): 433–60.

Viveiros de Castro, Eduardo. (2009) 2014. *Cannibal metaphysics,* edited and translated by Peter Skafish. Minneapolis, MN: Univocal.

———. 2010. "In some sense." In "History and Human Nature," edited by Brad Inwood and Willard McCarty, special issue, *Interdisciplinary Science Reviews* 35 (3–4): 318–33.

von Neumann, John. (1945) 1993. "First draft of a report on the EDVAC." *IEEE Annals of the History of Computing* 15 (4): 27–43.

———. 1951. "The general and logical theory of automata." In *Cerebral mechanisms of behavior: The Hixon symposium,* edited by Lloyd A. Jeffress, 1–41. New York: John Wiley & Sons.

———. 1958. *The computer and the brain.* New Haven, CT: Yale University Press.

———. 1966. "Re-evaluation of the problems of complicated automata—Problems of hierarchy and evolution." In *Theory of self-reproducing automata,* edited and completed by Arthur W. Burks, 74–87. Urbana: University of Illinois Press.

Wegner, Peter. 1998. "Interactive foundations of computing." *Theoretical Computer Science* 192 (2): 315–51.

Weizenbaum, Joseph. 1976. *Computer power and human reason: From judgment to calculation.* San Francisco: W. H. Freeman.

Whitby, Blay. 1996. "Turing test: AI's biggest blind alley." In *Machines and thought: The legacy of Alan Turing*, edited by Peter J. R. Millican and Andy Clark, 53–62. Oxford: Clarendon Press.

Wiener, Norbert. 1948a. *Cybernetics, or control and communication in the animal and the machine.* Cambridge, MA: MIT Press.

———. 1948b. "Cybernetics." *Scientific American* 179 (September): 14–19.

Wilson, Robert A., and Lucia Foglia. 2017. "Embodied cognition." *Stanford Encyclopedia of Philosophy*, Spring Edition. Accessed November 29, 2018. https://plato.stanford.edu/archives/spr2017/entries/embodied-cognition/.

Winograd, Terry, and Fernando Flores. 1987. *Understanding computers and cognition: A new foundation for Design.* Boston: Addison-Wesley.

Wittgenstein, Ludwig. 1980. *Bemerkungen über die Philosophie der Psychologie.* Vol. 1, edited by Elizabeth [G. E. M.] Anscombe and Georg Hendrik von Wright. Oxford: Basil Blackwell.

———. 2009. *Philosophical investigations.* Translated by Elizabeth [G. E. M.] Anscombe, Peter Hacker, and Joachim Schulte. 4th rev. ed. Chichester: Wiley-Blackwell.

Zuboff, Shoshana. 1988. *In the age of the smart machine: The future of work and power.* New York: Basic Books.

Zúñiga, Gloria L. 2001. "Ontology: Its Transformation from philosophy to computer science." *Proceedings of the International Conference on Formal Ontology in Information Systems (FOIS'01)*, 187–97. New York: Association for Computing Machinery.

Zuse, Konrad. 1993. *The Computer—My Life.* Translated by Patricia McKenna and J. Andrew Ross. Berlin: Springer-Verlag.

CHAPTER ELEVEN

Rhetorical Antinomies and Radical Othering: Recent Reflections on Responses to an Old Paper Concerning Human–Animal Relations in Amazonia

Stephen Hugh-Jones

Ever since Philippe Descola's (1986) and Eduardo Viveiros de Castro's (1996) seminal contributions, human–animal relations among the Indigenous peoples of Amazonia have played a central role in what would later become known as anthropology's "ontological turn." For convenience, and sometimes for rhetorical or polemical effect, the Amerindians' different understandings of these relations are often summarized in terms of a stark contrast or radical othering between "us" and "them." In this vein, Viveiros de Castro (1996: 479) contrasts our cosmology's postulate of a physical continuity and metaphysical discontinuity with the Amerindians' perspectival cosmology of metaphysical continuity and physical discontinuity, a contrast that Descola (2005) recasts as one between our naturalism's common physicality versus different interiority and their animism's common interiority versus different physicality. Viveiros de Castro's (1996) article also quotes Descola's (1986: 120) aphorism that, for Amerindians "the common point of reference for all beings of nature is not humans as a species but rather humanity as a condition."

In 1995, before the "ontological turn" really got going and acquired a name, I was invited to write a paper for a conference on the subject of meat and meat consumption (Hugh-Jones 1996). The meeting, partly inspired by French meat producers' worries about the threat to their livelihood posed by the rise of Anglo-Saxon vegetarianism, was attended by a mixed group of anthropologists, farmers, representatives of regional cultural affairs, and members of the public. For me, this slightly unusual context posed a challenge.

On the one hand, I was keen to use my experiences among Barasana, Makuna, and other Tukanoan-speakers living along the Rio Pirá-Paraná in Colombia's Vaupés region to explore issues that would be interesting and relevant to people who reared animals for meat and also ate meat themselves. As people in close daily contact with animals, did they have misgivings about eating meat, especially meat from their own animals and, if so, how did they cope with this dilemma?

On the other hand, I was keen to distance myself from another, more popular kind of radical othering. I knew from previous experience that, however hard one may try to avoid this, in talking to lay audiences about Amerindians' different ways of acting and thinking, one runs the risks of reaffirming deep-seated prejudices about "primitive savages who still have a very long way to go before they reach our level of civilization." To avoid this pitfall, I decided to try the opposite tack. Instead of talking about obvious differences between French beef producers and Amazonian hunter-cultivators, I decided to explore some points of convergence between Euro-American and Amerindian attitudes and behavior regarding animals.

At the same time, this would give me an opportunity to explore some of the variations, contradictions, tensions, and layered complexity that are often glossed over in the contrasts between "us" Euro-Americans and "them" Amazonians that frequently crop up in anthropological discussions of human–animal relations. These contrasts represent the sharply delineated ontological tips of large, misshapen ethnographic icebergs. Lurking beneath these tips lie lumps of raw and often quite contradictory data that are the daily bread of anthropological field research. At this ethnographic level, most would recognize that, for Amerindians, it is not usually all animals that fall under the rubric of humanity as a condition and certainly not "all beings of nature."

Quoting my own work on the Barasana (Hugh-Jones 1996), Kaj Århem's work on the Makuna (1991, 1996), and Gerardo Reichel-Dolmatoff's work on the Desana (1971, 1976), Viveiros de Castro (1996: 471) notes that, in respect of perspectivism and cosmological transformism "the cosmologies of the Vaupés area are highly developed." Reichel-Dol- matoff's Desana and their Master of the Animals also play important roles in Descola's (2005) discussion of animist ontologies. This is right and proper for, in some contexts, Tukanoan-speakers are dyed-in-the-wool animists. They tell perspectival stories about an unsatisfactory marriage between a human man and a Star-Woman—she wakes up when he wants to sleep—and about a woman who visits her dead husband—what he sees as a cooking pot she sees as a coiled snake.[1] They do indeed talk about game animals as people who suffer predation by human-jaguars and who, as a result, are sometimes prone to seek vengeance. For this reason, before their meat can be eaten, a shaman must remove the weapons, body paints, and other dangerous substances that animals hide in their flesh, ready to injure anyone who eats it.

As these examples suggest, this animals-as-people talk typically happens in the contexts of shamanism, ritual, and mythology. In other contexts, I have heard plenty of other kinds of animal talk. Some of this talk concerns the identification, behavior, and habitats of different animal species, their evident cunning and intentionality, and the different strategies that hunters use to try to outsmart them. The knowledge evident in this talk is based on detailed, long-term observation combined with information transmitted across the generations. Some of this is required to hunt and fish effectively but much of it is simply picked up during these and other activities and serves no immediate purpose. Although it is not phrased in the same terms, much of this knowledge overlaps with our own ecology, ethology, and zoology and is readily communicable to visiting scientists. In days gone by, other animal talk concerned the prices outsiders would pay for jaguar and otter skins; today, it is more about the prices that both neighbors and outsiders will pay for fish and meat. Finally, as among ourselves, much animal talk concerns the behavior of pets, here the host of dogs and other domesticated forest animals and birds that typically hang around Amerindian houses.

These different kinds of animal talk also correspond to a whole gamut of intellectual and emotional states, including investigation and enquiry,

---

1. These two examples were chosen by *kumu* ("shaman") Ricardo Marín when asking if we outsiders had a word for this kind of thought. I told him that we call it "perspectivism." His question followed an earlier query about "metaphor "and "analogy."

curiosity, respect, admiration, aesthetic appreciation, fear, horror, amusement, and affection. They also correspond to different kinds of behavior. In different contexts I have seen both wild and domesticated animals treated sometimes with empathy, warmth, and care; sometimes with an unthinking, businesslike attitude much like that applied to various kinds of food and raw materials gathered in the forest; sometimes with pain inflicted intentionally in order to train dogs; and sometimes with outright torture—this last usually at the hands of young boys and often condemned by adults. This is a world of practical compromise and often inconsistent or contradictory ideas, attitudes, opinions, and behavior, one that is only rarely the subject of prolonged, systematic reflection. It would be hard to square such over-determined ideas and behavior with one single animist ontology.

This inconsistent world is not unlike that of my Welsh Marches sheep farmer neighbors, another population with close, daily contact with animals in their guises not just as pets, fellow workers, stock, merchandise, or prey but also as the denizens of school biology classes, children's books, and TV documentaries. These are rational businesspeople who employ techniques, chemicals, medicines, and machines derived from science. But they do not fully understand the scientific knowledge on which they depend, are not usually given to systematization, and find no problem with the anthropomorphism of wildlife documentaries or the perspectival stance of the books they read to their children at bedtime. It is likewise hard to square all this with a unitary naturalist ontology.

But ontologies, fully fledged, came later. The aim of my 1996 paper was not to agree or disagree with other anthropological approaches, but rather to situate these in a wider context and consider issues that these approaches had tended to ignore. With reference to Eric Ross (1978) on ecologically sound food taboos—the larger animals that are subject to most intense restriction are also the slowest to reproduce; Reichel-Dolmatoff (1971, 1976) on energy conservation—exchanges between hunters and the Master of Animals bear some resemblance to Western ideas of ecology and thermodynamics; and Descola (1993) on animism, I wrote (Hugh-Jones 1996: 131), "I do not intend to comment here on the merits of these arguments except to say that if European attitudes to animals and to the consumption of meat are complex phenomena which reflect considerations which are simultaneously practical, sociological, moral, philosophical and ethical, the same is also likely to be true in Amazonia."

With this in mind I sought to make four basic points:

1. There is some common ground between Western attitudes to killing and eating animals and those of some Amazonian peoples, especially of the Tukanoans of Northwest Amazonia and the Xinguanos of Central Brazil.
2. This common ground involves awareness that, because humans and animals share anatomical, physiological, cognitive, and other attributes in common, the boundary between them is not always clear. This can result in unease about taking animal life for the benefit of human life.
3. In some respects, the religious, cosmological, or philosophical sources of Western ideas of animals' proximity to human beings are very different from their Amerindian counterparts. In other respects, they appear to be quite similar and would seem to be grounded in everyday observation and experience.
4. A focus on religion, cosmology, or philosophy ("good reasons") risks not only exaggerating differences between "us" and "them" but also overlooking variations, inconsistencies and historical changes within and between Amerindian groups.

I tried to make clear that my arguments were intended to complement rather than replace other approaches and that I did not consider Amerindian and Western attitudes to animals and the natural world to be directly comparable in all respects. In addition, I never intended to suggest that Amerindians always sentimentalized their interactions with animals and always treated them kindly. No one who has lived with Amerindians could make such a claim! But I did make the mistake of referring to unease or misgivings about killing and eating animals as "bad conscience." At the time, when put in juxtaposition with the "good reasons" anthropological discussions gave in terms of ecology, religion, and cosmology, this tidy antinomy seemed to have the right rhetorical effect.

Over the years, my paper has elicited two quite critical reactions, an early one from Descola (1998) and a more recent one from Florent Kohler (2016), the one chiding me for straying too far from ontology, the other for sticking too close. I shall comment on the two critiques in reverse order.

Kohler writes about Amerindians living in the Uaçá river basin on the Brazil–French Guiana frontier. Although certain of these peoples' ideas and practices might seem to fall under the rubric of Descola's animist ontologies or Viveiros de Castro's perspectivism, Kohler is keen to distance himself from this line of thought.

Kohler first raises various problems regarding the status of animals as persons or social subjects. For Uaçá peoples, they are persons mainly to shamans and only in a space-time removed from the here and now, contexts that cannot be extrapolated to human–animal relations in the context of ordinary people's quotidian hunting and fishing. Furthermore, insofar as animals might be considered to share human subjectivity and point of view, far from engendering any sympathy, such shared attributes are seen to pose a threat.

Second, Kohler argues that Uaçá peoples' statements about animals as persons are to be understood not as any confusion or ontological continuity between human beings and animals but rather as metaphorical statements in which social relations with distant, threatening others are being transposed to the level of ontology. Statements about "animals as people" should therefore be understood to mean their opposite, namely that "those foreigners are animals."

Finally, Kohler takes myself and others to task for our one-sided attention to ontology or cosmology, ritual, and shamanism. This leads us to neglect the everyday world of hunting and fishing where animals figure not as subjects but rather as quasi-objects. To underline this contrast, Kohler describes what happened when he protested about a man who was tying up a caiman in a manner guaranteed to cause it acute pain. The man replied, "But that's food! It's *not* a person!" Furthermore, this neglect of the everyday has serious consequences. Because anthropologists are so attached to ontological abstractions and systems of meaning and ecologists so concerned with species and populations, neither has anything to say about Amerindians' callous and brutal treatment of animals and both remain blind to the wholesale slaughter of animals happening throughout Amazonia. This neglect has moral implications but to call it cruelty would be ethnocentric, for cruelty implies thought in the form of a system of representations and values. Habitual, brutal behavior of this kind is literally thought-less. For Kohler, as far as the study of real animals in a nonritual context and concern for their well-being are concerned, ontology is a dead end.

I think that here and elsewhere, and like Descola below, Kohler may have been led astray by my ill-judged use of the phrase "bad conscience." This was intended as a shorthand to refer to an unease or malaise about taking animal life for the benefit of human life that I believed—and still believe—to be shared between Euro-Americans and Amerindians. But I never intended "bad conscience" to imply "good treatment" or to suggest that ideas about the personhood of some animals in ritual contexts had any necessary connection with how animals were treated in everyday practice. Barasana hunters do indeed sometimes mistreat animals in a careless or intentionally brutal way—I was amiss in not having made this clearer.

Kohler's position is closer to my own when he observes that the Uaçá peoples' cold-blooded treatment of animals is most evident in the case of reptiles, creatures whose own cold blood, aquatic habitat, and lack of mammalian features make them relatively distant from human beings and closer to fish. He notes (2016: 142) that this is one example of a near-universal human tendency to rank living creatures along a great chain of being. Compared with their treatment of most mammals and birds, Tukanoans also treat reptiles and fish in a relatively careless manner, one aspect of what I called their "hierarchy of foods" (Hugh-Jones 1996: 128). This hierarchy is based on relatively common-sense principles—vegetable versus animal and, if animal, its size, amount of blood, diet, manner of capture, and manner of cooking—criteria that have some obvious parallels in European thinking. However, while the chain of being to which these principles relate may be common to most of humanity, they still play out in specific cultural contexts. In the Tukanoan case, they come all-of-a-piece with shamanic considerations. Thus, like Uaçá peoples and for the same reasons, Tukanoans put caimans on the side of fish. But the vulture-like scavenging habits of these reptiles produce ambivalent attitudes to them as creatures and mean that their meat requires special shamanic treatment, different from that for other "normal" fish, before it can be eaten. A more general malaise about killing larger animals for food also means that, with each mammal having an equivalent in the domain of cultivated plants, shamanic spells can be used to transform meat down the food hierarchy and into fruit or vegetable (Hugh-Jones 1996: 129–30). Considerations such as these also enter into how animals are treated. For this reason, as far as Tukanoan ethnography is concerned, like Descola's animism and naturalism (see below), I find Kohler's (2016: 137) distinction between the conceptual animals of shamanic ontology and the real animals that are killed in habitual practices related to subsistence or commerce hard to sustain.

In addition to his more general point about anthropologists' neglect of the cruelty involved in everyday habitual practice, Kohler (2016: 140) cites the Uaçá peoples' record of failed conservation initiatives to take issue with my (1996: 140–41) suggestion that when Makuna shamans claim that their ritual dances ensure the reproduction of animals and fish, this and other similar notions have parallels with European ideas about stewardship of nature and about humans and animals existing in a single moral universe. I can only respond by saying that Janet Chernela's (1989) work on Kotiria (Wanano) protection of fish-breeding sites along river margins, Clara van der Hammen's (1992) study of "world management" by Yukuna shamans, and the results of collaborative research involving ecologically oriented NGOs and several Tukanoan and Arawakan speaking groups (Cabalzar 2005, 2010, 2016) all suggest that, for NW Amazonian populations, there is some good evidence that restrictions on hunting or fishing around sacred sites inhabited and controlled by spirit Owners can create refuge areas where fish and animals are able to reproduce free from the pressure of predation.

But I would not wish to suggest that sacred sites were somehow invented with this result in mind. This would be to repeat Ross's (1978) problematic use of an imputed effect of food taboos to explain their existence. NW Amazonian sacred sites are typically salient features in the landscape but this salience can take many forms. Sometimes it has to do with concentrations of feeding or breeding animals but mythology, shamanism, and ritual are always involved. In other instances, with the salience of a particular sacred site having to do with rocks that resemble people, animals, or human artifacts or the danger of a waterfall that sounds like thunder, it would be hard to discern any hint of what might look like "practical reason." As with the hierarchy of foods mentioned above, here too it is hard to keep separate what Kohler (2016: 137) calls the "conceptual" animals of shamanic ontology and the "real" animals and fish that are killed in habitual practices related to subsistence or commerce.

However, such counterexamples are really beside the point for, given differences not just in ecology, social organization, ritual practice, and cosmology but also in involvement with the outside world, I would not expect the Tukanoans' attempts at resource management to resemble, or have the same outcome, as those of the peoples of the Uaçá. Indeed, my argument concerning some measure of consistency between peoples' attitudes to killing animals for meat, their attitudes toward killing other people, and features of their overall social organization was intended as part of a more general argument concerning a diversity of ideas and practices within and between different Amerindian groups.

In sum, whereas Kohler draws a contrast between ontology—animals as subjects—and what we might call "practical un-reason"—animals treated thoughtlessly in the manner of objects—and takes me to task for a one-sided adherence to the former, I had sought to stress the complex, contradictory nature of human–animal relations, to emphasize a plurality of ideas and the relevance of context, and to nuance ecological or cosmological arguments concerning the personhood of animals and ambivalence about eating their flesh by suggesting that another source of such ideas about might lie in everyday encounters with these animals in their guise as four-limbed, warm-blooded, sentient, and intentional beings like ourselves.

If Kohler still finds that I am too closely wedded to a ritualistic or ontological approach, in Descola's view I stray too far from ontology. Descola accuses me of deriving attitudes and behavior regarding animals from individual moral concerns determined by an imputed universal "bad conscience," a notion that implies a specifically Western ethical framework of recent origin and one characterized by ideas not shared by Amerindians. Such an exercise would render any properly anthropological analysis impossible for it cannot account for the systemic, structural character of human–animal relations where attitudes and behavior are shared by members of the same group and vary systematically from one group to another in parallel with variations in attitudes and behavior toward other human beings (Descola 1998: 32–33, 35).

"Structure or sentiment," the title of Descola's (1998) paper, evokes Rodney Needham's (1962) *Structure and Sentiment*, a rebuttal of George Homans and David Schneider's (1955) critique of Claude Lévi-Strauss's (1949) theory of prescriptive marriage. Needham takes Homans and Schneider to task for reducing structural relations of affinity to the final cause of sentiments.[2] Descola's allusion to Needham suggests that he has misunderstood what I had to say, for I never intended to suggest that a "bad conscience" was the final cause behind what I too tried to treat as coherent, socially grounded cultural patterns. Interestingly enough, Viveiros de Castro (1996: 471) cites my paper as exemplifying perspectivism and, in it, I stated my general agreement with Descola's argument

---

2. Their argument suggests that, rather than being an expression of Lévi-Strauss' structural principle of prescriptive marriage, the statistical preponderance of matrilateral cross-cousin marriage found in some societies is one outcome of the avunculate. Put simply, this would be that, because they have special affective relations with their mothers and their brothers, men tend to visit these brothers and end up marrying their mother's brother's daughters, the girl next door.

concerning structural homologies between human-human and human–animal relations and its specific application to the contrasting Jivaroan and Tukanoan cases, and I went on to suggest the possible relevance of this to the Kalapalo's abandonment of meat-eating (Hugh-Jones 1996: 144–45). Although rhetorical antinomies such as my own "good reasons versus bad conscience" or Descola's "humans as species versus humanity as condition" can serve as useful shorthands, they can also mislead. When I wrote my paper, I was already aware that "bad conscience" risked introducing the distracting cultural baggage of Western ethics that Descola mentions. This is why I wrote (1996: 146): "'Bad conscience' evokes a morality of sin and guilt which is not readily transposed to an Amazonian context; perhaps Erikson's (1987: 105) more neutral 'conceptual malaise' would be more appropriate."

Descola (1998: 31, 35) comes closer to what I had in mind when he recognizes that a conceptual malaise concerning the eating of animal flesh could be linked with cognitive psychological studies of the construction of living-kind categories in infancy. Such living-kind categories are highly relevant to Amerindian and Euro-American categorizations of animals, both as species and as food. But if living-kind categories are part of a basic, universal human cognitive apparatus, they must also be shared across the different animist and naturalist ontologies that separate "them" from "us." Although Descola does not elaborate on this further, his (1986: 124) suggestion that the human tendency to anthropomorphize animals is as much a matter of "popular knowledge" ("*science populaire*" in the French original) as mythic thought also goes along similar lines to my own. This popular knowledge or empirical science comes to the fore in the practical contexts of hunting, fishing, and gardening and can generate fruitful collaborative research with professional scientists.[3] Nonetheless, hunting, fishing, and gardening still involve much ritual and shamanism and, as Lévi-Strauss (1966) suggested, this same popular science provides the basis of the concrete logic apparent in shamanic and mythological contexts where animist ideas are dominant.

I would take this further. I suggest that this conceptual malaise stems from a more general awareness of various morphological, anatomical, physiological, cognitive, and behavioral characteristics that are shared between humans and animals. This recognition of trans-specific

3. Cabalzar (2005), containing the results of research on upper Rio Negro fish by Brazilian ichthyologist Flávio Lima and Tukano and Tuyuka fishermen, is a case in point.

similarity-with-difference between human beings and higher mammals is probably universal even though its intellectual, behavioral, emotional, and ethical consequences will vary with respect to different cultural, individual, and situational contexts. However, while characteristics such as anatomy or physiology that are recognized as shared between humans and animals fall on the side of Descola's "physicality," cognition (including intelligence, intentionality, etc.) falls on the side of "interiority." That this recognition is common to both Euro-Americans and Amerindians becomes obscured when, according to Descola, "we" and "they" are opposed in terms of continuity/discontinuity along these same axes of "physicality" and "interiority."

Finally, it should be noted that awareness of these same, shared characteristics can also result in inconsistent or contradictory outcomes. The bullfight aficionado who sees a bull tormented before being put to death in the *corrida* probably finds no conflict between his enjoyment of this spectacle and the sentimental pleasure he derives from playing with his cherished pet dog. I suggest that neither activity would have much point if this man were unable to perceive some measure of similarity between himself and the animal concerned.

Given these clarifications, the key issue turns out not to be one of sentiments but rather one of ontologies. As explained above, while acknowledging differences between "us" and "them," my paper took the opposite tack and sought to explore common ground. This urge to highlight some similarities between "us" and "them" to a French audience concerned with eating meat sprang from two kinds of personal experience. On the one hand, that of interacting with Amerindians on a daily basis where, for much of the time, the animals-as-people talk went on alongside other kinds of animal talk, some of it already more familiar to me in my home context. On the other hand, that of talking to people at home who took my efforts to render strange Amazonians familiar as merely confirming what they thought they already knew—just how different those "primitive people" really are.

Against this, Descola (1998: 34) says that we should not be afraid of making Amerindians seem very different from ourselves—for that is indeed what they are. Although we may project human characteristics such as sensitivity, altruism, or maternal love onto animals, any similarity between this Western personification of animals and Amerindian animism is purely superficial because our anthropocentric attitudes are part and parcel of a naturalistic ontology that allocates humans and nonhumans to the two discrete and different domains of "culture" and "nature."

By contrast, in Amerindian cosmologies, "animals and to a lesser degree plants are perceived as social subjects possessed of institutions and behaviors perfectly symmetrical with those of men. For us the referent is man as species; for them it is humanity as a condition" (Descola 1998: 27, 29).

Descola intends his ontologies to be ideal-type models derived, in a classic structuralist manner, from an exhaustive examination of the logically possibly permutations of a set of relations, in this case a four-fold grid between physicality ("material processes"), interiority ("mental states"), identification, and difference (see Descola 2005: 323). Physicality and interiority are abstract, generic labels for the kind of phenomena that ethnographers deal with—such as particular cultural ideas about (what we call) the "bodies" and "souls" of humans and animals. But these models are not to be understood as descriptions of any particular ethnographic reality, nor are they intended as a method for classifying whole societies in terms of one or another isolated "world view" (Descola 2010: 338). Their purpose is heuristic, to allow the anthropologist to see the wood from the trees, to penetrate through the fog of ethnographic detail, to give some precision to familiar intuitions about differences in cultural style in different parts of the world, and to provide answers to questions such as "What is it about Amazonian societies and cultures that make them so different from those of Africa?" or "Why don't we find sacrifice or domesticated animals in Indigenous Amazonia?"; the kind of wide-ranging, comparative questions that much of contemporary anthropology seems to have abandoned.

This means that when people of society X are described as "animist" or as "having an animist ontology," this is to be understood not as suggesting that they are animist at all times, in every respect and to the exclusion of anything else but rather as a convenient shorthand for which mode of identification is dominant and most evident in that society's key institutions, practices, and ideas. In practice, Descola tells us, the most common situation is one of hybridity "where (one) mode of identification will slightly dominate over another, resulting in a variety of complex combinations." To illustrate such hybridity, Descola (2010: 338–39) raises the relatively trivial case of his readers—most probably naturalists—behaving occasionally as animists when talking to their dog or cat as if they could thus establish some sort of intersubjective relation with their pet.

But let us take a look at a rather more complex example, that of my Welsh sheep-farming neighbors who, day after day, rely on long-term and very effective intersubjective relations with their border collie dogs in order to herd their sheep, a situation not unlike Amazonians out hunting with their dogs. Here the synergetic farmer-dog pair would appear to take the point of view of the sheep, acting on assumptions about the interiority of these sheep in order to anticipate their movements and thus to outwit them. If situations such as these seem to fall outside naturalism, to describe this synergy between farmer and sheepdog as animism on a par with its Amazonian counterparts would seem to be stretching the model much too far. It is both quite similar to, and also has some of its roots in, the hunting that Descola (2010: 335) identifies as an experiential basis of animism. But it is not animism itself because it is not discursively systematized in myth or ritual. My farmer neighbors would certainly not suppose that their dogs have institutions and behaviors that are perfectly symmetrical with their own. But I am far from convinced that my Amazonian Barasana neighbors would make such an assumption at all times and in all contexts either. Yet, against the more usual situation of hybridity, Descola (2010: 339) suggests that Amazonia stands out as a region that evidences animism as a mode of identification in a very pure form. This may be true of the Achuar but not I think of Tukanoans. Amazonia is a large region and cultural diversity was a central theme of my paper.

In some contexts, Barasana certainly do talk and act in the classic mode of Amazonian animism. This is what Descola has in mind in discussing Tukanoan relations with the Master of Animals as an example of exchange, itself one of his three ways of relating to animal others within animist ontologies. In this context, mythology has it that humanity is the original default "spirit" condition of all sentient beings with today's animals, in their mundane, bodily form, the result of their subsequent fall from grace. But in the context of Tukanoan initiation rituals and in their stories of origin associated with patriliny, hierarchy, and ancestors, human–animal relations figure in a rather different guise.

To begin with, in these origin stories, animals play second fiddle to personified objects, something that already sets the Tukanoans apart from the Amazonian animist or perspectival norm (see Hugh-Jones 2009). Second, instead of a fall from grace, animality in the form of fish here figures as an original condition from which true human beings became progressively differentiated. On a journey of transformation, human beings became separated off from "fish people" (*wai masa*), a residual category of dangerous spirit beings who manifest themselves in bodily form as both fish and animals and who are united in a vengeful resentment of human beings for having left them behind.

In one sense, any resemblance between this Amerindian version of evolution and that of Western naturalism is entirely superficial, precisely because each is embedded within different overarching sets of knowledge and assumptions. But, in another sense, there is some overlap. While the Tukanoans' origin story is not wholly or simply about observation and experience of mundane contexts, it clearly draws upon knowledge derived from them. The story is partly about sex and gestation and here it builds on knowledge that conception involves watery fluids, that birth involves a passage from a watery ("riverine"), uterine state to a dry, terrestrial existence, and that, compared to human beings, fish and animals are both "lower" forms of existence. The story is also about naming, initiation, and the passage from infancy to adulthood. Here it builds on the knowledge that, to different degrees, fish, reptiles, and mammals share attributes in common and fit into some kind of evolutionary sequence—a literal gloss for *wai bükü*, the generic Barasana term for "game animal" would be "mature fish." This sequence corresponds to Kohler's "chain of being" or to my "hierarchy of foods" mentioned above.

The Tukanoans' origin story is one of several contexts in which, instead of humanity as a common condition, it is precisely the differences between humans and animals that are being stressed. Another such context is the habitual situation of hunting that Kohler has in mind. Here and on most occasions, even the jaguars that in other contexts are considered to be on a par with human beings are simply jaguars—especially when it comes to selling their skins. But when jaguars behave in an unexpected manner, some people, especially shamans, may assert that these jaguars are really other shamans in animal form. The shaman's authority to make pronouncements of this kind is underscored by a formulaic phrasing typically used to indicate a different, shamanic point of view: "You see it as X but a shaman would see it as Y." It follows from this that assertions about animals as people typically refer to shaman-others or imply some claim to shamanic expertise on the speaker's behalf. But such talk can also go in a reverse, "naturalistic" direction. I have witnessed occasions on which one shaman has said of another: "He claimed that that animal was a person but he was lying. Actually, it was just an animal."

Finally, there are situations where what might look like a shamanic animals-as-people statement turns out to be a case of straightforward anthropomorphism. Talking of two macaws, a man once said to me, "he's off back home with his wife." It was clear from the context that I was being told about macaw behavior: the man knew that macaws are monogamous and knew where the pair in question had their nest.

These examples—all instances where it is not humanity as a condition but rather man and animals as species that is being foregrounded—are offered in order to qualify the notion of a "pure" Amazonian form of animism—at least as it might apply in NW Amazonia. But to describe such instances as "naturalism," to describe sheep farmers who talk to their working dogs as cases of "animism," or to refer to either as cases of "hybridity" does not seem helpful. So much is being left aside that the model becomes overstretched and what remains is a systematization that is largely in the head of the observer.

My 1996 paper was written before the full flowering of anthropology's ontological turn. Although I nowhere referred to "ontology," Kohler is correct in identifying parts of my argument as ontological in tone. I based my argument on my experience among people who, in some contexts, are unquestionably animist or perspectivist in outlook. But the spirit of the paper was to explore diversity in Amazonia and to use ethnography to go against the grain of what I referred to as "a monolithic opposition between Western culture and tribal peoples" (Hugh-Jones 1996: 147) by seeking out common ground instead. Much of this common ground lies in the space between Kohler's "habitual practice" and the "ontology" to which it is opposed. With hindsight, I can see that using "bad conscience" as shorthand to characterize elements of this common ground simply muddied the waters. Let us stick with "conceptual malaise." Descola uses another binary contrast, this time between "us" or man as species and "them" or humanity as condition to critique a paper that sought to go beyond such oppositions. This contrast risks a confusion between the details of ethnography and the comparative heuristics of ontology, a confusion between trees and wood. My concern was ethnography and not with ontology in this sense.

References

Århem, Kaj. 1991. "Ecosofía Makuna." In *La selva humanizada: Ecología alternativa en el trópico húmedo colombiano*, edited by François Correa, 109–26. Bogotá: Instituto Colombiano de Antropología.

———. 1996. "The cosmic food web: Human-nature relatedness in the northwest Amazon." In *Nature and society: Anthropological perspectives,* edited by Philippe Descola and Gisli Palsson, 185–204. London: Routledge.

Cabalzar, Aloisio, ed. 2005. *Peixe e gente no alto rio Tiquié: Conhecimentos tukano e tuyuka, ictiologia, etnologia.* São Paulo: Instituto Socioambiental.

———. 2010. *Manejo do mundo: Conhecimentos e práticas dos povos indígenas do rio Negro: noroeste amazônico.* São Paulo: Instituto Socioambiental e São Gabriel da Cachoeira, Federação das Organizações Indígenas do Rio Negro.

———. 2016. *Ciclos Anuais no Rio Tiquié: Pesquisas colaborativos e manejo ambiental no Noroeste amazônico.* São Paulo: Instituto Socioambiental e São Gabriel da Cachoeira, Federação das Organizações Indígenas do Rio Negro.

Chernela, Janet. 1989. "Managing rivers of hunger: The importance of the blackwater river margin." In *Resource management in Amazonia: Indigenous and folk strategies,* edited by William Balée and Darrel Posey, 238–48. New York: New York Botanical Garden.

Descola, Philippe. 1986. *La nature domestique: Symbolisme et praxis dans l'écologie des Achuar.* Paris: Éditions de la Maison des Sciences de l'Homme.

———. 1993. "Societies of nature and the nature of society." In *Conceptualizing society,* edited by Adam Kuper, 107–26. London: Routledge.

———. 1998. "Estrutura ou sentimento: A relação com o animal na Amazônia" *Mana: Estudos de Antropologia Social* 4 (1): 23–45.

———. 2005. *Par-delà nature et culture.* Paris: Gallimard.

———. 2010. "Cognition, perception and worlding." *Interdisciplinary Science Reviews* 35 (3–4): 3–4, 334–40.

Erikson, Philippe. 1987. "De l'apprivoisement à l'approvisionnement: Chasse, alliance et familiarisation en Amazonie indigène." *Techniques et Culture* 9: 105–40.

van der Hammen, Clara. 1992. *El manejo del mundo: Naturaleza y sociedad entre los Yukuna de la Amazonia colombiana.* Bogotá: Tropenbos.

Homans, George C., and David M. Schneider, 1955. *Marriage, authority and final causes: A study of unilateral cross-cousin marriage.* Glencoe, IL: Free Press.

Hugh-Jones, Stephen. 1996. "Bonnes raisons ou mauvaise conscience? De l'ambivalence de certains Amazoniens envers la consommation de viande." *Terrain* 26 (March): 123–48.

———. 2009. "The fabricated body: objects and ancestors in NW Amazonia." In *The occult life of things: Native Amazonian theories of materiality and personhood*, edited by Fernando Santos-Granero, 33–59. Tucson: University of Arizona Press.

Kohler, Florent. 2016. "'Bon à manger': Réflexion sur la cruauté non rituelle envers les reptiles dans l'Uaçá, bassin de l'Oyapock, Brésil." In *Trophées: Études ethnologiques, indigénistes et amazonistes offerts à Patrick Menget*, vol. 1, edited by Philippe Erikson, 127–46. Paris: Société d'ethnologie.

Lévi-Strauss, Claude. 1949. *Les structures élémentaires de la parenté*. Paris: Presses Universitaires de France.

———. 1966. *The savage mind*. London: Weidenfeld and Nicolson.

Needham, Rodney. 1962. *Structure and sentiment: A test case in social anthropology*. Chicago: University of Chicago Press.

Reichel-Dolmatoff, Gerardo. 1971. *Amazonian cosmos: The sexual and religious symbolism of the Tukanoan Indians*. Chicago: Chicago University Press.

———. 1976. "Cosmology as ecological analysis: A view from the forest." *Man* 11 (3): 307–18.

Ross, Eric. 1978. "Food taboos, diet, and hunting strategy: The adaptation to animals in Amazon cultural ecology." *Current Anthropology* 19 (1): 1–36.

Viveiros de Castro, Eduardo. 1996. "Cosmological deixis and Amerindian perspectivism." *Journal of the Royal Anthropological Institute* 4 (3): 469–88.

CHAPTER TWELVE

Turning to Ontology in Studies of Distant Sciences

Nicholas Jardine

Until quite recently I was inclined to be dismissive of the so-called "ontological turn" currently sweeping into science and technology studies (STS) from anthropology. My supercilious attitude sprang in part from incomprehension faced with its pervasive jargon—"obviation," "dividuals," "infrastructural fractals," et cetera—and with such wondrous pronouncements as "ontology, as far as anthropology in our understanding is concerned, is the comparative, ethnographically-grounded transcendental deduction of Being (the oxymoron is deliberate) as that which differs from itself (ditto)" (Holbraad, Pederson, and Viveiros de Castro 2014: 1). I was baffled also by passages that appeared to imply that anthropologists, having "gone native," should (figuratively) stay out there rather than returning in order to communicate their findings in terms comprehensible to us. As for aspects of the ontological turn that I felt able to grasp, it seemed to me that it brought little real innovation to our field of STS. Its insistence that in interpreting others we should set aside our own "worlds" in order to immerse ourselves in theirs has a history in theory of interpretation going back at least to the eighteenth century (see Szondi 1995; Venuti 1995). Its "ecological" approach, focusing on the embodiment of persons in their environments and on their prereflective engagements and attunements with things, traces back to the works of, among others, Alfred North Whitehead (2011), Martin

Heidegger (1999, based on lectures in 1923), Jakob von Uexküll (1926), and James J. Gibson (1979). Further, its more specific recommendations seemed to me (wrongly as I now believe) to have been already accomplished through earlier "turns" in STS: its focus on practice rather than theory, and on interplay with tools and instruments, being anticipated by the "practical" and "material" turns of the 1970s and 1980s; and its recognition of the "hybrid" agency of complex alliances of humans and nonhumans being central to actor network theory (ANT) from its outset in the early 1980s.[1]

Crucial for my eventual grasp and present appreciative view of the ontological turn was my reading of Annemarie Mol's *The Body Multiple*, a work whose case studies of clinical, surgical, and pathological "enactments" of an illness are accompanied by a subtext spelling out central theoretical and practical tenets of the ontological turn (Mol 2002).[2] Guided by Mol, and helped also by Anna Lowenhaupt Tsing's *The Mushroom at the End of the World* (Tsing 2015), I was able on second reading to come to grips with works of such avatars of the turn as Marilyn Strathern (1988, 2004), Tim Ingold (2000), Eduardo Viveiros de Castro (2009), and Philippe Descola ([2005] 2013). So, as a prelude to my observations on the ontological turn as manifest in contributions to *Science in the Forest, Science in the Past*, let me run through some of the main points raised by Mol and Tsing.

In the opening chapter of *The Body Multiple*, Mol declares the general principle of her ontological approach: "It is possible to refrain from understanding objects as the central points of focus of different people's perspectives. It is possible to understand them instead as things manipulated in practices. If we do this—if instead of bracketing the practices we foreground them—this has far-reaching effects. Reality multiplies" (Moll 2002: 4). The following chapters explore the multiple realizations of an illness/disease, atherosclerosis, within a single hospital in different settings: clinical, pathological, and surgical. It is shown in detail how complex are the interactions of persons, bodies, body parts, instruments, reports, et cetera, in the processes that realize atherosclerosis in these

---

1. On the practice and material turns, see Law (2010) and Soler et al. (2014), and on ANT, see Callon (1986) and Latour (1987).

2. I am indebted to Jennifer Bangham for alerting me to Mol's book. On the connection of the ontological turn with study of the material practices of the sciences, I was helped also by Klein (2005), the articles in Woolgar and Lezaun (2013), and Boris Jardine (2017).

different settings, and how much of the knowledge involved is embedded in these practices. As Mol notes, this recognition of complex networks of persons and things is in line with actor network theory, but where ANT tends to focus on conflict and closure, Mol's emphasis is on "non-closure," on difference and mutual accommodation without conflict. Rather than establishing any general correlation of findings as symptoms of a disease, communications between the different settings are partial, involving context-dependent matches and mismatches. On the issue of scale, Mol follows other new ontologists in rejecting any straightforward spatiotemporal scaling. Though devoted to practices in a single Dutch hospital relating to a single (though multiply enacted) disease, the book cannot, Mol insists, be consigned to microhistory. For the materials, practices, and communications studied are connected to varying degrees with those elsewhere, some in adjacent rooms, some in other Dutch hospitals, some worldwide.

Likewise exemplary in its exploration of interactions of local and global worlds is Tsing's *The Mushroom at the End of the World.* The mushroom in question is matsutake, inhabitant of ruined northern hemisphere coniferous forest and a highly valued delicacy in Japan. The local worlds of forests, fungi, foragers, sellers, buyers, dealers, and consumers are presented in detail, and it is shown how these worlds are linked and sustained through international commerce in the mushroom. As with communication within Mol's Dutch hospital, so in these worldwide dealings Tsing shows how productive collaboration and coalition often involve not consensus but friction and compromise.[3]

Before considering how these aspects of the ontological turn as highlighted by the works of Mol and Tsing figure in the conference contributions on history and anthropology of mathematics, a moment's reflection on the general principle of the turn is needed. Proponents of the ontological turn are almost unanimous in breaking with the nature/culture division. In doing so they break with both strong realism, belief in the existence of a single coherent and exclusive truth about the world, and strong relativism, belief in the existence of many equally valid but radically different perspectives on the world (Paleček and Risjord 2012). Instead they are pluralists, prepared to recognize many worlds or many "dimensions" of reality. Precisely how such pluralism is to be spelled out

---

3. On friction, compromise, and collaboration, see also Tsing's (2005) study of the communities and organizations involved in exploitation and defense of Indonesian rainforests.

and whether it is tenable as a general philosophical position are conten-
tious issues. However, there are domains in which some such pluralism seems eminently plausible. The subject of Mol's book, the diagnosis,
treatment, and study of illness and disease, with its complex interactions
of scientific, practical, psychological, social, and ethical issues, is one such
domain. Mathematics is another. There are, indeed, those who maintain that unique numbers and measures exist entirely independently of
us, our languages, and our practices. But pluralism about numbers is a
well-established position; and it is relatively uncontentious to regard the
lengths embedded in the practices of Liberian tailors as different from
those grounded in the standard meter in Paris or the speed of light.[4] As
for the various fields of "science," the plausibility of pluralism depends
heavily on the ways in which science and its disciplines are defined. If,
as in Manuela Carneiro da Cunha's contribution, agricultural science is
taken to include all practices of plant cultivation and harvesting, then a
pluralist view of that science is in order. Similarly with chemistry, if that
science is taken to cover the skills involved in Indigenous practices of
pigment preparation. If, by contrast, science and its disciplines are more
strictly defined, radical ontological pluralism becomes deeply problematic. Consider the Wikipedia definition of chemistry: "Chemistry is the
scientific discipline involved with elements and compounds composed
of atoms, molecules and ions: their composition, structure, properties,
behavior and the changes they undergo during a reaction with other
substances."[5] On this definition, a modest pluralism with regard to current chemistry, as with many other strictly scientific disciplines, is appropriate (cf. Dupré 1993; Cartwright 1999; and Kellert, Longino, and
Waters 2006). Indeed, it has even been argued on historical and experimental grounds that phlogiston could be resuscitated (Chang 2012). But
the world of alchemical elixirs and the philosopher's stone has obviously
gone forever.

Guided by Mol and Tsing, let me now turn to mathematics in the
forest and the past. All of the relevant contributions move away from
classification of mathematics according to the mentalities, styles, symbolic forms, et cetera of different cultures. Rather than privileging explicit theoretical knowledge, they attend closely to the mathematics embedded in everyday transactions and material practices—that is, to what
in her contribution Strathern calls "invisible ontology." Further, there is

---

4. On Liberian tailors see Lave (1988); on standard lengths, see Zupko (1990).
5. https://en.wikipedia.org/wiki/Chemistry.

a general opposition to the overgeneral categories so prevalent in cultural anthropologies and histories. Thus, Karine Chemla and Serafina Cuomo resist the lumping together of "ancient Greek" or of "ancient Chinese" mathematics, and Agathe Keller contests the notion of a unified "Hindu/Indian" mathematics.

There is opposition also to stereotyping of persons. Aparecida Vilaça, for example, considers translations of our impersonal arithmetic into an adapted and extended Wari' language in which numbers are emotionally and morally loaded—for example, with 1, conveying loneliness, hunger and ineptitude. She also notes the "alternation" of personal identity involved as Wari' teachers, trained at an intercultural university, and their students switch between our register and their own. Keller comments on the long history of interaction between high and low Tamil mathematics. And Cuomo contests Marcus Asper's assignment of ancient Greek theoretical and practical mathematics to distinct cultures, emphasizing the mathematicians' capacity for "code-switching" between the theoretical and practical registers required in different settings (cf. Lave and Wenger 1991; Burke 2005; Asper 2009). In Strathern's terms (Strathern 1988), the Wari', Tamil, and ancient Greek mathematicians are not individuals but "dividuals," persons who assume different identities in different settings.

As recommended and put into practice in the works of Mol and Tsing, these studies focus on knowledge embedded in material and social practices: the uses of rods on calculating surfaces (Chemla); estimation of the fineness, purity, and value of gold (Keller); the establishment of kinship relations (Almeida). Again in line with the approaches of Mol and Tsing, though focused on particular mathematical practices, they cannot be classed as microhistories. For many of these practices are and/or were widely spread, either through direct communication or indirectly through their involvements in trade and commerce; and, as shown in the contributions of Keller and Chemla, certain of them have extensive histories of transmission and commentary.

The central methodological issues raised by contributions to the conference concern interpretation and translation. How, as historians, sociologists, and anthropologists are we to gain access to, and communicate to others, the sciences (or analogues thereof) of the forest and/or the past? As Lloyd, Keller, Strathern, and others make clear, the types of evidence—oral, textual, material—differ widely according to the type of science in question, whether it is past or present, and whether our encounter with it falls into a history of encounters or is a first. So the question arises whether, in the face of such diversity, there can be any general guidelines and criteria of adequacy for interpretation and translation.

Philosophers have proposed a range of general conditions of adequacy of interpretation under the headings of "principle of charity" and "principle of humanity" (Fitzgerald 2008). Donald Davidson, for example, has claimed that "charity is forced on us; whether we like it or not, if we want to understand others, we must count them right in most matters" (Davidson 1974: 19). Richard Grandy has proposed as a principle of humanity "the condition that the imputed pattern of relations among beliefs, desires, and the world be as similar to our own as possible" (Grandy 1973: 443). And David Wiggins has urged us in the name of humanity to so interpret others as to "diminish to the bare minimum the need for the interpreter to ascribe inexplicable error or inexplicable irrationality to them" (Wiggins 1988: 146). Sensible as they may sound, such principles are problematic on several counts.[6] They are applicable to forms of interpretation that engage primarily with systems of belief rather than actions and material practices; as such, they align with cultural rather than ontological approaches. They yield to what in his contribution Lloyd calls "the temptation to legislate," inviting us to impose on the beliefs of others what we know to be true, right, and rational. Thus they "familiarize," where what is often needed, at least at the outset of our interpretative enterprises, is "defamiliarization"—that is, recognition of the distance from ours of others' practices, norms, and beliefs. Further, they offer little in the way of practical guidance, Wiggins's principle of charity being generally unworkable, since negative existential claims are largely unverifiable, and the others being at a high level of generality and abstraction.

Building on Lloyd's contribution, let us turn to more down-to-earth guidelines, useful to ourselves as interpreters and to our audiences. As just remarked, there is the general requirement of preparedness to recognize radical otherness. Consequent on such recognition is the problem of access; and on this score the contributors' approaches to the sciences and mathematics of "others" are highly instructive. Keller and Mauro Almeida demonstrate ways in which our own nonstandard forms of mathematics can provide keys to understanding the mathematics of others. Chemla, Strathern, and Vilaça variously indicate ways in which indirect encounter, through engagement with the history of communications,

---

6. For a characteristically brisk and effective debunking, see Williamson (2007: chap. 8).

interactions, and appropriations, may facilitate access. And, taking "others" to include software systems, Alan Blackwell and Willard McCarty consider the grounds on which we understand and explain findings of artificial intelligences. In evidence also in several of the contributions are the opportunities provided by serendipitous matchings and analogies. Almeida, for example, notes the analogy between Tamil kinship structures and a form of non-Boolean algebra; and Lloyd points to the successful prediction of eclipses by the Babylonians as a way into their mathematics/astronomy.

Since the 1960s there has been ever more general recognition of the varying degrees of openness of texts to multiple interpretations and appropriations, and of the often-complex dependencies of texts on earlier ones.[7] Proponents of the ontological turn go along with this, opposing the identification of works with unique original texts and recognizing rather their multiplicity as clusters of texts, variously related to each other and to their readerships. The practical implications of this view are at once mild and onerous: mild in releasing us from obsessive quests for lost originals and unique best readings; onerous in requiring meticulous attention to textual reception and appropriation.[8] Close concern with reception and appropriation is evident in the contributions of Keller and Chemla, and an excellent example of its fruitfulness is Michela Malpangotto's study of the history of diagrammatic representation in versions of Theodosius's *Spherics* (Malpangotto 2010).

In accord with the ontological turn, the contributors show a marked move away from general schemes, systems of belief, epistemes, et cetera to close engagement with specific utterances, activities, and material practices. In this connection, let me conclude by offering an alternative to the principles of charity and humanity of interpretation. This is the principle that when we so interpret the actions, declarations, and material productions of others as to attribute to them success, whether practical or cognitive, it is incumbent upon us in cases where it is not obvious how it is achieved to provide explanation of that success.[9] Consider, the

---

7. The classic work on such openness is Eco ([1962] 1989).

8. For reflections on the philological and philosophical implications of pluralist conceptions of works, see Gurd (2005).

9. Compare with the passage in Cicero's *De divinatione*, in which Cicero's namesake Marcus, faced with Quintus's endorsement of testimonies of remarkable divinations, chides him for his failure to produce "arguments and reason" (Cicero 1927, II: 27).

following attributions: to Babylonians, successful prediction of eclipses; to Cambodian immigrants in Oregon, successful harvesting of matsutake mushrooms; to ancient Chinese mathematicians, successful calculations using rods, blocks, and diagrams. In all such cases, those who make the attributions should follow the example set by contributors to this volume in explaining how those remarkable feats were achieved.

As for the practice of translation this principle is consistent with "foreignizing," exploiting the flexibility of our language and the admissibility of neologisms, as opposed to "domesticating," confining the wording of translations to literal use of our current vocabulary.[10] For the domestication required by this principle lies not in translation, but in the explanatory exegesis of the passages translated. The focus on success rather than failure is pragmatically motivated; for, as the saying goes "truth is one, error many," and the possible explanations of failure are innumerable compared with those of success. Further, in achieving such explanations of success, whether of Babylonian successful prediction of eclipses or of Etruscan accurate estimation of field areas, we may greatly enrich our understanding, capturing the modes of existence that constitute others' worlds. Conversely, failure to find an explanation may cast doubt on the initial interpretation. To take just one example, the ethnobotanist Richard Evans Schultes spent many years in Amazonia failing to find a complete resolution of "Schultes's enigma," the supposed ability of inhabitants of Northwestern Amazonia to distinguish at a glance specimens of the same species of plant that produce different kinds and degrees of hallucination (Schultes 1986). This surely raises doubts about Schultes's interpretation of the relevant actions and utterances of the Amazonians he encountered.[11]

This demand for explanations is proposed not out of condescending charity toward those we interpret, but out of respect for those who hear and read our interpretations. For however deep the understanding we may achieve by "going native" in the forest or the past, we owe it to ourselves and our audiences to provide comprehensible interpretations.[12] So I call it "the principle of responsibility."

---

10. On the long traditions of foreignization and domestication in translation, see Venuti (1995).
11. My thanks to Merlin Sheldrake for introducing me to Schultes's ethnobotanical work.
12. For witty reflections on the problems of returning from the past to the present, see Hexter (1954).

Acknowledgments

My thanks for guidance to Jenny Bangham, Boris Jardine, Marina Frasca-Spada, Lydia Wilson, the participants in the conference and, especially, Aparecida Vilaça and Geoffrey Lloyd.

References

Asper, Marcus. 2009. "The two cultures of mathematics in ancient Greece." In *The Oxford handbook of the history of mathematics*, edited by Eleanor Robson and Jackie Stedall, 107–32. Oxford: Oxford University Press.

Burke, Peter. 2005. "Performing history: The importance of occasions." *Rethinking History: The Journal of Theory and Practice* 9 (1): 35–52.

Callon, Michel. 1986. "Some elements of a sociology of translation: Domestication of the scallops and the fishermen of St Brieuc Bay." In *Power, action and belief: A new sociology of knowledge?* edited by John Law, 196–223. London: Routledge and Kegan Paul.

Cartwright, Nancy. 1999. *The dappled world: A study of the boundaries of Science*. Cambridge: Cambridge University Press.

Chang, Hasok. 2012. *Is water H_2O? Evidence, reason and pluralism*. New York: Springer.

Cicero, Marcus Tullius. 1927. *De Senectute, De Amicitia, De Divinatione*. With an English translation by William Armistead Falconer. Cambridge, MA: Harvard University Press.

Davidson, Donald. 1974. "On the very idea of a conceptual scheme." *Proceedings and Addresses of the American Philosophical Association* 47: 5–20.

Descola, Philippe. (2005) 2013. *Beyond nature and culture*. Translated by Janet Lloyd. Chicago: University of Chicago Press.

Eco, Umberto. (1962) 1989. *The open work*. Translated by Anna Cancogni. Cambridge, MA: Harvard University Press.

Dupré, John. 1993. *The disorder of things: Metaphysical foundations of the disunity of science*. Cambridge, MA: Harvard University Press.

Fitzgerald, Gareth. 2008. "Charity and humanity in the philosophy of language." *Praxis* 1 (2): 17–29.

Gibson, James J. 1979. *The ecological approach to visual perception*. Boston: Houghton Mifflin.

Grandy, Richard. 1973. "Reference, meaning, and belief." *Journal of Philosophy* 70 (14): 439–52.

Gurd, Sean Alexander. 2005. *Iphigenias at Aulis: Textual multiplicity, radical philology.* Ithaca, NY: Cornell University Press.

Heidegger, Martin. 1999. *Ontology–The hermeneutics of facticity.* Translated by John van Buren. Bloomington: Indiana University Press.

Hexter, Jack H. 1954. "The historian and his day." *Political Science Quarterly* 69 (2): 219–33.

Holbraad, Martin, Morten Axel Pedersen, and Eduardo Viveiros de Castro. 2014. "The politics of ontology: Anthropological positions." Theorizing the Contemporary, *Fieldsights*, January 13. https://culanth.org/field-sights/the-politics-of-ontology-anthropological-positions.

Ingold, Tim. 2000. *The perception of the environment: Essays on livelihood, dwelling and skill.* London: Routledge.

Jardine, Boris. 2017. "State of the field: Paper tools." *Studies in History and Philosophy of Science* 64: 1–11.

Kellert, Stephen H., Helen E. Longino, and C. Kenneth Waters, eds. 2006. *Scientific pluralism.* Minneapolis: University of Minnesota Press.

Klein, Ursula. 2005. "Shifting ontologies, changing classifications: Plant materials from 1700 to 1830." *Studies in History and Philosophy of Science* 36 (2): 261–329.

Latour, Bruno. 1987. *Science in action: How to follow scientists and engineers through society.* Cambridge, MA: Harvard University Press.

Lave, Jean. 1988. *Cognition in practice: Mind, mathematics and culture in everyday life.* Cambridge: Cambridge University Press.

Lave, Jean, and Etienne Wenger. 1991. *Situated learning: Legitimate peripheral participation.* Cambridge: Cambridge University Press.

Law, John. 2010. "The materials of STS." In *The Oxford handbook of material culture studies,* edited by Dan Hicks and Mary C. Beaudry, 171–86. Oxford: Oxford University Press.

Malpangotto, Michela. 2010. "Graphical choices and geometrical thought in the transmission of Theodosius' *Spherics* from antiquity to the renaissance." *Archive for History of Exact Sciences* 64: 75–112.

Mol, Annemarie. 2002. *The body multiple: Ontology in medical practice.* Durham, NC: Duke University Press.

Paleček, Martin, and Mark Risjord. 2012. "Relativism and the ontological turn within anthropology." *Philosophy of the Social Sciences* 43 (1): 3–23.

Schultes, Richard Evans. 1986. "Recognition of variability in wild plants by Indians of the Northwest Amazon." *Journal of Ethnobotany* 6 (2): 229–38.

Soler, Léna, Sjoerd Zwart, Michael Lynch, and Vincent Israel-Jost, eds. 2014. *Science after the practice turn in the philosophy, history, and social studies of Science*. London: Routledge.

Strathern, Marilyn. 1988. *The gender of the gift: Problems with women and problems with society in Melanesia*. Berkeley: University of California Press.

———. 2004. *Partial connections*. Rev. ed. Walnut Creek, CA: Altamira Press.

Szondi, Peter. 1995. *Introduction to literary hermeneutics*. Translated by Martha Woodmansee. Cambridge: Cambridge University Press.

Tsing, Anna Lowenhaupt. 2005. *Friction: An ethnography of global connection*. Princeton, NJ: Princeton University Press.

———. 2015. *The mushroom at the end of the world: On the possibility of life in capitalist ruins*. Princeton, NJ: Princeton University Press.

Uexküll, Jakob von. 1926. *Theoretical biology*. Translated by Doris L. Mackinnon. London: Kegan Paul.

Venuti, Lawrence. 1995. *The translator's invisibility: A history of translation*. London: Routledge.

Viveiros de Castro, Eduardo. 2009. *Cannibal metaphysics*. Translated by Peter Skafish. Minneapolis: University of Minnesota Press.

Whitehead, Alfred North. 2011. *Science and the modern world*. Cambridge: Cambridge University Press.

Wiggins, David. 1988. "Truth, invention, and the meaning of life." In *Essays on moral realism*, edited by Geoffrey Sayre-McCord, 127–65. Ithaca, NY: Cornell University Press.

Williamson, Timothy. 2007. *The philosophy of philosophy*. Oxford: Blackwell.

Woolgar, Stephen, and Javier Lezaun, eds. 2013. "A turn to ontology in science and technology studies." Special issue, *Social Studies of Science* 43 (3).

Zupko, Ronald Edward. 1990. *Revolution in measurement: Western European weights and measures since the age of science*. Philadelphia: American Philosophical Society.

CHAPTER THIRTEEN

Epilogue: The Way Ahead

Geoffrey E. R. Lloyd and Aparecida Vilaça

The contributions to this volume range over a vast variety of topics. To some readers this may seem somewhat bewildering, but we consider it to be one of its great strengths, for our explorations are limited neither in time nor space nor intellectual discipline. The topics in question relate to many different kinds of practices, knowledge systems, interactions, issues of understanding and misunderstanding, whether between different language communities or within a single one, all separated in time or place or both. However, one obvious consequence of our wide-ranging discussions is that there can be no question of trying to draw up a neat balance sheet of concrete conclusions. Rather, it is more useful to highlight certain recurrent themes that can yield some guidelines for future work.

Each study exemplifies one or another mode of the problem of making sense of what is often represented as the *radically other*. All raise, to a greater or lesser degree, the question of the evidence available to us, the source material we are dealing with, with all of its limitations and possible biases, exhibiting the risk of prejudicing from the outset any interpretation we might propose. Even more fundamentally we have to question the very conceptual framework in which we conduct our inquiries. Given that a totally neutral framework is an impossibility, we have to probe the presuppositions we bring to the task with particular determination, especially when, as so often, these reflect typical preoccupations of Western modernity or even postmodernity. Such a critical examination of some fashionable current assumptions—concerning both ontology and science in particular—is, indeed, we would like to claim, one of the achievements of our project.

Let us focus here on three recurrent questions of special importance: (1) the issue of the diversity of ontologies; (2) the problems of translation and mutual intelligibility; and (3) the political ramifications of the issues that our studies raise.

(1) It soon became abundantly evident in our discussions and explorations that however fashionable the idea of ontologies has recently become in social anthropology and in science and technology studies, quite what that term implies is far from clear. Some contributions underline the difficulty of assigning a single coherent ontology to any given group, and how indeed is any relevant "group" to be defined (Cuomo)? Are ontologies a matter of certain beliefs or of certain practices or of both, where problems of scale are deeply implicated (Strathern)? Where ontology corresponds to nothing in the actors' own explicit categories, who or what is to be taken to be its spokesperson (the question of evidence, stressed by Hugh-Jones in particular)? What kind of ontological commitment is implied by the actors' understandings and lived experiences of such other fundamental concepts as person (Vilaça), or law, or time (Strathern)? Do such commitments extend across the entire lived experience of the population concerned—a point pressed by Stephen Hugh-Jones in his exploration of the similarities, and the similar complexities, in the lives, attitudes, and practices of NW Amazonians and Welsh sheep farmers. Where "time" is concerned, Marilyn Strathern spells out the ontological implications of the contrast between an evolutionary and an episodic apprehension of it—where, however, those ontological differences may not be perceived as such by the actors concerned. That would mean that in such instances, ontology is as it were below the radar of an investigation of so-called cultural divergences—with corresponding consequences for the universal viability of the concept of "culture" itself.

Several contributors do not just issue something in the nature of a health warning concerning the use of "ontology" so much as implicitly recommend bypassing it altogether (Carneiro da Cunha). Thus, Serafina Cuomo, having examined the pluralism in the ways of doing mathematics in the Greco-Roman world raises problems for any view that would treat them as hermetically sealed entities, emphasizing the risks of framing the analysis in terms of "cultures," "traditions," or indeed "ontologies." She mounts a strong case for an alternative framework in terms of situated learning and the possibility of code-switching. Nicholas Jardine, in turn, while not rejecting "ontologies" in toto, argues for a refinement of their use, to focus on practices rather than on objects. Mauro Almeida's tactic is different again. Accepting plural ontologies in mathematics still leaves room, in his view, for intertranslatability between them if one concentrates on the pragmatics of their application.

Surprisingly, perhaps, one context in which it is comparatively unproblematic to say that we are dealing with a plurality of "ontologies" relates to the world of computing, where, as Alan Blackwell shows, it is the job of artificial intelligence engineers not to discover ontologies but rather to invent new ones. To be sure, the assessment of those innovations poses plenty of issues for the present and more especially the future. Pursuing that question and taking his cue from the pluralism of the anthropologists, Willard McCarty engages in deeply suggestive explorations for the differences that may be in train in modes of reasoning and in our understanding of intelligence. What, for instance, might be the price that has to be paid to meet the demands of what McCarty calls "complete consistency and absolute explicitness"?

(2) Several contributions, including those of AI specialists, give startling examples of the problems of translation and of mutual intelligibility that arise. There can, of course, be no perfect translation from one language to another, nor indeed a perfect rendition of the sense of any given speech act in other terms in the same "natural language." Aparecida Vilaça's Wari' assimilate what they are taught by missionaries and educators, but, in ways that those outsiders may themselves not be aware of, contrive to preserve their own Wari' understandings alongside those extraneous lessons. Agathe Keller's Tamil and Sanskrit practitioners can be brought into communication with one another and yet may have or have had very different views on the substance of the problems they in some sense share. Strathern, too, suggests that local Indigenous peoples may have been more aware of their divergent understanding of key parts of experience that we gloss as "time" and "law" than the original Australian officials and settlers when they first arrived. Pressing the relationship between intelligibility and ontology, Strathern argues forcefully that mutual interaction and interchanges are possible without mutual intelligibility, where the divergence—indeed, clash—between ontologies is not necessarily visible to the actors themselves. The challenging conclusion, in her own words, is that "the world plays back to people what they apprehend about it through the supports it gives to their ideas."

But examples of potential misunderstandings are not limited to those that involve more than one natural language. Cuomo illustrates such tensions by different mathematical practitioners who all share Greek. Karine Chemla, too, discusses the variety of mathematical practices in different texts that all use the Chinese language, and concludes that in that case ontology cannot be said to be determined by language. Blackwell explores the ambiguities of "objective function" used by computer engineers and the ways in which they and nonspecialists (or specialists in other disciplines such as philosophy) may be radically at cross-purposes in their use of the same terms in the English language. McCarty examines how, in order to use the calculating capacities of computers, the problems have to be reformulated in their language—with a consequent loss of elements of text through the process of digitalization.

Over and over again our contributors have challenged the terms in which we talk of what we assume to be well-defined intellectual disciplines. What we should understand by "mathematics" and what by "science" has to be radically problematized if we are to do justice to the variety of practices, experiences, and knowledge that we encounter in the field and in history. Making the most of developments in modern mathematics, Almeida shows the pervasiveness of mathematical structures and pragmatic applications across widely divergent domains, including Indigenous kinship systems. As Jardine points out, a narrow view of "science" excludes much of what has been accepted as knowledge by other peoples and at other times. We work, therefore, toward a broader conception of "science," a pluralist one that avoids the twin pitfalls of universal relativism and of a narrow strong realism. Joining forces with Strathern, he argues for a "foreignization" of our analytic framework to accommodate a principle of responsibility to the peoples we investigate. Manuela Carneiro da Cunha probes the underlying assumptions at work in what might seem the relatively unproblematic term *agriculture*, both challenging in particular our current dominant models that assume an evolution from foraging to domestication, and in the process restoring the claims that can be made on behalf of Indigenous knowledge practices.

(3) As that last remark already indicates, the political repercussions of our investigations underlie most of them and come to the fore in several. Carneiro da Cunha reveals the narrow-mindedness of many of our common assumptions about agricultural practices and shows how mistaken the policies of governments and NGOs have often been, even when their aims have been ecological conservation and sustainable productivity. Strathern and Vilaça, too, point to the threats that the imposition of

Western concepts and practices poses to the groups they study. Keller charts the interference of nationalist agenda in the representation of the varieties of mathematical pluralism in India. A different but still very tangible danger is present in the current, often overhyped debates about the future of artificial intelligence, where, as both McCarty and Blackwell point out, it is not just an understanding of rationality that is at stake but even some assumptions about what makes humans human.

Every contributor stresses the amount of further research that needs to be done to make the most of the opening up of study to which they bear witness. Our efforts here are avowedly provisional and preliminary. But the way ahead we envision involves not just individual disciplines but also their joining forces. We believe *Science in the Forest, Science in the Past* offers a model for fruitful cross-disciplinary exchanges on some fundamental problems that we face today.

Contributors

Mauro W. Barbosa de Almeida is Professor Emeritus in the Department of Social Anthropology at the Universidade Estadual de Campinas, Brazil. He has field experience in the Brazilian Northeast (rural communities, chapbook literature) and wrote his doctoral dissertation on Amazonian Indigenous and migrant rubber tappers. He was part of the task force that designed and initiated the first extractive reserve for forest dwellers and played a leading role in the design of the University of the Forest (now the Forest Campus of the Universidade Federal do Acre). He has led several projects involving local researchers and has produced many reports supporting the territorial and cultural claims of Indigenous peoples and traditional communities. He coedited the *Enciclopédia da floresta: O Alto Juruá* with Manuela Carneiro da Cunha and has published articles on forest peasantries, traditional knowledge, and Indigenous mathematical and scientific practices, including "On the Structure of Dravidian Relationship Systems" (*Mathematical Anthropology and Cultural Theory*, 2010); "Symmetry and Entropy: Mathematical Metaphors in the Work of Lévi-Strauss" (*Current Anthropology*, 1990); and "Local Struggles with Entropy: Caipora and other Demons" in *The Anthropology of Sustainability* (eds. M. Brightman and J. Lewis, Palgrave Macmillan, 2017).

Alan Blackwell is Professor of Interdisciplinary Design in the University of Cambridge Department of Computer Science and Technology. Drawing on his previous career in professional engineering, he has developed undergraduate and graduate curricula applying practice-led and craft perspectives to the design of software as a material. His historical and cultural research focuses particularly on the influence of artificial intelligence in the software industry from the 1960s to the present. He has conducted his fieldwork in California's Silicon Valley and in the Silicon Fen of the Cambridge Phenomenon laboratories and companies and is now extending his research to carry out fieldwork with computer scientists in sub-Saharan Africa. He has published in journals that apply critical theory to technology design, such as *Transactions on Human-Computer Interaction* and *Personal and Ubiquitous Computing*, with recent contributions applying artificial intelligence and information theory, published in *Critical Theory and Interaction Design* (eds. J. Bardzell, S.Bardzell, and M. Blythe MIT Press, 2018) and *Marx200: The Significance of Marxism in the 21st Century* (ed. M. Davis, Praxis Press, 2019).

Manuela Carneiro da Cunha is Professor Emerita of Anthropology at the University of Chicago and the Universidade de São Paulo, Brazil. Her research and publications deal with Indigenous Amazonian cultures, the return of freed slaves to West Africa in the nineteenth century, and the history of Brazilian legislation and policies toward Indigenous peoples from the sixteenth century to the present, focusing on ethnicity, history, and myth. She is deeply involved with Indigenous rights in Brazil and is currently conducting a multidisciplinary project on the contributions of Indigenous peoples and local communities to biodiversity in Brazil and the policies that affect them. Among her books are *Os mortos e os outros* (Hucitec, 1978); *Negros, estrangeiros: Os escravos libertos e sua volta à África* (Companhia das Letras, 2012); *Cultura com aspas e outros ensaios de antropologia* (Cosac Naify/UBU, 2009); *Savoirs autochtones: Quelle nature, quels apports?* (Fayard/Collège de France, 2012). She also edited *História dos Indios no Brasil* (Companhia das Letras, 1992).

Karine Chemla is Senior Researcher of Exceptional Class in the Sciences, Philosophy, and History Laboratory (SPHERE) of the Centre National de la Recherche Scientifique (CNRS) and the Université de Paris. Her work uses an historical anthropology viewpoint to focus on the relationship between mathematics and various cultures in which it is practiced. In particular, she is interested in the different mathematical cultures that can be identified in ancient China as well as in modern Europe and in the ways in which the diversity of mathematics has been approached in past historiographies. She published *Les Neuf Chapitres* with Guo Shuchun (Dunod, 2004) and edited *The History of Mathematical Proof in Ancient Traditions* (Cambridge University Press, 2012); *Texts,*

Textual Acts and the History of Science, with J. Virbel (Springer, 2015); *The Oxford Handbook of Generality in Mathematics and the Sciences*, with R. Chorlay and D. Rabouin (Oxford University Press, 2016); *Numerical Tables and Tabular Layouts in Chinese Scholarly Documents* (*East Asian Science, Technology and Medicine*, 2017); and *Cultures without Culturalism: The Making of Scientific Knowledge*, with E. F. Keller (Duke University Press, 2017).

Serafina Cuomo is Professor of Ancient History in the Department of Classics and Ancient History at Durham University in the UK. Previously, she held positions at Imperial College London and Birkbeck, University of London. Her main area of research is Greek and Roman antiquity, in particular the history of science and technology. She has published three books: *Pappus of Alexandria and the Mathematics of Late Antiquity* (Cambridge University Press, 2000); *Ancient Mathematics* (Routledge, 2001); *Technology and Culture in Greek and Roman Antiquity* (Cambridge University Press, 2007); and several articles on Hero of Alexandria, Frontinus, Volusius Maecianus (a Roman jurist who also wrote a treatise on units of currency for the emperor), and Nonius Datus (a Roman military engineer active in North Africa). She is currently completing a monograph on numeracy in ancient Greece and Rome and is Area Editor for Science, Technology and Medicine for the Oxford Classical Dictionary.

Stephen Hugh-Jones taught for many years at the Cambridge University Department of Social Anthropology and is now Senior Research Associate. Over the past fifty years, he has carried out ongoing field research among the Tukanoan-speaking Barasana, Bará, Makuna, Taiwano, and Tatuyo peoples living in the Colombian Amazon and acted as consultant in their research-based program of culturally-appropriate education. The foci of his research and publications have dealt with mythology, ritual and shamanism; kinship and architecture; the interface between Indigenous economy and capitalism (rubber gatherers, gold miners, and cocaine producers); Indigenous knowledge of animals, plants, astronomy, and other aspects of the environment; and books, writing, and systems of memory. He has also conducted research on books, printing, and paper-making in Tibet and Bhutan. He is the author of *The Palm and the Pleiades* (Cambridge University Press, 1979); "Yesterday's Luxuries, Tomorrow's Necessities: Business and Barter in Northwest Amazonia," in *Barter, Exchange and Value* (eds. C. Humphrey and S. Hugh-Jones,

Cambridge University Press, 1992); "Shamans, Prophets, Priests and Pastors," in *Shamanism, History and the State*. (eds. C. Humphrey and N. Thomas, University of Michigan Press, 1994); "Bride-Service and the Absent Gift" (*Journal of the Royal Anthropological Institute*, 2013); and "Writing on Stone, Writing on Paper: Myth, History and Memory in NW Amazonia" (*History and Anthropology*, 2016).

Nicholas Jardine is Professor Emeritus of History and Philosophy of the Sciences at the University of Cambridge. He has worked on early-modern astronomy and natural history as well as philosophical issues relating to the formation and transformation of scientific disciplines and agendas. His publications include: *The Scenes of Inquiry* (Clarendon Press, 2000); *La guerre des astronomes*, with A. P. Segonds (Les Belles Lettres, 2008); *Christoph Rothmann's Treatise on the Comet of 1585*, with M. A. Granada and A. Mosley (Brill, 2014); and *Worlds of Natural History*, ed. with H. A. Curry, J. A. Secord and E. C. Spary (Cambridge University Press, 2018). His current interests are the history of cross-cultural communication in the sciences and the problems of interpretation of schemes of classification and scientific practices far removed from our own.

Agathe Keller is a researcher in the Sciences, Philosophy, and History Laboratory (SPHERE) of the Centre National de la Recherche Scientifique (CNRS) and the Université de Paris. She works on Sanskrit mathematical commentaries, having published a translation and analysis of Bhāskara I's commentary (629) on the mathematical chapter of the Āryabhaṭīya (a sixth-century astronomical text). She is currently editing Pṛthūdaka's (fl. 860) commentary on the mathematical chapter of the Brahmagupta's Brāhmasphuṭasiddhānta (628). Her research also deals with the historiography of science in South Asia from the nineteenth century to the present, and she has an interest in ethnomathematical activities. She is the author of the two-volume *Expounding the Mathematical Seed, Bhāskara and the Mathematical Chapter of the Āryabhaṭīya* (Birkhäuser, 2006). As a slow-science advocate, she is a member of the Bradygolist Academy. She is codirector of the Springer collection Why the Sciences of the Ancient World Matter.

Geoffrey Lloyd is Professor Emeritus of Ancient Philosophy and Science at the University of Cambridge, where he was Master of Darwin College from 1989 to 2000. Trained originally as a classicist, his interests in ancient Greek and Chinese philosophy, science, and medicine have increasingly drawn him into comparative studies drawing on social anthropology, evolutionary psychology, ethology, and cognitive science. He has authored or edited some thirty books, including *Polarity and Analogy: Two Types of Argumentation in Early Greek Thought* (Cambridge University Press, 1966). Those comparative themes are particularly prominent in his *Demystifying Mentalities* (Cambridge University Press, 1990); in *Cognitive Variations: Reflections on the Unity and Diversity of the Human Mind* (Oxford University Press, 2007); in *Being, Humanity and Understanding* (Oxford University Press, 2012); and most recently in *The Ambivalences of Rationality: Ancient and Modern Cross-Cultural Explorations* (Cambridge University Press, 2018).

Willard McCarty is Professor Emeritus of the Department of Digital Humanities, King's College London. His research is focused on the development of digital computing and its potential to become a discipline of the human sciences, especially with regards to the questions of reasoning and intelligence. To aid in this focus, he draws on whatever disciplines offer help, especially historical, philosophical, and psychological studies of the sciences, anthropology, and the cognitive sciences. His publications include essays on simulation in *The Shape of Data in Digital Humanities* (eds. J. Flanders and F. Jannidis, Routledge, 2018); on modeling in the journal *Historical Social Research* (2018); on interdisciplinary studies in *A New Companion to Digital Humanities* (eds. S. Schreibman, R. Siemens, and J. Unsworth, Wiley, 2015); and on digital humanities in *Companion to New Media Dynamics* (eds. J. Hartley, J. Burgess, and A. Bruns, Wiley, 2013). His monograph *Humanities Computing* (Palgrave MacMillan, 2005) established modeling as a central concern of the field.

Marilyn Strathern is Professor Emerita of Social Anthropology, Life Fellow of Girton College (both Cambridge University), and Hon. Life President of the UK Association of Social Anthropologists. She had the good fortune to begin her research career in Papua New Guinea, which led to work on law, kinship, and gender relations. In the UK, she subsequently became involved with anthropological approaches to new reproductive technologies, intellectual property, and audit cultures. She pairs *The Gender of the Gift* (University of California Press, 1988), a critique of anthropological theories of society applied to Melanesia, with *After Nature* (Cambridge University Press, 1992), a comment on the cultural revolution at home. *Partial Connections* (AltaMira Press, 1991) looks askance at comparative anthropology. Her recently published work *Before and After Gender* (HAU Books, 2016) is also one of her first texts, written in the early 1970s. Her most recent book is *Relations: An Anthropological Account* (Duke University Press, 2020).

Aparecida Vilaça is Professor of Social Anthropology at the Museu Nacional, Universidade Federal do Rio de Janeiro. Since 1986, she has worked among the Wari' people of southwestern Amazonia, Brazil. She specializes in the study of sociocultural changes among Indigenous peoples, with an emphasis on first colonial encounters, conversion to Christianity, and schooling. Her current research on how Wari' children and young people learn science in school seeks to understand the equivocations produced in the encounter between different ontologies, especially regarding the idea of nature. She is the author of *Strange Enemies: Indigenous Agency and Scenes of Encounters in Amazonia* (Duke University Press, 2010); *Praying and Preying: Christianity in Indigenous Amazonia* (University of California Press, 2016); *Comendo como gente: Formas do canibalismo* wari' (Mauad X, 2017); and is coeditor with Robin Wright of *Native Christians: Modes and Effects of Christianity among Indigenous Peoples of the Americas* (Ashgate, 2009). Her most recent book is a literary essay on the life of her Wari' father, *Paletó e eu* (Todavia, 2018).

Lightning Source UK Ltd.
Milton Keynes UK
UKHW012023100221
378573UK00001B/1

9 781912 808410